MASTER YOUR $TOCKBROKER

WALL STREET SECRETS

by

Patrick G. Finegan, Jr., Esq.

The Palindrome Press
Hartford, Connecticut

First Printing

Proudly Printed and Bound in the United States of America.
10 9 8 7 6 5 4 3 2

The author and publisher have exhaustively researched the materials in this book to accurately present the material. This is not a book on how to invest in the stock market. It does not offer individual investment advice, tax or legal advice, and encourages readers to get individual advice they can trust from competent professionals. For investment advice, the book urges readers to do their own research and seek out a good investment counselor. The same is true for taxes. Readers should seek reliable tax advice from a competent tax professional about their particular situation. As for legal advice, the author and publisher strongly urge readers to develop a relationship with their own personal attorney and get his/her opinions regarding any questions the readers may have. The book is intended for informational and educational purposes only. The author and publisher assume no responsibility for errors, inaccuracies, or omissions or any other inconsistencies in the text. All hypothetical situations and other characterizations are based on general practices, traditions and usages and are not based on individual persons. The opinions expressed herein are those of the individual author.

Finegan, Patrick G., Jr.
Master Your Stockbroker.
ISBN: 1-878905-00-7 hardcover
1-878905-01-5 softcover

Library of Congress Catalog Card Number: 90-61322
includes index.
stock brokerage

Dedication

Over deep, salt seas,
Through hours of hard duration,
In laughter,
Always and everywhere,
For my Mary Elizabeth.

About the Author

***

Patrick G. Finegan, Jr., Esq.

Attorney Finegan graduated from Fordham College in New York City, then took his JD Law Degree from New York Law School. He went on to earn a Master of Laws Degree in Corporations from the New York University School of Law, whereupon he served four years as a Captain in the Judge Advocate General Department, United States Air Force, prosecuting and defending Courts Martial and other matters around the world, which he summarizes as a "great four years!"

Next: "Wall Street." He was the Assistant General Counsel for a Member Firm of the New York Stock Exchange for 8 years.

He handled well over 100 securities arbitrations, numerous regulatory investigations and dealt with professionals throughout the financial community on intricate problems. He held major securities licenses by the time he left the financial world for private practice:

Registered Representative (Stockbroker)
Associated Person (Commodity Broker)
Registered Options Principal
Branch Manager
Compliance Officer
Supervisory Analyst
General Principal
Financial and Operations Principal
Municipal Securities Principal.

He practices law, writes and lectures in Washington, D.C.

ANOTHER PALINDROME BOOK BY THIS AUTHOR:

Master Financial Statements

Table of Contents

INTRODUCTION

A GOOD BROKER,

is like gold: shining, valuable, without tarnish. A good broker saves you from hazards you probably don't know exist, such as the insatiable dollar appetite of the "Home Office." A good broker will educate you, gather information and explain it to you, identify investment opportunities and warn you against fads. A good broker earns every cent in his paycheck because he delivers you service, service and more service. He can't give guarantees, but he will help YOU make informed decisions based on relevant information. Be grateful!

A BAD BROKER,

is a voracious rodent.

PREFACE

Rodents, Regulators, and You

The United States Bankruptcy Courts are becoming brokerage experts as big houses and little ones go under from the excesses of the 1980's. You should be concerned.

This book was originally intended for lawyers, proceeding on assumptions that the reader would already understand definitions of equity securities and bonds, references to statutes, and advanced concepts of partnership taxation and corporate procedure.

During the outline stage, a nagging observation became a curiosity, then took hold of the direction I had wanted to travel and became an inescapable barrier: while I have met sophisticated attorneys who practice in the pure finance area, very few professionals or civilians understand the daily workings of the brokerage business - *this includes the staff of the Securities and Exchange Commission!*

This is NOT a book about how to make millions in the stock market. It may, however, save your financial life by making you wonder why any retail customer gets involved with the market through a bad broker, when good brokers ARE out there. I want to help you understand how to "read" the signs of a bad broker. My original outline was set aside for another time in favor of a more relevant and readable book intended to open your eyes (yes, the public) to the frightening and fascinating reality of how the retail securities industry works - or doesn't work. It's about con-men, churners, switchers, rodents, marketeers - Wall Street.

Drexel finally died in 1990. Put on your life preserver, as more firms slip under the waves of financial history.

Let's examine the problems by unveiling:

- *the predatory reality of retail sales,*
- *the brotherhood of silence,*
- *the shocking entente wherein the government regulators are actually the industry's best friend!*

INFORMATION IS THE BEST DEFENSE - Heed this warning: watch out for CANNIBALS and BOGEYMEN - they <u>do</u> exist, they <u>are</u> everywhere, and they're out to get <u>YOU.</u> It's nothing personal, but the average investor is a VICTIM of spreadsheet anonymity, meaning that in the logic of modern brokerage cash flow, you are as unidentified and fungible as a single grain of sugar within an old, grand recipe for baking sweet pecan pie.

Marketing has defeated morality, because morality doesn't pay this month's rent. In comparing brokerage house planning to the solar system, next month is as far away as Mars, next year is like the edge of the planetary system, and beyond that takes one into the theoretical: it doesn't matter, even if it does exist. Heavy duty public relations, served up by some of the best on Madison Avenue, coupled with the firepower of statistical decision-avoidance, has been grandly installed within the inner sancta of Wall Street, with all the vengeance of militant, religious conversion.

Unlike other industries that supply genuine needs to the general population, Wall Street has decided, since 1945, that IT WILL EXIST on a retail basis, that it can be profitable, and that even if consumer-investors don't need them, the Street can seduce individuals to render large amounts of their money in tribute to the transactional beast. Retail Wall Street continues to exist by sheer force of its own will and the trusting servitude of the investing public who believe that the famous regulators are making the Street a safe place for investment.

And YOU - if you are an investor who is fed up, and you fire Brokerage House "ABC" where do you go? "DEF?"

You may get more of the same!

"DEF" really is the same as "ABC," so don't look for solutions by taking a walk to a new brokerage house. Look for the solution in YOURSELF. The old motto remains sound:

BE PREPARED!
FIND A GOOD BROKER!

Tired of listening to your BAD stockbroker talk in endless circles of excuses, making promises routinely left unfulfilled? Had enough of the broker's hot enthusiasm to use YOUR money for his sport, where YOU end up with the old line, " Well, the market giveth and the market taketh away," if you get any response at all?

Study this book!

Take notes in the margins, underline, dog-ear parts that you want for ready reference, and let your broker know that you have it; use the letters in Appendix F in the back of the book! Your broker will not treat you the same again because the relation will have changed completely - YOU will be the MASTER, just as it should be, and that's only if YOU want any account at all! This book will help you to think twice about future investments through Wall Street, especially through a full service brokerage firm.

Remember - timing and the selection of investments are the foundations of portfolio management for the professionals who run the great institutional fortunes you have heard of so many times in the past.

The big guys know the game. They have information and make decisions in ways beyond your present means, using late breaking news and trading floor action. The bad broker doesn't need this book, and will probably cringe to know you have it.

YOU need this book! NOW!

This isn't a sensational expose - it's more practical. I want you to read this book, then re-read and study it. I want you to be comfortable with the long, long history of mercantile dealings, derivative finance and the evolution of the modern wire house. If you don't know the facts, you should get ready for a devastating, blindside hit.

I want you to be able to look up information on your own, see your own limits and be able to recognize the difference between a quick sale and a bona-fide investment profile. Use this book to help you burn right through the fog, hype and disinformation, so that you can watch out for Number One - you!

About 60% of all transactions on the New York Stock Exchange are done by institutions: that's right, experienced professionals. A lot of the remaining activity is done by sophisticated individuals, such as stockbrokers for their own accounts. The percentage of professionals is going up as the trading volume goes down.

How can YOU possibly compete against these forces? Do you think even an honest stockbroker has an investing chance against the institutions? Flip through the Chapter headings: are you ready to fight against program traders and NYSE members trading for their own accounts as I later describe that multi-headed monster?

Don't let events go by another day - take control, and, with personal authority, YOU can feel genuine triumph as you MASTER YOUR STOCKBROKER! You cannot afford to let bad brokers stay in the driver's seat any longer!

You cannot put your savings under the control of pretenders, gurus, chart-benders and houses that disappear when the bankers refuse to make short term loans. You can't trust an industry that has been and remains out of control, and quite possibly out of its financial mind.

PGF, jr.
5/90

FORWARD

extracted from Marcus Tullius Cicero, Against Verres, translation, liberally, by PGF, jr., May, 1990.

Marcus Tullius Cicero was born in 106-105 BC in central Italy in the small town of Arpinum. He was educated within the Roman interpretation of classic Greek curriculum, emphasizing Rhetoric, then Roman History and the Humanities. He studied in Greece as a young man, eventually became a lawyer and began his public career with bureaucratic service in Sicily.

In approximately 70 BC, he prosecuted a former Governor of Sicily, a despot named Verres, before the Senate in Rome, because the people of Sicily had protested in the extreme that Verres had financially wrecked the Province through extortion and theft. The Senate appointed several of its members to act as a court, much as today, our Congress works through committees and sub-committees. Think of it as the Watergate Hearings and an Impeachment Court rolled into one tribunal, with the power to inquire, reach a verdict and hand out a sentence.

Rome's then pre-eminent barrister, Quintus Hortensius, represented the Accused Verres. The opening rounds of the Defense effort were marked by political intrigue, attempts to get different judges, influence Senators, fire Cicero as prosecutor, and rearrange the Court Calendar with deadly delays - all to avoid going to trial. It didn't help; the trial went forward. Verres left Rome before the trial was finished because he sensed the inevitable, but, under Roman procedure, the trial was concluded in his absence. He was found liable for all claims, stripped of his rights as a citizen, and banished. All his property was confiscated.

It was a great triumph for Cicero. The polemic against Verres has matured through history as a measure of the moral standards expected of people who serve the public trust when deciding the fate of the most wealthy and evil individuals of an era. I have extracted a small part of this very special speech.

What should prevail: wealth or law? Where does honor weigh in the prosecution of corruption? What is integrity?

Does history sound oddly current? From a distance of two thousand years, Cicero speaks:

*** ***

The Roman people are watching you, the Senate, in this case to see how you will persevere in matters of conscience and law. Rome knows that in recent times but one Senator has been found guilty by you of any offense, and he was personally insolvent. The people are not criticizing that case, but they aren't impressed by it, either. You see, one's honesty is not worthy of great acclaim unless it weathers serious attempts at its corruption. Your decision in this case will set the standard, for Rome shall judge this Senate based on its verdict - will this Senate convict a criminal if he is wealthy?

...I start this case by asking that my prayers be answered, that apart from the defendant, whose outrages are infamous, that there not be another insincere member within this court. Be confident, and I ask the Roman people to be confident, that if there is dishonesty here aside from the defendant, before all heaven, I would sooner die than fail in the tenacity and courage needed to punish such treason!

*** ***

Cicero, who spoke publicly against Verres, Julius Caesar, Marc Antony, the Conspirator Cataline, and others of enormous wealth and power, and who wrote so prolifically about life's meaning, was assassinated at the age of 64, in approximately 42 BC.

The Greek Historian Plutarch tells us that after the death of Julius Caesar, when the Roman Government was in turmoil before Augustus became Emperor, two Centurions, one a former defense client of Ciccro's, under orders from Antony, cut off Cicero's head and hands, and brought them to Antony in Rome, thus finally silencing one of history's great commentators.

Antony had the gruesome body parts nailed up for public display, offering an obvious message to idealists concerned about the rule of law, a final consequence for honesty.

We need a Cicero in our national government! We need people with ideals unrelated to their careers and incomes, who act courageously for the common good. We need heros who do not compromise in the face of powerful corruption.

Thank you, old friend.

PGF, jr.
5/90

As You Read This Book...

FIRST,

1. Review the Appendix. Read the glossary terms in Appendix D. You will see them again, in small doses, after each of the first eight chapters. They are essential. Glossaries are some of the most ignored parts of any book - please, read this one!

2. Consider the questions in the self test in Appendix C. After you have read the entire book, their importance should be clear.

3. I refuse to put in a mere chapter on margin and then one on options, because each is worthy of a long book. I didn't want any reader to come away with a feeling that they could command the two subjects without thorough, specialized study. Margin and options are discussed in context throughout the book. These two concepts cause the most harm to retail investors every year. You must understand the risk involved in these areas to deal with Wall Street. See Appendix E. Stay away from margin and options unless you can handle the extreme risk.

4. Get used to demanding written information from your broker. Telephone discussion is not the answer. Sometimes you have to get it on paper. See the letters in Appendix F.

5. Take notes as you are reading!

NEXT,

6. If you are an investor, you MUST find time to use the library.

7. Keep on reading and searching for answers!

Good Hunting!

CHAPTER ONE

EVOLUTION OF STOCK
WHAT IS A BOND?

Adventure, Danger, Slavery
Heads Roll
Unlimited Liability

Among the most ancient cuneiform tablets bearing the first evidences of writing are inventories from warehouses which were situated in the area of modern Iraq about five thousand years ago.

Sumerians, Babylonians, Egyptians, Assyrians - each culture developed, from the fruits of agriculture and war, a system of surplus inventory and trade that depended on the ability to fulfill a promise to pay for goods if delivered, and an ability to gather and ship items, awaiting payment when delivered elsewhere. Once farmers produced a surplus crop, beyond their own requirements to survive, professional traders developed to figure out what to do with the surplus. While governments certainly took their share as taxes, some was left over.

If you have extra grain, but want meat, how do you get it? How do you pay for the army that stands watch over the slave labor that is building your pyramid, and then, how do you feed both the army and the slaves (and yourself and an immense household staff) while still paying for the delivery of gigantic stone blocks? The solution was commerce. Kings who cannot pay their bills have the highest incidence of coups, or, put another way, a king who doesn't pay bills desperately needs an expert taste tester, who, if anyone, must be paid in advance.

The great, long lasting kings in history have enjoyed solvency at home, either because they were great administrators who could stretch value to the maximum, or because they went on a path of successful conquest and, while spending a lot on war, netted a vast profit when they stole everything the losers had.

The Phoenicians and Minoans were creative heralds of the modern financial world because they were dynamic traders from small countries who had to depend on venture capital, credit, inventory receipts, high speed communications and changing commodity, currency and personal consumption markets.

They serviced the entire Mediterranean basin by carrying goods back and forth, thereby providing market liquidity to owners of surplus products. Trade was conducted by barter (grain for meat, grain for wine) or based on hard quasi-currency (grain for precious metals like gold or silver or jewelry stones). Coins were used, but were accepted for their gold content, not a mere promise to pay later from a foreign government. The personal risk from storms, pirates or plain business failure was immense!

That was a little over three thousand years ago.

The Roman Empire was like nothing the West had seen before. The ancient empires of Egypt and Babylon were neither as geographically extensive nor long lasting. The Greeks never went beyond city states and a few colonies of localized power, and even the Persians, who were on the way to a large, mercantile society, declined rapidly due to the harsh fortunes of war with Alexander the Great.

War has always been expensive: if you lost in ancient times, you lost on a grand scale, effectively going out of business. The heads of the Heads of State were lopped off, so, in battle, worried monarchs threw in everything they had, without regard to cost. Survival, not cost, mattered.

The Romans burst out of central Italy to the south in about 500 BC and went to war for the next 900 years, but most dramatically, from 240 BC until 50 BC they subjugated entire populations throughout Europe and the Middle East, and brought incredible wealth back to Rome in the form of commodity tributes (grain, livestock, raw materials, etc.), slaves, gold, silver, jewelry and just about anything that could be detached and transported (stolen) by the conquering Legions.

Life became untenable for Roman farm workers because of slave labor pouring in from the successful wars of expansion. Speculators, looking for investments with all this new war wealth, were simultaneously driving up the price of grain and creating huge farms manned by all that cheap slave labor. Absentee landlords, a novelty for Rome, became tremendously powerful by purchasing great areas of the best land. The Roman bakers were squeezed by grain price manipulation, with the result that their working-class customers were too poor to buy any bread! Grain was being held in storage or sold overseas within the empire for higher prices, or bartered for valuable products like jewelry or glass, which were subject to further speculation.

By 135 BC, speculators and urban poor were literally fighting it out in the streets of Rome. Various guilds were demonstrating and engaging in boycotts, riots and strikes. About 25% of the population of the City of Rome was slave labor. Unemployed Roman citizen-workers were starving to death.

This led to the separate assassinations of the Gracchus brothers during street riots in 133 and 121 BC. They were champions of the then-controversial "power to the people" movement that relied on old Roman traditions of a true republic and land reform. In the first Gracchus assassination, hundreds died; in the second, thousands. The division caused by economic power redefined the Roman tradition of a united people. The republic fell to the dictators and the public lost its traditional role in a society of equals.

We know the aristocrats won, but we also know that Roman wealth maintained its power by thereafter subsidizing the life of the urban poor (the infamous "bread and circus") in order to keep the growing and restless urbanites from rebellion or anarchy.

The most famous Roman financier, Marcus Lucinius Crassus, derived his wealth from this misery. He had more capital than he could possibly need, so the unnecessary funds went into investments in real estate, import/export of foodstuffs, and a personal army, to further increase his wealth. He personally financed the Roman Government at times, much as the later, famous House of Rothschild financed the European Monarchs of the 19th century. Crassus was the soldier/financier who defeated the slave revolt of 71 BC, made famous by the movie "Spartacus." Crassus even bankrolled Julius Caesar in his drive to supreme power in Rome.

According to fairly reliable accounts, Crassus started a private fire department in Rome, the only such brigade aside from the Palace Guard, which was responsible only for the Government buildings. When fires broke out around the city, Crassus' agents would hustle over to the buildings and start buying them up from the owners as the flames seemed to be destroying the structures. The deal done, the Crassus Fire Brigade would arrive and put out the fire. Crassus became the biggest single landowner in the city. No one has shown he engaged in arson; he didn't have to because Rome had frequent fires. He died in 53 BC, leading his troops in the disastrous battle of Carrhae. One thought about Crassus: if he was a man of tireless ambition, he certainly paid the highest personal price.

Roman aristocrats had tremendous wealth and often got together to put on commercial ventures. By the birth of Christ, the start of the modern era, Chinese silk was for sale in Rome, as was African grain, Greek wine, Egyptian Jewelry and so on. There was no insurance as we know that practice, but there was an understanding of shared risk, that is, of not putting all one's eggs in one basket. Ten or twenty investors might pay for a shipment of grain, each able to bear his part of the loss if the ship went under. In the port of Ostia, speculators bid on the price of grain en route from Africa before it arrived.

****

But, if you were a businessman who could not meet his debt when due, you went into slavery. Not just embarrassment, not court proceedings - slavery!

****

There was no bankruptcy protection, and no salvation from "cruel and unusual punishment." Slaves had no rights and were typically murdered or severely beaten (leading to probable death) for little cause, often for amusement. Roman cruelty in this area is well documented: it was extreme.

The concept of venture capital was, therefore, deadly serious, highly personal business. Because the risk was so great, the expected rewards had to be at least as great - and they were! Immense, lasting fortunes were made and merchant houses became as influential as the Emperor (causing various Emperors great distraction). Semi-private armies were the norm! It should be noted that heads rolled, families went into slavery, and the rich and famous became subject to the financial envy of the Emperor, with no real rights of due process under law after approximately 60 AD.

When the Emperor was broke, which was often, he sold honors and offices, ambassadorships and titles. Occasionally, with artful maneuvering, an Emperor could single out a wealthy target, gather secret allies, and then fabricate allegations of treason. Conviction on treason led to confiscation of all property to the Emperor!

The Emperor would have to share a part of the spoils of success with his secret allies to make the practice palatable. No Emperor ever wanted to go so cash poor that he missed the payroll for the Praetorian Guard, German Mercenaries who formed the personal Imperial bodyguard. When they became unhappy, the Emperor was in physical danger.

The Romans made very few scientific innovations; science and philosophy were the glories of Greece. Rome left a legacy of war, surplus wealth, bureaucrats, businessmen and authors.

When the Roman Empire lay in bureaucratic ruins after the "barbarian" invasions, so did European commerce. Bridges crumbled, pirates returned to the Mediterranean, and national boundaries became barriers to trade.

Latin became a "literary" language, declining as the common language of commerce and the second language of the masses. Scholars debate the existence of any intellectual "Dark Ages" pointing to notable achievements in art and social structure, but the fact remains that international trade decreased after 400 AD in the West, which was splintering, then reacting to the threat of further invasions.

The Empire, when dying, had resorted to debasement of the coinage. The central government, which controlled the mints, purposefully put in less gold and more copper. When the population found out, the currency was subject to inflation, then was ignored in favor of barter or gold based transactions. Intra-Empire tarriffs were tried out, with disastrous results. The Emperor couldn't get credit to buy enough arms to equip armies in 400 AD, much less feed and pay for the troops. When foreign armies moved on Rome, the central government was powerless to stop them after 400 AD because the bureaucratic machine broke down. If success can be said to breed success, then failure certainly compounds, yielding deeper, more serious failure.

Don't assume that we are any smarter today. There is nothing magical about our study of economics that was not within the working knowledge of the Romans. True, they did not have vast data bases, but they knew that cold calculation and logical application of experience often prevailed over emotion. They knew that debasing their currency would hurt, but they did it anyway. They knew that internal tarriffs would stall commercc, but thcy did that, too.

Why? Probably because the decisions were made by stressed politicians reacting to the pressure of certain groups within Rome who wanted quick fixes through "easy" cash for the government.

Debtors in Prison

Did the Renaissance bring about modern Nationalism or was it Nationalism that made the Renaissance possible?

In the end, who really knows?

City-states of Northern Italy were firing up the engine of creative capitalism, as their trading fleets and merchants were everywhere, selling objects produced at home in Italy, fighting with the Moslems, and speculating on foreign products being delivered into their home markets by their returning sailors. Marco Polo left Venice for the East in 1271 AD. Merchant associations were popping up like Spring flowers with extensive commitments of speculative money, making it possible to outfit ships and hire crews for voyages that were years long. Guilds formed based on capital, not just traditional skills such as baking, carpentry, or weaving. Modern Banking had begun (or at least, had been resurrected) and the merchant class kept growing as the opportunity for trade remained open.

Prison still loomed for debtors, but not slavery. This was a major change, because the greatest risk of speculation was reduced from slavery and death to mere prison! Prison was horrible, but it was a significant step up.

If the Roman Catholic Church was opposed to charging interest because it was "sinful," secular scholars would get around the Church by making discount loans, that is, not charging interest on top of the loan payments, just taking out the charge at the front end by handing over $90 on a $100 loan.

Investors put funds into ventures in the hope of sharing in the final profit, becoming equity owners in the project as much as the project's promoters.

Wealth, while still concentrated, began to spread out into a merchant class, separate from the Church, the bureaucrats, or the monarchs. Nations were rising on new capital strength, even though small territorially, going back to the Phoenician model.

Financial methods accelerated over several hundred years so that as Thomas Jefferson was obtaining a scientific patent for a greatly improved, but still horse-drawn plow, most of the cash instruments of mercantile finance were far along to maturity, useful for new opportunities. Insurance and early corporations, financial "Companies," were created. The Dutch had risen, then fallen as the powerhouse of European Finance. Spain had risen on the strength of New World gold, and then collapsed, bankrupted by spending on unsuccessful war with Protestant Europe. Even Russia, after the Battle of Poltava with the Swedes in 1709, spent the 18th century trying to break into western commerce with a navy, trade routes and banking credits. (Absent from serious international commerce since 1917, Mother Russia is trying to make a comeback in the 1990's.)

And then?

Mass warfare in Europe in the age of Napoleon (1769-1821) brought misery and mass migrations to the New World by displaced workers and dissident idealists. The influence of Theology faded, Rationalism was ascendent and Capital survived quite nicely, financing industrial products such as the railroad, the steam engine and steam ship, the ironclad warship, the cotton gin and sewing machine, and the telegraph. Nationalistic politics adjusted to massive capital in the American Civil War, the Franco-Prussian conflict - stop! Too fast?

After the Renaissance (14th through 16th centuries), unlike after the demise of Rome, a class of independent, professional merchants arose who did not manufacture anything, but who made it possible to take the product of one market and sell it in another, picking up a cargo for the return, and selling that in the home port, or maybe yet another intermediary port on the way home.

Language, customs and religion stood aside as capital became the voice of commerce. The merchants needed money to get their operations going, and independent, professional bankers were happy to oblige, eventually opening the door to smaller, private investors, acting in groups to spread the risk. It continues to this day. Empires rose and fell - but unlike the Roman collapse, commerce did not wither.

Progress occurred.

While the politics of Europe in the 14th and 15th century brought sudden fragmentation, the 16th and 17th led to nationalism. Small nations like the Dutch and Portuguese enjoyed their moment of glory, becoming powerful beyond the expected norm of their population and geographical endowment.

In economic terms, their per capita productivity shot up markedly, their standards of living rose in corresponding fashion and the local strengths of their little, national economy were surpassed by the strength of their international trade. Without significant military conquest, they brought vast wealth and new ideas home.

One dynamic idea was democracy.

Democracy compels the distribution of power and wealth from the monarch to non-, often anti-royal activists who are concerned about their own political objectives and the protection of their personal commercial activity. Commerce became an active expression of political theory, witness the Boston Tea Party wherein the Sam Adams gang reacted politically to a peculiar and actually beneficial mercantile system which made tea cheaper in Boston than London, but tied the American Colonies more and more into the ex-parte control of the British Parliament. Democracy tends to distribute wealth by opening up the avenues of political power to different groups, often causing governments of compromise power, not authoritarian rule.

I respect serious arguments against that position; I am not trying to paint an ideal world under the banner of democratic capitalism. Eastern Europe is demonstrating that perfection is not the day's topic. Food, clothing, shelter and opportunity to improve one's life are highly motivating aspects of every day life throughout history.

Political liberty is another motivating factor that commands respect, yet it does not appear in texts on economics.

Eternal Corporations
Limited Liability
Professional Managers

Out of the mercantile explosion of the Renaissance came the concept of "companies."

The Dutch and English embraced the idea. Partial colonization of the English New World was done by companies formed for profit, speculating on tobacco agriculture. These companies were managed by professional businessmen who sought investment for the purchase of ships and equipment to send the settlers to the colonies to farm or obtain furs for secondary European trade. European cloth and hardware would then be traded to the colonials so they could continue to farm. The investors included, but were not limited to, the Monarch, which meant investors had a chance to make a profit. The company would not die when the managers died, because, as a "company", it had its own life.

This offered continuity of purpose and form when the average life expectancy was only 32 years, and disabling disease was rampant.

On January 8, 1675, the Governor and Council of New York, still a colony, issued a corporate charter to the New York Fishing Company, with shares costing 10 Pounds each.

Adam Smith, author of the Wealth of Nations, which was first published in 1776, described the use and acceptance of companies, especially in exploration and banking where one of the real difficulties was raising permanent funds to keep an enterprise going that might not generate profits right away, but which looked like an otherwise profitable, long-term activity.

In partnerships, everyone is liable for everything and when one partner dies, the others have to pay out his share, dissolve and then reform, if that is practicable. Key man life insurance did not exist until this century, although insurance was available for cargo and ships in the 18th century. How do you pay out a deceased partner's estate when the ship and equipment with 99% of the group's assets is on a voyage of 3 to 6 months to the New World and hasn't been seen for a while?

A "company" business form offered great advantages, even defeating death to an extent. If an investor in the company died, no payout was needed and no reorganization was required. The ownership interest was transferrable to the next-of-kin, the government, or it could be sold. Business went on, with a new ability to raise funds without total reorganization. A business could sell shares. Because the business had permanent capital and would be able to live longer than individual promoters, it was easier to borrow money.

Addressing Business Failure

Ventures fail for a number of reasons, but the historic Roman dilemma was that failure and insolvency led to slavery and death. The subsequent development of debtor prison was not much better, but at least one had a chance to pay off and get out if family and friends had charitable feelings about the debtor and loaned money to repay or get a satisfactory payment plan in place. Investors had to consider that they entrusted their partners with their lives, which is a combat commitment, not just a business decision.

Then a revolution occurred.

In the 16th century the concept of limited liability became established in small areas, spreading in the radically democratic 17th and 18th centuries, even turning up as an oblique reference in the United States Constitution, which gives Congress the right to make laws regarding bankruptcy. Congress didn't have to pass such laws, but it could.

In 1800, in the United States, you could still go to jail if you personally owed money to your grocer that you couldn't or wouldn't pay; but, you could also invest in a company, and if the company went under, you did not go to jail - provided you fully paid for your shares and did not otherwise engage in any wrongdoing. Limited liability existed, and its spread was slowed only by the sluggish activity of legislators in passing corporate laws in the various states. This was an age where entire state legislatures voted on individual bills of divorce. Lawmaking was a very slow process, and legislatures had to approve each corporate charter as though approving an individual statute, by full vote!

While no one could have predicted that the corporate form of business would become the master of modern capital, in hindsight, it was natural. Remember: it didn't die if a manager or "owner" died. It spread around the risk of investment. It used professional managers who could be replaced. It worked on democratic principles of control by vote, and if it failed, an investor didn't go to jail or into slavery. What a deal!

If it engaged in dangerous activity and people got hurt, the corporation paid - not the investor. Shares could be transported across boundaries in your pocket, given to friends or relatives, or even sold directly or through brokers.

The NYSE is Born

According to many authors, the New York Stock Exchange was founded in May, 1792 by 24 brokers who signed a written agreement binding themselves to create a restricted physical market for the trading of shares. The agreement limited who these traders would do business with, and where it would be done. In 1800, Thomas Jefferson was publicly defaming the "stockjobbers" who were ruining the nation's morals and credit in a frenzy of greed.

He regularly went to them to arrange finance to run the US Government, however, no matter what his public stand, because they were a principal source for government funds. Jefferson had no choice.

Since that time, the world has seen tumult in major warfare, and social upheaval unknown since the Mongol expansion from China to modern Poland in the 13th century. Rather than the collapse following the demise of Rome, business has grown, as though it prospers on disaster.

A Piece of the Action
Reduced Risk

A share of stock represents the ability to participate in a business venture to a large or small degree without having to be an expert in the field of activity, without having to go to the location of the activity, and without having to lose any more than the investment in the share if the business goes under, and the further ability to control the activity in proportion to the amount of shares you own compared to all the other shares owned by other investors. It makes you an owner without historic ownership horrors. You have a piece of the action!

This vicarious sense of daring has been, and remains, thrilling for those investors who identify with the venture's activity; for others it is just mathematics, always looking to profit. You can buy a share because the business looks profitable, because it sounds daring, because it is local or because your brother works there, because you like the name, or actually use what it makes - any reason at all! And you are not responsible if it destroys civilization! It's like going to the movies for an adventure extravaganza, except you might make a profit, and there are no special effects - or are there?

Suppose you own 500 shares and there are 20 million other shares out in the market besides yours - how much control do you have? Suppose the company tells you what it is doing by way of a balance sheet or income statement, but not in plain English? Suppose you think the professional managers who run the company should be fired, because you see them wasting your company's assets or because they worry about themselves and their salaries before the interests of the company?

This is modern capital, where big companies that build lots of large machines or provide enormous levels of service in certain industries turn their many owners into passive sheep, and the former advantage of corporate immortality can become finally corrupted into management immortality.

Now that you own the 500 shares of the common stock of a company, and don't have to worry about going to prison if the business fails, what exactly do you own, and what is it really worth, if anything?

1933: The Federal Intervention

Prior to 1933, companies were free to sell their stock to the public with little regard for precision in the format of sale, that is, the markets were often flooded with worthless stock, watered down stock, counterfeit stock, promoter's shares that had been withheld in the past, classes of common and classes of preferred. Individual lawsuits coming after financial disasters tried to clarify liability issues, but had little effect in creating an orderly market for public participation.

Whether the Stock Market Crash in October, 1929 caused the Great Depression is open to scholarly debate. Congress thought the markets had responsibility for it, and so, in 1933 Congress passed the "Truth in Securities Act" which gave a structure to how stock could be issued, what information had to be provided, when it had to be provided, and what consequences would arise if this wasn't done right. We'll cover this more in the chapter about the Securities and Exchange Commission. This is referred to as the "1933 Securities Act," or "the 1933 Act."

Kinds of Stock
Common Stock

Common stock gives you ownership according to the amount of shares you own. It usually is viewed as offering the greatest chance to participate in the growth and profits of an enterprise, because after all the bills are paid, you share in what's left. If the ship comes back and the cargo is sold for an immense profit, you can make a lot of money, because you are part owner. Your share of the profits comes to you as a dividend, and in the increased value of the company if they keep a part of the profit as a retained earning for use in other projects.

If the ship goes down, well, the most you can lose is your investment. You can't be assessed for a reverse dividend.

It's democratic, because you get to vote for management elections and on major issues facing the company at annual and special meetings. If you can't show up, you can usually vote by proxy, that is, by giving your vote by mail or through another person.

You get a certificate to show how many shares you own. Your name, or your nominee's name will be entered on the books of the corporation as an "owner." You generally can't be kicked out of your ownership by the other stockholders, except that majority shareholders can decide to sell the company even when a minority dissents. It makes sense.

You even get exceptional rights to protect your ownership interest by legal action in the courts, not just yelling and screaming, to stop bad managers from wasting assets on limos and condos, or from committing the firm's assets to one big shot at a dumb venture - but in these situations, you have to act through lawycrs, which is expensive. Institutional investors will consider this kind of extraordinary control when danger appears, but retail investors are often powerless because of their size.

The stock certificate is negotiable, that is, you can sell it. The price depends on how good the company is doing, or perceived to be doing by the buyer.

On modern certificates, if you look at the back side, you will see a printed seller's endorsement similar to certificates of title for a car. This anticipates that holders will want to sell stock, and the printed endorsement makes it easier. You can also attach an endorsement called a stock power, which does the same thing.

When you do sell to the market, donate to a charity, or give it to your child as a gift, the share gets returned to the company by the new owner so the company can issue a new certificate in the new owner's name. This procedure is handled by a transfer agent in most public companies, typically a bank that does the work for a fee. Morgan Guaranty and Chase Manhattan Bank are huge transfer agents located in New York City. The largest banks in your home state are probably transfer agents for local companies. Occasionally a company does its own transfer work to save money and make sure that its shareholders receive the best service, although the large banks do an excellent job. Another reason for in-house transfer is to keep track of who is doing what with the stock.

In the early part of the twentieth century it was not uncommon for investors to have stock that looked like it was fully paid for, but, in fact, was not. The issuing company often gave this to its promoters or organizers. They got stock that said it had a par of $10, but they paid only $1 to the company. It was a kind of bonus to these "insiders" before the age of stock options. In theory, they still owed $9 to the company for each share. At times they repaid it, sometimes not. If you bought the stock, you could get stuck for the $9. In the modern world, since the 1933 Act, if you buy stock as a member of the public on a licensed Exchange, you will not see this kind of stock, but if you dabble in foreign or obscure, pre-1933 issues you may come across a label, "assessable" meaning that the company has the right to get more money from the holder. Don't buy it unless you know what you are doing.

Shares should be fully paid and non-assessable. Most are marked just that way.

"Par," means that the company cannot issue the stock for less than the par amount. If it is $10 par, then the corporation must get at least $10 when it first issues the stock. The market price may drop later, but the company has to get the $10 when it sells the stock the first time.

It is possible, although rare, for a corporation to have several classes of common stock, but only one class will vote. If there are several classes of common stock, be very careful, and make a cautious investigation so that you know what is going on before you invest. What does the other class of common get? Does it share in all dividends? Why does it exist? Does it ever get to vote?

Most modern issues of common stock are no-par, that is, they have no set price on the company's books. When issued and first sold, they are sold for whatever the company can get for them. The capital account will not show a number tied to "par."

The company's books will also tell you how much of this common stock is legally authorized for sale, and how much has already been sold. This allows you to see if your interest could get watered down by subsequent sales of more of the same stock by the company. Look for this in the corporate charter. The charter is a public document filed in the company's home state. It is also called the "Articles of Incorporation." You can get a copy at low cost from the home state's Secretary of State.

You'll see how much is "authorized" and how much has been "issued" and remains "outstanding," that is, in the hands of owners other than the company itself. The company can hold its own shares for a number of valid purposes. This is called "treasury stock." Treasury stock has been issued, but the company bought it back. After the 1987 crash, big public companies did massive re-purchases of their own stock. It's legal.

Watch out for how the voting rights work. You might think it works like any election, but it doesn't. In political elections, you get one vote for each open office. In corporate elections, it might work that way, which is called "statutory" or it might work on the "cumulative method."

Suppose you go into a local governmental election and there are 10 offices on the ballot. You can vote once in each office election. In corporate life, that would be described as 10 statutory votes. If you have these 10 votes, why not be able to put all 10 behind one candidate, not even voting in the other races, or break it up, five for one and five for another, but nothing in the remaining races. Sounds crazy? It's serious! When cumulative voting is in place, you can vote all your shares based on the number of questions. Example: are six directors up for election? Your one hundred shares has six hundred votes, and you can put them all behind one candidate! Cumulative votes indicate management shenanigans, institutional politics, or an unwelcome outside takeover shaping up, and your influence as a retail stock buyer will be greatly reduced in a company with a lot of shares outstanding.

Market data available from a number of services can further tell you how much of the outstanding common is held by institutions and how much therefore makes up the "float," the amount that is subject to trading. Institutions tend to trade on the moment, but they also sit and wait for a long time before that right "moment." The "float" tells you how much of the stock trades, that is, how much of the stock is not "restricted" or otherwise kept off the market.

An Aside: Shark Repellent
An Editorial

In my opinion, if you see cumulative voting, expect to find a management that has circled the wagons to defend their jobs. Really good managers are in demand no matter how the economy is doing, but other ones aren't. They know it. The first act of a worried manager is to wreck a company. The second is to make himself "immortal" by loading the board with reliable pals, staggering the elections so that a few serve for several years instead of just one year, and start to have cumulative voting. Most companies don't start there, but a lot end up that way, because many shareholders don't vote at the annual elections. The management knows that, and they sneak in cumulative voting and other "management immortality" devices at these annual elections.

A company can be controlled by a small percentage of the voting common stock because people don't take enough interest in their investments. We know that voters stay away from regular political elections in droves, so it follows into corporate America. Management knows this and uses it to the maximum.

Another tip: find out how much of the common stock is owned by the company's employees; no, not just directly owned. Find out how much is owned by the employee retirement plans. The employees don't usually understand this. Here's how it works. If I am a manager and am afraid that if my company is bought I will be unemployed, I circle the wagons. I quietly get cumulative voting approved at an annual meeting while I still have control, along with a stacked board and staggered director's terms for future, annual elections. I also get the pension plans to buy a lot of the stock because I can indirectly influence those shares.

On top of that, I get the pension plans changed so the plan can buy more of the stock whenever the plan feels it "appropriate" in the open market, and I further get the company lined up so that it will provide the funds to the pension plans to buy the stock whenever I dictate. The company will borrow cash, which puts debt on its balance sheet, making it less attractive to a takeover. The cash gets put into the employee retirement plan to buy up the company's stock in the open market, thereby supporting the price of the shares, maybe driving that price up.

This has nothing to do with giving the employees a share in the fortunes of the business. The employees are told that fairy tale, and may actually believe it. In the situations publicized thus far, I have seen no litigation or objections coming from the employees to stop this imposition on their retirement funds. Consider this: the employees work at a company and invest their time and effort in a paycheck and growth of the company to keep that paycheck coming. Now they are investing in the company with their retirement benefits. If the company goes under, they lose the paycheck and the value of the stock falls to nothing. No paycheck, no retirement.

View me as the corporate maestro; let an outsider try to get me out of my job as President-for-life. I vote my own and my cronies' stock, and the employees will give me their vote from the pension stock, because I can convince them that a takeover means they will be laid off. My pals are in control of the board for the next 3 years.

If an outsider-shark says he is going to try to get control, I can buy up more stock with the company's credit and the employee's retirement funds. To get me out, you'll have to blast me out, and I am willing to wreck the company's credit and the employee's retirement to stay in! So, come and get me, because, like a cockroach, I can survive any assault. I'll have the company take on debt to raise the cash to give to the pension fund so it can buy stock with no regard for the price! I'll drive the price up, far beyond what it's worth, with the pension funds! It won't cost me a personal cent!

Banzai! I'm an emperor!

This bunker mentality is in place all through corporate America, and many investment bankers make a living telling paranoid corporate "leaders" how to do it. Find out if a company is set up like this before you invest. If it is, you have no real vote. Many of your rights as a corporate owner have been stripped away and the management no longer has to respond to shareholders. If you still want to buy the stock, be sure it's worth the increased risk of management incompetence. Buyer beware! An entrenched management can put itself first, before your interests. We'll discuss "financial royalty" later, in the chapter on the Securities and Exchange Commission, wherein William Douglas is reviewed in detail.

Preferred Stock

Preferred stock is a hybrid between a bond and common stock. Don't touch it unless you are a professional. With preferred, you get ownership interests, but you do not get to vote, except in cases where the dividend isn't paid on time for several due dates AND this feature is described in the original prospectus. You also get a dividend which is like an interest payment, but different. When preferred is issued, it might have a par value or it may not. If it is a 5% preferred, that 5% must be paid if there are profits. No profits - no payment. A bond requires payment whether there are profits or not. A bond doesn't vote. A bond holder only wants his money, on time, in the right amount.

If there is a dissolution of the company, the preferred shareholders get the par value of their shares if there are sufficient assets, but if the shares are "no par," they get paid according to the board's judgment, which means litigation will ensue and no one gets paid except lawyers.

Bond holders are paid before the preferred because bonds are debt. The real advantage of a preferred stock is if you think the company might grow while having profits, you may get paid like a bond and have growth potential like a common. The company is loathe to pay dividends to the preferred for tax reasons. If you want to cover those same bases with a bit more clarity, buy the common and buy a bond from the same company. Preferred is not as liquid as common or bonds. Stay away from preferred stock unless you study the subject and feel you understand the stock, the pitfalls and the liquidity of the issue. Stay in control as much as you can!

Then there is convertible preferred. This is a preferred that can be changed into a set number of common shares. If the price of the common goes up, the convertible preferred might seem more attractive because you could convert, get the common, sell it and make a profit. The issuer used this device because convertible preferred usually carries a lower "dividend" since it has the potential to rise with the common. The company pays a smaller dividend because the buyer thinks the conversion potential has value which makes up for the reduced dividend.

There are other kinds of preferred, but they are too obscure to be worth mention. Watch out for the effect of Shark Repellent on Preferred. You can see it coming, but you can't vote to stop it.

What is a Bond?

Bonds haven't changed much over the years.

If I borrow money, $100, from a person or a bank, I am expected to sign a paper that describes how much I owe and how I have to pay it back. The parties negotiate it between themselves so that payment might be due in one big lump sum at the end (maybe $110 for a 1 year loan at 10% simple interest), or in equal payments during the course of the term. The term is the lifetime of the note, and it can be 1 year, 10 years or anything negotiated; it can be days, weeks or months. The actual paper this is written on is called a note. The paper should have all the relevant terms on it, telling who owes how much to whom and when it has to be paid.

That note, the actual piece of paper, has value.

If I have borrowed from you, you might take that paper and try to sell it to get immediate cash before I have to pay you under the terms of the note. The person or company you try to sell it to will probably pay a little less than the face value of the note, because they want to make a profit. If they have reason to think there may be any difficulty in getting me to pay, they might pay a lot less: a steep "discount." If the note was for $100, and your prospective buyer isn't thrilled about my credit rating, but is willing to take a risk, then the buyer might offer to pay you only $75. You might not like this, but if your need for cash is critical, you may have no choice, because that buyer may be the only one you can find in time. This happens to junk bonds.

You might have lent me the $100 when I was in good shape, but now, with my business down, it looks like I can't pay on time - same problem. If you go to sell the note, you won't get $100 for it.

If I don't pay, you can't have me sold into slavery. If I really meant to pay the note when I made the deal, and if I didn't lie to you about my assets at the time (if you remembered to ask me) you can't have me arrested for fraud, either. You can sue me, but if I have no money, you can't collect. If I have a little, but not enough money, I can go into Bankruptcy and you may get a few cents on the dollar.

A wise lender will ask for security. If the note is not paid on time, the security can be sold to pay the amount due. The security should be examined and accepted only if it has value. A pawn shop works on this theory. If I own a working color T.V., and want to borrow 10 dollars, I take the set into the pawnshop. I get my $10 "loan" because the shop owner believes that even if I do not pay the loan back in the 30 days we agreed on, he can probably sell the T.V. for more than the $10. He doesn't care about my credit rating - he is secured to the absolute maximum because he anticipates selling the security.

If you own a house, you probably used a mortgage to buy it. This is a note and a pledge of the real estate as security. Cars and boats are common purchases made by note and a pledge of the item as security. If you don't pay, the holder of the note can go against the security. Notice I didn't say the "lender" because the original lender may have already sold the note to a new "holder." The ability to sell a note to a new "holder" makes it a negotiable instrument, a certificate that can be used for value in commerce. Everyone has made an unsecured loan: a friend needs $5 to buy lunch. He doesn't have it, so you "lend" it to him. He will pay it back after he has a chance to go to the bank and get cash at lunchtime. You trust him. It is unsecured and not even in writing. Is it a risk? It's only $5.

How about $1,000? How about lending him $10,000? Now the element of risk comes in. Before you would lend a lot of money you would probably start acting like - a bank! You would check out his credit, ask for security, even ask that a person sign the note in addition to him so there would be another party, a co-signor with assets, who would pay in the event your friend could not. You would be very careful, using the "belt and suspenders" approach, because, just as we have all been short term lenders to friends for a few dollars, we have all had friends forget to repay us.

Corporate Bonds; Other Species

If a corporation needs money for a project, it can raise funds by going to a bank for a loan, by issuing and selling stock to select, sophisticated individuals, or the public, or it can issue and try to sell bonds.

These bonds are the same as your note when you bought your house, or when you bought a car on credit. It is a promise to pay a certain amount to the holder of the paper at a certain time. Corporate bonds issued to the public are not individually negotiated - they are put together as a package. As an investor, if you don't like the package, don't buy the bond. You have no chance to negotiate on the terms of the note, only on the price you feel willing to pay.

The incidentals, such as amount and terms of payment are set out at length, yes, in small print, because a corporate bond issue may seek to raise millions of dollars, and will exist as serious debt for a long time. The bond does not offer ownership, only set payment. A bond holder does not vote on corporate matters. If the corporation doesn't pay on time, well, go back to the example of what happens when I don't pay the money I owe you on the $100 note: no one goes into slavery, jail or any place bad. Lawsuits are a possibility, as is bankruptcy. YOU MAY NOT GET REPAID.

These days corporations seek bankruptcy protection with shocking regularity, even as a tool to deal with unions. Bankruptcy can be complete and terminal. The company does not survive; its business is wound up, bills paid, and whatever is left is paid out to the shareholders. I have a special chapter on brokerage bankruptcy, later.

Filing for bankruptcy is easy. Put the forms together, file them in the local United States Bankruptcy Court, and you are "in," probably under Chapter 11, seeking reorganization. Chapter 7 is for final dissolution. A company can file under Chapter 11, then go into Chapter 7, or it can file under Chapter 11, change its business around, and come out, alive.

Bankruptcy can be structural, that is, the company survives, but comes out looking different; your 10 year bond at 10% may now be a 20 year bond at 6%, courtesy of the US Bankruptcy Court.

A big-time corporate bond is just like a note from any other debtor, and should be treated as such. Look for a reliable debtor, with hard, reachable security, and maybe a co-signor.

Very short term corporate debt (less that 270 days) that is unsecured is known as "commercial paper." This is used by financial companies to get funds for day to day use.

Most corporate bonds are long term, and are issued with an "indenture," which is the agreement that covers what happens if the bond is not paid on time. They are usually sold in certificates of $1,000 minimum denomination, and are registered in the name of an owner. The issuer sends a regular interest payment to the owner. A bank is usually a trustee under the indenture, and is supposed to watch for timely payments and maintenance of promised reserves, if any. Long term bonds are part of the company's capitalization, and appear that way on the balance sheet.

Bonds can be sold, and it is important to get the new owner properly on the books to have the interest payments remain current.

Certain bonds are sold with coupons attached. Ever hear of wealthy people spending the day clipping coupons? This refers to the practice of sitting with bonds and literally clipping off coupons which have a dollar value per time period. The specific coupon is presented to an accepting bank or brokerage house; the bank or broker gets the money from the issuer and gives it to the presenter. Service-oriented banks and brokers will clip them for you if you let them hold the bonds. A few will pay in advance because the redemption takes only a few days. But, if you lose the coupon, watch out. It's like losing money. Can it be recovered? Yes, but at a cost, because the issuer has to be protected against anyone else turning it in and demanding payment. "Bearer" bonds have the same problem. If you lose it, you may get a new one if you provide an insurance policy to protect the issuer against a claim by another holder that they are the rightful owner. This insurance policy is also called a "bond," but it is an entirely different usage of the same word. It can be quite expensive. Don't lose a coupon or a bearer bond. Lock them up as securely as possible! It could cost you $400 to buy an insurance "bond" on a lost $10,000 corporate bond.

If a bond is not registered in your name, it is probably "bearer." This was a very common form for municipal bonds, and yes, a standard of the money laundering business is to use "bearer" bonds. For tax reasons, they are disappearing. New ones cannot be issued by municipalities, and corporations have to issue 1099 forms to record bondholder income for the IRS. If a bank or brokerage house holds your bonds in their name, they will issue the 1099 Form.

If you buy a bond for $1,000 that pays 9% per year the day it comes out, the value of the bond can drop if interest rates change. Let's say rates go to 10%. Your bond only pays 9%. If you want to sell it, no one will pay you $1,000. If rates go to 8%, your bond is worth more than $1,000 because it pays more than the prevailing rates. There are bonds that pay varying rates of interest, usually tied to the rate of one of the US Treasury issues. If rates change, then the value of a bond will change. Rates change all the time. You CAN lose money on bonds.

Junk
More Junk

Bonds represent risk.

Know what you are buying! Sophisticated issuers pay to be rated by Standard and Poor's or Moody's. These services analyze the corporate balance sheet, and give a letter rating to describe the financial condition of the company. This is the "triple A" you have heard of, or the BBB, BB, etc. It helps the company raise capital. States pay to be rated, too.

This rating tells the likelihood that the company will be able to pay the bond interest or "maintenance" when due, and the principal when the bond matures. The best companies are rated "AAA" and they pay the lowest interest because they are the most reliable borrowers. Move down many ratings, to "C" and an issuer will have to pay higher interest on its bonds because it might not pay back at all! Would you buy this kind of debt? It's called a "junk bond", or a "high yield" bond by the promoters that sell them. Any book on bonds will explain the way S&P rates. Do you own bonds right now? Do you know the rating? If you don't know the rating, you shouldn't own the bond.

If you buy a bond, make it "investment grade," that is, make sure the rating is not lower than S&P BBB, which is four ratings down from AAA. You can buy a bond that is A rated one day and find it C in a short while because the company is in trouble. A "C" rated bond is junk. It will not sell at par; it sells at a discount. Its liquidity may be severely impaired by changes in the bond market.

Put another way, if you were solicited to buy "junk," would you? A lot of people did. Don't feel lonely. A lot of institutions did, too. The US Government, courtesy of the Savings and Loan debacle is the largest holder of junk bonds. If they start selling, watch out!

The current yield on a bond is calculated by taking the interest paid per annum and dividing it by the present market price of the bond. Don't be fooled by brokers that tell you to buy only yield in a bond and fail to mention quality. Junk bonds can offer great yield, but have little quality. US Government bonds have the highest quality, but they have less of a yield than more risky bonds.

<u>Another very important item</u>: the yield on short term debt will fluctuate more than the yield on longer term debt when the market moves, but the price on long term debt will fluctuate more than the price of the short term debt.

There is more risk as time goes further out because the bond will exist longer. In simpler terms, drop a rock from your hand into a pool of water: it makes a little splash. Drop the same rock from the top of a tree, it makes a bigger splash. Same rock. The drop from the tree is like the drop over time of a long term bond. The price of long term debt can fluctuate wildly, seriously. Many professional investors will not go out beyond a 7 year bond life because the yield curve traditionally flattens out at 7 years. The Japanese watch the time duration of bond investments very closely, and they demand higher yields the further out they go. If they can't get the higher yield, they won't go.

You can get seriously hurt investing in bonds or in mutual funds that invest in bonds. They are not like money sitting in a savings account that draws interest until you take it out. Bonds exist for a set time. That time existence affects their value every time rates change.

Incidentally, the debt market dwarfs the stock market in dollar value when US Government debt trading is included. The US Government is the largest debtor with the most frequent turnover of notes.

Instruments issued by the US Treasury are the safest investment you can get, because they usually cannot be called back prematurely, and, if you hold the paper until it matures, you have the word of the US Government that you will be paid back in full. Investors are willing to buy these debt instruments from the US Treasury at a higher price than they are willing to pay for IBM's debt, because as good as IBM's reputation is, the US Treasury's is better. The US Treasury has a public auction almost every Monday for its short term debt, and schedules separate auctions for longer term paper. There is a network of 44 Primary Dealers. You can buy direct from the US Treasury at the auctions by making a written bid through the Treasury Direct Program administered by your own, local Federal Reserve Bank.

The United States is divided into different districts under the jurisdiction of a local Federal Reserve Bank, where you can bid with the big guys and buy as the debt is issued. For specific information about the program call your local Federal Reserve Bank, listed in the US Government section of the Yellow Pages, but you can also call the Richmond Federal Reserve, tel. (804) 697-8372. They have a book for sale that tells the whole story, including how to set up an account with the Fed; ask for their free brochure.

The Fed will carry an account for you, send you statements, and send you reminders of maturity dates and interest payments. It's great. They don't charge a cent for the service. They won't disappear!

Federal Debt

Treasury bills are short term. They are notes from the US Government that mature in one year or less, and are sold at a discount, that is, you get $100 in six months when the particular T-Bill matures, but you only paid $96 for it. You made $4 interest. If you hold one at the Fed, you can't trade it until you move the position to a brokerage house, which is not difficult. If you buy it through a broker you can trade it. Trading T-bills is heavy duty action because most individuals buy to hold to maturity. Institutions trade this debt all the time, taking even small profits in hopes of an aggregate home run after a lot of trades. T-bills come in minimum denominations, $10,000, with $5,000 increments up. They are traded in the Over The Counter Market, and are quoted according to yield, not price. If you want to buy one in the open market, you state the yield you will accept, which is then translated into price. The broker will charge you a commission.

Treasury Notes have maturities of 2 to 10 years. If under 4 years in duration, the Notes will be issued in $5,000 minimums with $5,000 increments. Above 4 years in duration, Notes will have $1,000 minimums and $1,000 increments. Notes trade by quote based on a percentage of their face value, in increments of 1/32.

Treasury Bonds are debt with a term over ten years to as long as thirty years. A few are callable a little before their face maturity. Watch out for these. Regular T-bonds are not callable. All Treasuries are now book entry, issued in $1,000 minimums with $1,000 increments.

Liquidation Priority

If a company goes out of business, it liquidates. This can follow success or failure. Failure is obviously time to cut up the remains and hand them out. Special companies formed for just one purpose, such as a treasure hunt for a specific wreck, are good candidates for profitable liquidation. The Government gets paid first for taxes.

Government is always first, and they have a 100% right to payment of their full amount. Senior Bond Holders with their security go next, then unsecured priority debt owners, then any subordinated debt holders get paid. Next come the preferred share holders, and finally the common stock holders. That's it.

The Common gets anything left over, which can be a lot, or nothing. The US Government has the best position; it survives a bankruptcy! Notice the classes of debt: some have priority and some are subordinated. Know which one you have before you buy it. Don't guess at it - know! The way you find out is to read the indenture for the bond or the prospectus for the preferred.

How do you get a copy of the indenture or the prospectus? From your broker. Make him work. Tell him to get you documents before you invest so you can make an informed investment decision. If you cannot read and understand the prospectus, don't buy the security, no matter what it is!

Plain English
Knowledge is power

Are you getting used to the interchangability of words such as "debt," "paper," "bonds, "notes?" Part of the residue of knowledge this book will impart is language, "Street" lingo, so that you get the gist of what your broker is saying, and the confidence to tell him to stop, and speak in plain English when you do not understand. That's right: when you don't understand what the broker is saying, tell him to explain the story again, IN PLAIN ENGLISH!

I do it. I have not encountered anyone with my licenses and law background anywhere in the securities business, and I see new terms pop up all the time.

When I talk finance with professionals, discussions range all over the lot. If a new term is used, I ask for an explanation of "who, what, when and where," all the detail I can get. The best way to learn: LISTEN! I cannot emphasize education and self study enough, but one of the best sources of information, with the least effort and best response, is to ask questions. Don't hold back. I've learned to respect men and women who are so confident in their abilities and experience that they don't hesitate to ask: "why?"

Ignorance of a specialized activity is nothing to be embarrassed about; we are all ignorant of mountains of information about life, science and philosophy. Learn! Listen! Most of all, ask questions and find answers, rejecting hot air while remaining cautious and determined.

Knowledge is power! A wise man recognizes and remedies his ignorance before placing himself at risk. A fool revels in his ignorance, displaying it proudly and continuously. The old saying is true, "A fool and his money are soon parted."

In my opinion, the retail brokerage business is a firm believer in that powerful little maxim, trusting that most investors are too lazy to think, to ask, to research, and be anything other than a collection of sheep in search of a ram. Relying on the allure of their seductive, empty promises, for each investor who wakes up and walks out the door, the industry has always believed another was just a cold call away. The theory is that retail investors are so greedy, they can't resist. That's you, the retail target. It is a poor image.

In the following material, we'll explore more detail about stock and bonds. It pays to get a little grounded in history, then in the fundamental makeup of securities, and next, a discussion of what an exchange is. Our goal is to be comfortable with the function and concept of investing in order to control it. It's not magical. If firms are all selling the same products, or essentially the same products, you can go to the one that offers the best combination of service and price, giving thought to both factors. The lowest price may not offer the best service.

Reject the sound, color and lingering image of commercials as the pre-meditated intrusions on your logic they are intended to be. Marketing people don't have to know the target product cold. They can still sell it! They can take the reality of a brokerage firm and create a synthetic theme of compelling fantasy. Investors at first don't want to believe they have been wronged, then they get angry, then embarrassed at having been fooled when they are confronted with all the statements and confirmations sent to them about all THEIR activity. We'll explore that in more depth.

It's "just business" to the Street. Keep it business. The broker is not your friend when it comes to handling your money. He's a professional, trained and capable of valuable service or devastating harm. Let me remind you that certain professions take an oath of service, of fidelity in their actions and dedication in their responsibility.

Stockbrokers take no such oath.

Key Definitions: Office Fundamentals

Author's note: after each of the first eight chapters, I have set out definitions, small glossaries, of key terms. There are fifty definitions, all included in Appendix D. My purpose: a few definitions at a time are easier to use than a long list. I want to help you be as comfortable as possible with later text where these terms are developed at length.

i. Churning occurs where a broker takes control of an account, acting on either written discretion or unwritten discretion, or by so dominating the customer relationship that trading occurs of such a frequency and for no apparent legitimate reason other than to generate commissions for the broker. The account does not have to have any losses. Churning is often marked by marginally profitable trades.

ii. A Self Regulatory Organization, SRO, is a body licensed under the 1934 Exchange Act through the Securities and Exchange Commission. It has powers to license, investigate and discipline its own member firms and employees of those firms. There are many SRO's. A brokerage house may be subject to the jurisdiction of several SRO's at one time because it does business under each, such as the American Stock Exchange, The New York Stock Exchange (NYSE), the National Association of Securities Dealers (NASD), and others.

iii. A Stockbroker is an individual who works for a licensed Broker-Dealer. The stockbroker, no matter what the firm calls him, is a Registered Representative. He must be licensed by each state he does business in, by the NASD and, if he works for an NYSE firm, he must be licensed by the New York Stock Exchange.

iv. A Branch Manager is the local supervisor of a stockbroker in a branch office of a brokerage house. The Branch Manager must have special licenses from the NASD and the NYSE if an NYSE member firm. He is responsible for watching what the stockbroker is doing, for approving new accounts of all kinds and for receiving customer complaints. He recruits from other firms. He trains new brokers in his office.

v. A Regional Manager works in a larger brokerage house and has control over several branch offices. He watches to see what the branch managers are doing. He also recruits stockbrokers from other firms, and deals with the big producers in his region on special issues, following their production closely.

vi. A Cash Account is a securities account where no credit is used. If a security is bought, the money must be in the account or deposited within five days of the trade. The securities must be segregated by the brokerage house and may not be used by the house as security against bank loans to the house.

vii. A Margin Account involves the use of credit. The amount of credit available is determined by rules promulgated by the Federal Reserve. It can vary. When an account is on margin, the customer uses leverage which involves a higher degree of risk and sophistication. If the account is on margin, it must pay interest each month.

viii. An Options Account is used where a sophisticated customer elects to use options as part of an investment strategy that is suitable for high risk. Options are not suitable for most investors. All option customers must get a 73-page brochure from the Options Clearing Corporation that discloses the risks involved in this trading, Characteristics and Risks of Standardized Options. Options accounts must be approved by the branch manager and, at an NYSE firm, by the firm's Compliance Registered Options Principal or Senior Registered Options Principal.

ix. A Market Order is an order to buy or sell at the prevailing price available in the market. There is no limit on the execution price, except that it must be the prevailing price at that time.

x. A Limit Order is issued to buy or sell a security at a specific price or better price. If an order to "Buy 100 shares at 100, Limit" is given, the shares can be bought for 99, but not for 100 1/8. A sale order works in the reverse. "Sell at 100, Limit" means the sale could go off at 101, but not at 99 7/8.

Please - Take a fast look at Appendix D.

CHAPTER TWO

You Need an Exchange: Liquidity

If you own a stock or a bond, there will probably be a time when you think about selling it. The alternative is to hold a stock forever, or, in the case of a bond, until it matures. Why do that? After all, wasn't the idea of liquidity, the ability to raise cash at any time, one of the reasons that you considered investing in stock? You need a place to buy "it" and then sell "it" - you need an exchange.

Liquidity

If you want to buy a house, take a vacation, pay tuition or a hospital bill, your investments represent value that should be liquid enough to turn into cash or a cash equivalent. If they are not liquid, then it should result from a situation where you understood that possibility when you made the investment, but decided to do it because the investment was worth it.

If the investment was not liquid when you bought it, the price should have gone in your favor just because of that. Price depends on many things, but one of the key considerations is liquidity. It is more important than inherent value; for example, what good is 1000 shares of IBM stock if you cannot sell it and you have a tuition or hospital bill to pay? If it is not liquid, it has no value, no matter what anyone tells you, unless you have sentimental attachment. What good is owning paper that was supposed to be an investment, but can't be sold? If it has value, then an investor or speculator will buy it, at a bargained price. That price may be depressed because the potential buyer will take advantage of your need to sell. Think of the times you have heard of a death or divorce forcing the sale of a house - the price suffers, but the house is still liquid even if at a lower price.

Never buy an investment unless you can turn around and sell it.

Repeat - never, never, never, never, never buy unless you absolutely, positively understand that you might be locking up your cash with no way out. Always ask about liquidity, and be sure you can get out. A lot of brokers will slide that by you when they show an investment, usually indicating that the opportunity is so marvelous that the "lock" on your cash, the lack of liquidity, doesn't matter because the investment will be so great, how can you lose, why would you ever want to sell it, and then come the magic words, "so, trust me!"

The irony of the situation: if you buy an illiquid investment in a company, it will usually take the form of a note. You will be lending your money to the company. The company promises to pay you back.

The investment will be a special note, and it will say the note doesn't have to be repaid by the company for a while, unless there are earnings - and those aren't guaranteed. It won't be co-signed by any of the corporate officers, it certainly won't be co-signed by your broker, and it may say that it is not transferrable to anyone for a period of time. It is not a freely negotiable instrument any longer.

Remember, the terms of the note are paramount; they set the rules for the transaction.

Yet, the day after you invest, the owners could sell the entire company. The officers probably own most of the company stock, so they might profit on such a sale.

You might be "locked," by the terms of the note, yet the company could be very, very liquid - with your money! Worse - it might all be set out in the proverbial small print on the investment, right on the prospectus, indenture or note itself.

When you complain, the lawyer for the brokerage house will routinely say you signed a receipt declaring you read and understood all the small print, so it's tough! He'll even send you a copy of the page you signed under the anti-transfer language, which might make you feel pretty low; then you'll be upset because you are staring at a real, live tuition bill that can't be held off, and you can't raise the cash.

Exchange prices may have many origins. Remember the Shark Repellent we discussed earlier? Suppose you watch the price of a stock and see it go up. It attracts you by its action alone. Movement in the animal kingdom draws attention, and it carries over to Wall Street. How do you know if the movement is due to the profitability of the company, or to company managers playing with the employee pension funds to make the price go up before the annual meeting so they can look good to the shareholders? Shark Repellents hurt liquidity because they make the stock less attractive to informed investors and potential control groups. Their reason: why buy the stock if unattractive management is entrenched? Shark Repellent can hurt your investment while it makes entrenched management happily secure.

Pay very close attention to the chapter on Direct Investments, and avoid being locked into the wrong investment.

Having viewed a bit of history, you might guess that there have always been exchanges, because people are always buying and selling. Exchanges for special products like rugs, crops, horses, farm animals, etc. have existed side by side with other markets from the dawn of time. There is nothing sacred or supernatural about them.

Don't treat them with respect unless they merit your praise, and that can't happen unless you understand how the market works. The various securities exchanges are made of a membership that controls the trading of approved shares in a physical location.

What is a Market?

A market is a place frequented by sellers and buyers for the purpose of exchanging value for an item of different value.

Imagine a flea market that specializes in New England antiques. On the appropriate Saturday, participants arrive with their inventory, pay their exhibitor fee, agree to abide by the rules of that flea market, and they are off to set up shop. The flea market maintains order in the facility, people transact business with the dealers throughout the day, and, at the appointed hour, the market closes. If an exhibitor was cheating people, he'd be thrown out, and if he had arrived with phony or stolen items for sale, he would have been denied admission. Most buyers offer money, although they might offer to trade items of their own as a "swap." Each side offers value to the other. If accepted, a deal is struck, then executed right there with a cash or swap transaction.

Think of auctions: the price is closely monitored by interested observers. If you are in the audience and think an offering is a bargain, you'll set a mental price limit and make bids. Other bidders may offer more. Auctions run until the bid on an item gets so high no one bids more, then the auctioneer closes the deal with a bang of the gavel and a cash transaction follows. Everyone has a chance at the bid.

Fabled Asian bazaars show the function of a market as a place to buy and sell with no set price. The price reflects the complete environment, that is, quality, scarcity, currency value, desire, utility, need, etc.; the identical item may have different prices within minutes, or from seller to seller, perhaps at drastic increases or decreases, because of skilled negotiation, ignorance, or need for cash. What would you do if you found yourself in this Asian Bazaar, with strange people, mystifying language and foreign products? You'd be wisely cautious, probably not buying at all, until you felt a bit of control. If you had time, you might listen, learn how it worked and then try small purchases for fun; but, sober caution would rule the day. You'd expect to be a target for a shoddy product or hyped sale.

The New York Stock Exchange

Let's explore the New York Stock Exchange. You know the 1792 story from the prior chapter. It is a physical place in lower Manhattan, located at the corner of Broad and Wall Streets. It "lists" world-class securities in that physical location, and has restricted membership, restricted access and historical momentum.

The New York Stock Exchange has been the subject of numerous books, television shows, government inquiries and its own publicity. Lots of the latter. The publicity image of the NYSE is familiar: men wearing little jackets scurrying about under and around racks of video tubes and computers, writing on scraps of paper, waving their arms, and generally acting like bees in a larger than life hive. Then a person stands on a balcony and rings a bell. The market closes and the scene quiets down. The NYSE claims it works for the betterment of society by providing liquidity for investments.

What do you think? Is it part of a government? If so, which government - Federal, New York State or New York City?

Does it have a license? From whom? Do you have any idea of its Rules, who its senior officials are, or what its finances are? Does it make a profit, and if so, how? Why are certain stocks listed on the NYSE and others listed elsewhere?

Do you believe the New York Stock Exchange has an influence on you? How much? Who let that happen?

Unless you have been involved in the operational side of the securities industry, it is almost impossible to be familiar with how the NYSE works. Individuals are correctly impressed by the name, "New York Stock Exchange," because we hear media people sound serious when they mention it, and Presidents, Members of Congress, and Governors of the Federal Reserve sound equally serious when they discuss the New York Stock Exchange. They must all know what the NYSE is about - right? No.

The New York Stock Exchange is not a part of any government. It is a non-profit corporation. That's right, it is not intended to make a profit.

It has officers that are elected by its 1366 members. Non-profit corporations are all around us: universities, churches, temples, little leagues, professional and fraternal societies. Importantly, a non-profit corporation offers limited liability to its members and officers, and it offers the other asset of corporate form - virtually eternal life for the entity. Non-profit corporations are supposed to serve the public good; that's you.

The NYSE has a license from the Securities and Exchange Commission under the 1934 Exchange Act to function as a place where public securities transactions can occur. The 1934 Act was the companion to the 1933 statute we looked at earlier. The 1933 Act defined securities and how they could be created if intended for public sale. The 1934 Act dealt with how they could be traded and handled after they got to the public.

You probably have a driver's license issued by the motor vehicle department of your state, and perhaps other licenses. Ham radio operators have licenses, so do electricians, plumbers, airline pilots, lawyers, doctors, and private detectives. There is no monopoly in any of those licensed activities, merely qualification standards. Each licensee performs the activity for a profit or personal desire.

The New York Stock Exchange, under its formal license, has responsibilities to establish and maintain an honest market, to make sure that prices are available for both sides, buy and sell, and that accurate information is available to the public about what goes on with those buys and sells. Theoretically, if it did not do its job, the NYSE would lose its license as a Securities Exchange, and close, leaving a lot of people who work there without jobs. By the way, NYSE employees are well paid, far above Federal Government rates, have almost assured tenure in their jobs, and enjoy a great retirement plan. The NYSE doesn't operate at a profit, so who promotes it as necessary? The

Exchange would say that everybody benefits, therefore everybody promotes it. Cicero would enjoy the pure rhetoric of that statement.

Don't worry about NYSE employees losing their jobs. When the securities industry staggers under a bear market and has massive layoffs, NYSE employees still get their yearly bonus. It has plenty of long term employees who are bureaucratic experts in their respective areas, in fact, many of the best financial experts in raising capital work for the Exchange.

The Securities and Exchange Commission makes sure the NYSE is doing its job. To a small extent, the US Congress occasionally probes by asking Exchange people to offer testimony on market activity, but the general presumption is that the SEC is on the job, and that the NYSE is part of the team. We'll discuss that misplaced confidence later.

All NYSE Members are human beings, not corporations. When you hear that Merrill Lynch is a Member of the NYSE, that's incorrect. It is a Member Firm, but not a Member. One of its employees is the titled owner of a "seat" or Membership and holds the seat as an individual. Merrill Lynch paid for it and the employee probably signed an "ABC" agreement, a contract stating that the employee acknowledges Merrill paid for the seat and that Merrill has the right to cause the transfer of the seat to another person. The employee cannot sell it. He must sign transfer papers when asked by Merrill. It's an important ritual restraining the transfer of the seat by contract.

Merrill can control numerous seats, as many as it wants to "buy." For all its size, it doesn't need more than a few; there is no requirement that a Member Firm needs "x" number of seats per number of brokers in its employ.

Charmingly, Members still have a gratuity fund, a kind of self-insurance policy that goes way back to times when insurance was not readily available. If you are a Member and die, your estate gets $100,000 from the fund. If you are over 60 years old and have priced renewable term insurance, you know the cash value of that benefit.

Under IRS Rules, an employee can only get $50,000 tax free life insurance benefit from an employer. If there is more coverage, the market value of the coverage is taxable to the employee if provided free by the employer. The Members pay dues to the NYSE each year. The gratuity fund is a separate assessment. Member Firms usually pay for the employee-Member's assessment. There is a private dining room (though not ostentatious) for "Members only" in the 11 Wall Street building and the trading floor is accessible only to Members and their designated employees and other specific personnel necessary for the trading function. It looks like a big gymnasium set up for a computer convention.

There are Members who trade only for their own account on the floor: there are no commissions for them. Other Members work for firms and trade for the benefit of public customers, ranging from human beings to gigantic institutions.

Since there are a limited number of "seats" or Memberships, 1366, the number of Member Firms is not all that great. Consider the number of auto dealers in the U.S. - many thousands. Think of the number of colleges throughout the US - thousands. There are 535 Members of the United States Congress, with 435 Members in the House of Representatives and 100 in the Senate. The number of Member Firms of the NYSE, while it varies, is approximately 550. It depends on the market, Bull or Bear.

Member Firms go out of business all the time. Partnerships used to be the norm until the 1960's, but now are like dinosaurs because of personal liability considerations. Today, Member Firms are usually corporations, a few publicly held and others closely held, but there is nothing immortal about any of them. Although many Member Firms hire analysts to critically review the management of public companies, Member Firms won't directly, negatively comment on each other, even though a few of the big ones are publicly held companies, and thus, should be the target of hard scrutiny. When they go under, these masters of investment analysis usually fail because of a lack of investment acumen. Poor management on Wall Street is fair game to the press, but not to research departments of other Member Firms. The New York Times devoted pages to the demise of EF Hutton, dissecting all the financial and management problems in detail. Hutton's stock was listed on the New York Stock Exchange, so it was fair game for analysis, yet the Street was silent, perhaps because they would be holding themselves up to the same mirror, displaying their own faults.

While the NYSE claims existence from 1792, how many Member Firms do? There have always been Members of the Exchange, but the Member Firms come and go. They merge and "die" outright. Others unwind as their promoters go separate ways. The New York Stock Exchange, however, goes on.

Being a Member or a Member Firm offers a special advantage, the right to go to the floor direct to execute trades in listed stocks and bonds. If you are a securities broker, but not a Member Firm or Member, then all executions for listed securities must go through a Member, then to the floor or the floor based computer.

If not on the "in," that non-Member is "out."

Exclusive membership is a matter of idle interest when discussing a country or luncheon club, but it is of the highest economic importance when considering daily, massive economic discrimination tantamount to monopoly. A market for necessary items, enjoying a government license, with limitations on membership has a control over your financial well-being. Monopoly control. When a security is listed on the NYSE, Member Firms cannot actively buy and sell the stock except on the floor of the NYSE. They can go overseas to do it, but the NYSE controls the US market. Member Firms must use the Exchange's specialist system, antiquated as it is. Many stocks trade on the NYSE and regional exchanges, but the only place to get volume is the NYSE where the big specialists work and where the institutions trade.

Most of the Exchange's employees do not work on the trading floor. They work in the back room in numerous departments offering direct support to the floor or in the investigative, enforcement, arbitration, marketing, and even the bureaucratic secretariat of the NYSE, itself. There are people who give tests, examine Member Firms and their offices, and there are computer programmers who anticipate future support demands. A few employees are tour guides for the excellent public display that enters on the 20 Broad Street side of the complex. The tour of the NYSE is free. It's first class marketing that leaves you with a good feeling, while telling you nothing about the real workings of the organization. If you are in the New York City area, take this book along and go for the tour. After that, go up to 4 World Trade Center, about 6 blocks up on the West side and take a look at a real live commodity exchange, the Comex.

IBM Common Stock is traded on the floor of the NYSE in what is called a double auction method, that is, buyers and sellers put up their bid and asked prices for all to see and are matched by price. A commodity pit works on the open outcry method where a seller or buyer is one of many traders standing around each other and talking directly, even over several yards distance with hand signals, with anyone who will sell or buy from them. The sales are direct. There is no specialist to get in the way or create an "orderly" market. It looks different, works faster, and sounds more like a "market."

You can rent a seat from an NYSE Member. If you are interested in the price of a seat or the cost of a rental call the NYSE and ask for Membership Seat prices. The prices are not set. They are dictated by supply and demand like any other item in commerce. Rentals are handled there, and are subject to the same price influences. A seat can cost hundreds of thousands of dollars, even a million, and a rental price will typically compare with the return on a bond. If a seat costs $500,000 and the prime rate is about 10 % you might expect a seat rental to be approximately $50,000 per year with wide swings from day to day. In 1987, before the crash, seats sold for over 1 million dollars. In 1990, you could get one for about 390 thousand dollars.

Have you heard of the expression, "the price of a seat on the New York Stock Exchange?" This refers to the transferability of a seat. If you own a Membership, you can sell it or rent it to people who are approved by other Members. That means most of the general public is not eligible to buy a seat because they would never get approved. They don't know enough about finance or the mechanics of the NYSE. After this book, I would never be allowed in as a Member.

This raises intriguing questions: does this sound like a non-profit corporation? Can you imagine buying, selling and renting profit-making "seats" in the American Legion, a not-for-profit hospital, or your town library? Why not? They're non-profit corporations, too.

Another: if you live in Dallas, Atlanta, L.A. or Seattle, why send your financial business to New York City?

A third: if any wire house stockbroker can send business to the floor of the NYSE from anywhere in the country on electronic lines, why bother to buy a seat whose value fluctuates?

Because, for all the talk about the NYSE being open and fair, the electronically responsive center of finance, it's not. It never has been. It's a false rumor, a snippet of public relations aroma, fleeting as a phantom. It's a closed, membership market.

Members buy seats to make a profit, even though the NYSE is a non-profit corporation. Traders on the floor have a distinct advantage in seeing what is taking shape as it happens over the public who must settle for reports of what has already happened. The Members' profit comes from riding the wave of public investment, charging a commission for entry and exit from investments, and trading on forming currents before the public can see them. Not only is it legal, it is affirmatively licensed by the SEC!

Time has become more and more important, not in terms of days, but in minutes. The use of computers has allowed the development of program trading to move from the theoretical into the reliable execution phase.

There are other, licensed exchanges sprinkled around the United States, but they collectively do not have near the impact of the NYSE. The Midwest Stock Exchange is in Chicago, the Pacific is in San Francisco, the Boston, Philadelphia, and Cincinnati Exchanges are in those respective cities. Those membership "seats" cost a fraction of NYSE Membership. And, don't forget the American Stock Exchange which is located behind Trinity Church, off Wall Street. The Amex is second in importance to the NYSE, but the disparity is on the widest possible scale. NYSE Members look down at the Amex, and a lot of media doesn't bother with coverage. In New York City, the NYSE reigns supreme, with no competition for business trading the "listed" securities. The Statistics Chapter explains how big the NYSE is in dollar terms, compared to the other exchanges.

There are over 110 exchanges throughout the world, all of them connected through information data banks so that trading is going on all the time, every minute of every day, and men and women trained in the same methods and traditions are in charge, no matter the country. There are but a few giants. The NYSE is one. The biggest exchange is in downtown Tokyo.

Let's Get Technical
Who Makes the Floor Work

House brokers work for their employer Member Firms. They are on the floor executing trades for the benefit of public customers of the Member Firm. This broker is on salary and a bonus based on performance. He doesn't trade for himself.

Two Dollar brokers are also on the floor. They do not handle orders for the public, only for other brokers. They get paid per transaction by their broker customers. There are times where the House brokers cannot cover all the trades on their books, or they have technical reasons to go to the Two Dollar brokers because of conflicts in executions for pension and other fiduciary accounts.

Specialists are usually Members. They have their own accounts and risk their own money. To get the position, they apply to the NYSE and get approved based on financial ability and market experience. Specialists are usually small firms, not individuals. A specialist covers one or more stocks and must stand ready to buy or sell the stock at any time, and, indeed, must be ready to buy even if the market is declining and sane investors would refuse to buy. He doesn't have to buy much of the stock he covers, just an occasional 100 shares. The specialist exists to keep an orderly market in the stock under his watch, but don't imagine he is supposed to support a falling price! He is supposed to help liquidity, not support falling prices or slow down any runaways going up. These are very, very professional people, risking their own funds to take on a dangerous job. Why?

If the specialist can average a few cents profit on every trade in the stock he covers for a day, he can make a lot of money. No one knows the action in a stock better than its specialist, who is not there as a matter of public benevolence. The specialist is after a profit, and makes it by taking in stock from House and Two Dollar brokers, then selling it back to other House and Two Dollar brokers at a slightly better price. The specialist is a middleman, adding no inherent value, only liquidity.

He works at a set place - a "post" during official Exchange hours, and he keeps a "book" which is a list of orders to buy and sell that displays the price liquidity of a listed security. The specialist knows what the last sale price is, and knows how many shares are bunched up, at what price, all the way up and down the buy/sell line. This information is also displayed on a screen at the post, but the specialist works just that post while the various brokers drift around. The data avalanche is everywhere, in such abundance that it obscures the important facts by the sheer magnitude of ALL facts. The specialist knows the pulse of his stock in a way that no House or Two Dollar broker can, certainly in ways that a stockbroker in the field cannot possibly know. Your stockbroker doesn't talk to the specialist. Only restricted telephones go to the floor.

The specialist, therefore, works as a broker, a dealer from his own inventory and an auctioneer by keeping his post open and functioning. In 1986, as a group, specialists earned revenues of 159 million dollars, but their profits from dealer activities, buying and selling from their own accounts, amounted to 64% of their revenue. Right before the 1987 crash, there were 422 individual specialists, covering an average of 3.7 common stocks each, working in 554 specialist units. Most importantly: no stock is assigned to more than one specialist.

Traders are Members who wander the floor, trading for themselves, as they see fit from moment to moment. They are registered with the NYSE to be sure they have sufficient funds and experience, and they see the action as it occurs. They can make a profit on very small movements of a stock because they pay no commissions, only the regular assessment on their Membership and trader status.

Does this sound like a non-profit corporation?

Floor governors are like traffic cops. They don't have to be there in quiet times, and they have the power to slow-up trading in particular stocks or, when several agree for good reason, to literally stop trading in a specific stock. They are similar to referees in modern NFL Football, almost invisible until events go wrong. They do not trade. When program trades go off and people scurry around to get fast execution, the floor governors issue citations for gouging, clipping, pushing, and other unsportsmanlike conduct in the trading crowds around the posts. They break up occasional physical jostling and rare fights.

Jostling? Fights? Imagine a stock collapses. Like a shiny lure in a school of mackerel, it draws predators! Traders and floor brokers rush to the post to get orders in, but like rushing for an exit in a fire, they push each other, and if the pack gets big enough, "crowding out" occurs. The big guys push the little guys out of the way, floor governors try to restore calm, and the market shows its greatest defect: it is a physical place, with anachronistic, physical limitations that impede requirements of mass liquidity.

"Upstairs" block traders work in houses, putting large transactions together, usually between institutional clients who are moving a lot of stock at one time. A block is a 10,000 share piece of stock. Blocks make up a lot of volume each day, so much that an average day's blocks today are greater in number than all the block trades for 1962.

The block is positioned and moved by telephone by the traders "upstairs" at the houses, then sent to the exchange for technical execution - but it is all prearranged. Several firms are registered with the NYSE as block positioners to enable them to package and execute this kind of trade on the floor. There is an interesting wrinkle here: the trade may not have to go to the NYSE floor if the security was listed on the NYSE after April 26, 1979. In that case, the whole transaction may take place upstairs.

It's made to crash. It's like a movie house with limited entrances and exits, orderly when people are calm, panicky when a chorus yells, "fire!" The General Accounting Office is reviewing the utility of this physically restricted trading floor system. The SEC's Division of Market Regulation is also looking at the system. Where has the SEC been for the past 50 years? The physical floor system has been a strangle-hold, a choke point in the flow of finance since it was started over two hundred years ago.

Discipline Inside the NYSE

The NYSE spends a great deal of time investigating the finances, ability, and integrity of these floor personnel, and then a lot more trying to figure out what they are up to when activity is scrutinized. If the Exchange feels a foul has occurred, floor people can be suspended, kicked out or fined.

The NYSE also has jurisdiction to investigate and discipline the employees of its Member Firms from the president of the firm to the janitor. When I say "discipline," I don't mean they can lock anyone up. The only discipline they can enforce is the ability to do a lock-out. They can kick the offender out, not just out of the Exchange, but out of the business - the entire securities industry.

If the NYSE "fines" a Member or an employee of a Member for an infraction, there is no enforcement in the courts. A failure to pay the "fine" means that the individual can be kicked out of the Exchange until he pays the fine. Under the 1934 Exchange Act, that means the bad guy is statutorily disqualified from working for any firm licensed under the 1934 Act, anywhere in the country. He is called an "S.D." and cannot get back into the securities industry until the SEC approves.

There is an intricate, formal disciplinary procedure that mirrors administrative practice in the Federal Government with rights of representation by counsel, due process hearings and appeal within the Exchange.

The NYSE Enforcement Department puts the case together and tries the matter. It is heard in the Disciplinary Department, which acts independently from the NYSE Secretariat, and can issue penalties that are ultimately reviewed by the NYSE Board of Governors. The NYSE Disciplinary Reports, published as digested case reports, are great reading. The Reports describe who did what, where the bad guy worked, when the case was heard and what penalty was applied.

If a stockbroker churned your account, lied to you, caused you untold grief and sleepless nights, he might get suspended for three years. If the same stockbroker stole a typewriter from his wire house office, he'd be bounced completely from the industry, for life. Theft from a customer account gets a lifetime bar, too.

Churning is a kind of theft because it works by a broker trading your account for the purpose of generating commissions, not for your investment advantage. The commissions are paid with your money. It's fraud in the extreme, but for churning a customer's account, a broker does not get a lifetime bar. Don't assume there is a sentencing schedule of recommended or mandatory sentences as in the Federal Courts. The NYSE has total discretion in the matter, going from just a censure, through fines, suspensions, and ultimately lifetime bars from the business.

My opinion - when a finding of churning is made, the broker should be kicked out for life. It's theft. It isn't a one shot deal where one might argue mistake or irresistible compulsion.

Churning happens over a period of time, by design. It happens on purpose and is committed by intelligent criminals, that's right, criminals. Securities fraud is a crime, not just innocuous play. It doesn't happen on the moment. It is pre-meditated, vicious and deserves prosecution, not just a suspension from the club for a few years.

Why isn't it prosecuted? Probably because it never has been. It should be. A bar from the club is not the answer, in fact, when a "suspension" is the penalty, the risk is minimal.

A good stockbroker doesn't have to churn because he has real clients who do real business; but a bad one, a stockbroker who has no profitable clients and can't otherwise make it in the business, what does he have to lose? Nothing. What does a possible "suspension" do to stop him before he hurts you?

Levels of Sin

The worst thing a broker can do is steal from an employer or customer. The next worst is an action tantamount to theft from the employer. Coming in a poor third: churning the public or making unsuitable trades. Coming in fourth is the schoolboy stuff: using unauthorized telephone lines, reporting late to the tape, failing to respond to Exchange demands for information, etc.

Based on what I have seen, my opinion is that the most important concern of the NYSE is the welfare of its Members and Member Firms, not protection of the public. The Member Firms are in it for a profit. There is nothing technically illegal with that! When you understand the NYSE's purpose, you know where you stand; you are on your own.

Let's Follow an Execution

A 2,000 share order for the purchase of Exxon common stock is supposed to start with the customer, unless the customer has given discretion to the broker. The customer gives telephone direction to a Registered Representative, which various Member Firms call Financial Consultants, Account Executives, Financial Planners, or other PR titles. The NYSE calls them Registered Representatives, "RR's" and "Reps."

The broker takes the verbal order and writes it down on a multi-copy order ticket, a form about the size of a big traffic ticket, then takes the physical order ticket to the secured "cage" in his branch office, and keeps one copy for his own, short term use in matching the execution with what he sent in. The cage is secured from the public and branch staff because it may have cash, certificates and other valuables, and because it has the internal order wire system for use by the key-punch operator.

The wire operator in the cage reviews the order ticket for essential trading information and electronically sends the data to a central desk in an operations center for execution. The cage does not review for anything other than data. They do not look for use of wrongful discretion, shortage of cash, manipulation, or exercise supervision.

A "limit" order for more than 1,000 shares of a common stock listed on the NYSE will usually go to a New York Listed Desk, where the data is next sent to the House broker on the floor. The House broker will go to the specialist working the "Post," where that particular common stock is handled. The House broker may try to get the specialist to sell directly, or the House broker may ask the specialist to "stop" the stock at a set price for a short, specific time, while the House broker tires to get the stock from another broker on the floor. If the House broker can't get the shares any cheaper from the "crowd" around the post, he returns to the specialist and does the trade. The specialist makes the appropriate note in his book, and the House broker does the same. The House broker returns to his "booth" where he sends a message back to his operations desk about the specific execution, which the desk relays electronically back to the branch office.

The broker may have a mail slot at the cage, or he may have waited at the cage window to get the report of execution back. The wire operator takes the incoming multipage wire, puts one copy in the broker's slot or hands it to him, and staples the other to the original order ticket he got from the broker. If the order was a "market order" for an amount under 1,000 shares, it would have been sent from the cage, to an automatic system past the New York Listed Desk that would have dumped the order into another automated system, matched an execution with a seller, sent an automated notice of execution back upstream, ending in the broker's mail slot. The NYSE calls this small order, automatic execution system "Super Dot."

The Designated Order Turnaround System, or "DOT," is an automated, computer system that links all the Member firms with the NYSE floor to provide direct transmission of orders for execution. Your brokerage house has to have its own computer to get into the system at the NYSE; once there, the NYSE takes over. The order goes right to the trading post for the stock on the floor, and you can get electronic execution by "comparison," faster than a speeding bullet. DOT can handle orders before and after the market opens, in different maximums. If you put in a market order after the market has opened for under 30,000 shares of a NYSE stock, you can go through DOT. If you buy a 1,000 share piece, go through a desk to get a feel for the price. YOU DON'T HAVE TO DO MARKET ORDERS. The time of execution, from the broker hanging up the phone until getting the report of execution back, can be one to several minutes. That's nation wide, under ideal circumstances at most big houses. When the broker gets the execution report back, he compares it to his original order ticket to make sure he got 1,000 shares and not 10,000, which does occasionally happen. He compares the order ticket to the report, to re-check the price.

At the same time the execution notice is being sent to the broker, the information is being sent to the firm's "P&S" or Purchase and Sale Department. This section notes the particulars of the trade, and prepares and sends the confirmations to the customers. The trade information goes to the Margin Department where the clock starts ticking on the payment due date. The information also goes to the Stock Record Department which is an archive where lists are kept of all securities in the firm's possession - the lists explain where every security is at any time.

Physical securities are kept in the Cashier's Department under lock and key in a safe. If you deliver stock or bond certificates to your broker in a branch office, he hands them over to the branch cage; the cage has a courier service securely deliver the certificates to the home office cashier department. If you give certificates to your broker, get a receipt. Always get a receipt. Until the branch cage gets the certificates, there is no record of delivery on the books of the brokerage house. You don't get a confirmation for delivering securities - only for trades. Deliveries of securities will show on your monthly statement, so compare that entry to what you actually delivered. Note: a verbal order was never signed by the customer, only written out by the broker, and on subsequent wires and book entries. The customer gets a confirmation, which looks like a credit card receipt, in the mail a few days after the execution. This very important piece of paper declares that a specific trade took place in the customer's account, that the trade resulted in a charge or credit of an exact amount, and when the customer has to pay, if it was a purchase.

Are securities and cash ever stolen? Sure. Protect yourself by using checks made payable only to the brokerage house and NEVER, NEVER make it payable to the stockbroker. Always get receipts when you deliver securities.

The customer pays on settlement date, typically five business days after the actual trade date. It is possible to pay later if a good reason exists and if the house has agreed to late payment, but otherwise, the broker will sell out the position if not paid. If the original trade was a purchase and if the price of the shares declined between trade and settlement dates, the broker will have a loss on the sellout, and will try to collect from the customer.

Editorial Position

The NYSE was started by men making mutual promises to trade certain securities within only a select group of Members. It was an exclusion system that was legal in its time. The requirement to trade only on the Exchange was "state of the art" just as the 100% hand sorted post office created by Benjamin Franklin was state of the art at roughly the same time. The present, centuries old requirement to trade listed securities on the floor of the NYSE has survived because the NYSE was licensed as an Exchange under the 1934 Exchange Act. Historic tradition is the reason it legally exists today while monetary advantage is the reason it continues to exist in practice. If the "Membership" was unlimited, not set at 1,366, and if the floor could be entered electronically by firms around the country, the specialist system would disappear. There would be no "post," because any firm could become a market maker in the stocks of its choice. Competition would be intense, not structured. Alas, the electronic market would render the actual floor obsolete. The discrepancies between stock and stock index futures prices would be fewer and smaller. We'll deal with program trading in a later chapter where you will understand arbitrage and stock index futures. As you go through the book, remember that the NYSE is a physical place and that most of the dollar market value of United States public companies calls it "home."

It is time for the presently-configured NYSE to die. The eighteenth century cannot be allowed to impede the twenty first. Will it resist? In the extreme. The physical floor is a strangulation of commerce, not an assistance. It is a constriction on the artery of finance, with a prognosis of probable, future heart attacks. It serves an elitist, restricted Membership of 1,366, not a nation of 250,000,000 people.

No matter the resistance, it is time for massive change.

No organization should have such a hold on finance. Think about it! Be concerned, even alarmed about it; but, no matter if you agree or not, understand the problem and take a position. If you are an investor, you are giving business to the NYSE. You have little choice.

Key Definitions: Deciding and Reporting Activity

xi. A Confirmation is printed and sent to the customer after every trade. It is usually put together in the home office, but the branch may be able to print them on special occasions. Sometimes the home office will send the information electronically to the branch office where the confirmation is printed and mailed. You get the confirmation in the US Mail. It looks like a credit card receipt. Because they are printed by computer, be very cautious if your confirmation has any overstrikes or erasures. It is supposed to be printed very carefully, not "fixed up." If it is fixed up, call the firm's compliance department at once. Forget the branch manager - go right to the compliance department. If you deal with a small firm, go right to the president: tell him you have a suspicious confirmation. Demand an explanation. Don't just ask - demand. You have to read your confirmations carefully. If you don't, be prepared to be a victim. If you get confirmations for trades you didn't authorize: go to the compliance department or branch manager right away! If you directed a trade but you don't get a confirmation, get in contact with your broker's branch manager right away. If you don't get the confirmation in short order, then go to the compliance department or the firm president. Study the small codes on your confirmation, because it tells you if the firm acted as your agent, as principal, whether the trade was solicited by the broker or not and the price, commission, etc. Study the confirmation. It will be waved in your face by the firm, if you later complain about unauthorized trades, to indicate the firm told you about ALL the trades. The confirmation CAN hurt you and help the brokerage firm. Don't be a fool and a victim at the same time. Get the confirm; understand it! If it's wrong, suspect foul play! Don't be shy about demanding explanations and solutions.

xii. The Monthly Statement is sent to you by your firm to show you what happened in your account. It will show the way the account looks at the end of the month, after the dust settles from any activity. The brokerage month is not exactly a calendar month because of the five-day settlement rule, so the June statement from your firm may show all activity that occurred from May 26 through June 25. The exact dates depend on when holidays fall. When the monthly statement comes, look at it closely. <u>If you can't read and COMPREHEND your statement STOP EVERYTHING.</u> Learn to read it! You cannot be in a position where the monthly statement is unintelligible. Are you embarrassed if you can't read the monthly statement? Don't be. I have examined witnesses from the operations area, branch offices, regulators and lawyers who couldn't read certain entries on monthly statements. Statements are designed by your firm, not the SEC, NYSE or NASD. Formats change for marketing purposes by adding color and flash - seldom clarity! They are printed by computer at the home office and you should get them in the US Mail. Examine the statement: there should be no erasures and strikeouts. You should recognize all the entries. Are you on margin? Can you tell from the statement? Learn how to read every entry. Keep all the statements.

xiii. <u>Discretion</u> is given by a customer to the broker to allow the broker to make trades in the customer's account without calling the customer before the trades are entered. Discretion is usually required to be in writing, except where a customer gives discretion as to time and price of the execution. Don't give discretion to the broker because you don't understand the market; that's exactly the WRONG reason to give discretion. Give discretion only when essential. Don't trust your broker to do the right thing while you are ignorant of the style of trading, how the security works, or how the account is set up. A bad broker will murder your account with the deadly weapon of discretion. If you have positions in your account and you are going on vacation, only give discretion in writing. If you travel on business a lot and can't get to your broker, only give discretion in writing. If your broker asks for discretion but says he doesn't need it in writing, don't bother talking to the broker anymore about it - talk to the branch manager right away and report the conversation. "Time and price" unwritten discretion is only for real players - people that know exactly what they are doing and are limiting the situation to one or two trades that are going to happen shortly in a volatile market. It's not for retail investors.

xiv. <u>Wrongful Discretion</u> occurs where the broker does a trade in your account that you did not authorize in advance. The broker can cause the trade to go off because the whole brokerage business works on the telephone and will continue to do so. The broker fills in the order ticket, gives it to his cage, and the trade goes off. The broker gets paid his commission. The house can't tell that the broker used wrongful discretion. The branch manager has no way of telling from the execution that the broker didn't talk to you about the trade. The assumption is that the broker did have permission to do the trade. You'll know about the trade when you get the confirmation. If you miss that mail, you'll see the trade on a monthly statement. If you see a trade in your account that you didn't authorize DO SOMETHING. Call the compliance department or branch manager right away. Send a note in writing to make a record of the complaint, but make sure you COMPLAIN. Forget all the usual excuses from the brokers - get that trade out of your account, fast! If a trade goes off in your account and you don't complain, it will look like you ratified the trade. Ratification means you may not have authorized the trade in advance, but once you saw it you said, "O.K.," and you are stuck with it. If you find wrongful discretion, fire your broker. REPEAT. If you find wrongful discretion, fire your broker. No excuses, forget the apologies, don't be a sucker - fire the broker. Get the trade out of your account!

Special Note: Options and Margin Alert!

Are you doing options? Do you understand how they work? Have you studied options in any reference books or other materials? Do you understand you can lose everything? Are you on Margin? Margin and Options are like phosphorous and oxygen - explosive! Beware! Option trading requires close attention from the customer and the broker to follow prices of the underlying securities and the separate option price which includes time value. Margin and options are discussed later. They are for very sophisticated retail or professional use. In the wrong hands they are like dynamite.

Don't use these brokerage "products" unless you could stand up in front of a classroom filled with brokers and "teach." You don't learn on the job with these products. Know what you are doing BEFORE using options or margin.

CHAPTER THREE

The Stockbroker in History

This chapter discusses the changes in technology that allowed for the creation of the mass-retail securities industry, which is a "new" development that has been on a rise in its power from the end of the Great Depression until 1990. Stockbrokers as we know them today are far different from their recent ancestors. You, as a customer, are a new creation as well. Will the brokerage industry change, yet retain its power, or will it fade as the Venetians and Hanseatics, whom we'll discuss below? What phase comes next for the retail securities industry? I think they will try to become money managers, deriving income from fees as opposed to transactional commissions. Money Managers typically charge a fee of 2 or 3% per year of the account value under management. It can be the same people.

Things Change

Let's examine brute economic force in ascendance and decline, then discuss how things, profound or minuscule, change.

We took note of ancient Sumer at the outset. Their commercial cuneiform dates from 3500 BC. Her sister city-states of Kish, Lagash, Umma, Ur and Uruk grew from 3,000 BC on but were taken by into servitude by Sargon of Akkad in 2400 BC. Then Ur took Elam and Assyria in 2100 BC. Where are they now? Why did they fade? Why do nations and institutions rise and fall so reliably?

The German Hanseatic League was a joint venture among merchants of the modern cities of Cologne and Lubeck. The League rose to prominence in northern Europe beginning in the early 13th century.

Their object was a commercial union, run by merchants, not politicians. The "empire" spread by use of two principal weapons: boycott and monopoly. The boycott meant they would approach a prospective member, make the usual offer, and, if membership was refused, a strangling boycott against the target was put in place. No food was allowed in and no purchases of the target's wares were permitted in the surrounding community under Hanseatic control. The League eventually controlled the fur trade between Russia and western Europe, the fishing industry of Sweden and Norway, and the wool industry of Flanders, in addition to the internal trade of north-central Europe. Through monopoly on these industries, they exerted great economic force tantamount to an invisible military siege. If you lived in Sweden and wanted wool, all you could get was Hanseatic-approved wool.

Denmark, no weakling, decided to militarily finish them off in 1370. The League must have seemed an easy target for a professional army because the League used commercial coercion, not military force; they had a set of maritime and commercial laws, but not much formalized government beyond that. The result - in 1370, a Hanseatic fleet seized and occupied Copenhagen! A very profitable war!

By the end of the middle ages, as power and wealth were shifting to the west coast of Europe, the launching area for New World colonization, the League fell apart. They dropped out of sight quicker than Ur.

One more view of financial transformation.

We have briefly examined medieval Venice, but it merits more depth. Venice was founded in a swampy area of several islands in about 400 AD by Italians fleeing the barbarian destruction of the Roman Empire. Venice was a smelly, bug-filled place. The Venetians did manage to hide and scrape by. If you live on an island, you get into shipping. By 1202 the refugee Venetians were the quartermaster corps for the Fourth Crusade. Finally, in 1308 they defeated their arch commercial rival, Genoa, thereby taking military control of Northern Italy, Crete, Cyprus, the Dalmatian Coast (Yugoslavia) and Genoa. She reached the pinnacle of her power.

The Hanseatic League was running the North, the Venetians were running the Mediterranean in the South. Both are now "history."

The aggressive natures of their commerce and investment power changed because the Old World was reacting to the New World bonanza of gold and silver. The center of economic power shifted from the Mediterranean to the Atlantic. Columbus "discovered" America in 1492.

Accept Change

Change is inevitable. It goes on all the time. A wise friend once told me that because a butterfly lives only a few days, it sees the world in permanence, unchanging. Trees are in full foliage during the butterfly's entire, brief life; grass is always green. Its life is so short there can be little time for learning or critical observation. The butterfly can only react on instinct, restricted by its life span.

In geological terms, where each tick of the clock is a million years, people live for a tiny instant. In our own experience, there is never enough time to become expert in more than, perhaps, a few disciplines, usually the trades or professions we practice and maybe a special hobby. I'm not referring to superficial familiarity, but rather, insightful expertise drawn from knowledge and experience.

History teaches us to be careful; don't appreciate the context of what we see as "unique." Whatever the situation, it probably is not unique. Humility teaches us to accept our strengths and shortcomings, to realistically assess ourselves. If we accept the lessons of history and humility, we can beat almost any opponent, no matter how overwhelming he may seem. He may start out bigger, faster and apparently smarter; compete on your terms, at the time and place of your choosing, and you seize the advantage.

Who Wrote the Investment Rules

"They" did: The professionals who make their living from it. They enjoy amazing power and have changed radically over the past 100 years. It's their field and their ball. They set the hours, they control admission to the playing field and the amount of information you can get, and how you can get it. The professionals are in complete control.

The only thing you bring to the "field" is your money, which "they" desperately want to turn over for transactional-based commission income. It wasn't that way at the turn of the century, but it has come to that end as the securities industry has evolved from a small club of combatants to a web of mass retailing, all over America.

In the whole of creation, if you want to sell a block of IBM stock, the New York Stock Exchange has continually tried to force you to come to it, right in New York City, for execution. Why does it open at 9:30 AM and close at 4 PM? Is that for your convenience? Is your work day the best time for you to take a break to run your brokerage account? Of course not.

Your lack of physical or electronic access makes you rely on the stockbroker and the proclaimed integrity of the market. It's like Hanseatic wool. If you want the product, you have to go to the approved, controlled source. They control the time and place.

The Agent.

In the law, there are masters and servants, principals, agents, and independent contractors.

The master usually employs the servant, describing the job to be done with detail, maintaining control over the action of the servant. Because of this control, legal tradition (the Common Law), has held the master responsible for actions of the servant, provided the servant acted in the scope of his employment in the business of the master. That's why Finegan's Parcel Service might be liable if one of its drivers negligently got into an accident. It may be a great firm, looking to safety first, training and screening its people, but as a master, it will be held liable for the negligence of its servant. It makes for careful masters who carry a lot of insurance.

An agent is a kind of servant; a principal is in charge. The principal has described the mission to be performed and gives power to the agent to commit the principal to the transaction. While the agent has partial independence, he is under the control of the principal. Agents may employ sophistication beyond that of the master because the agent might have professional licenses or special experience. Principals regularly employ attorneys, accountants, scientists and others to do things on the principal's behalf which the principal couldn't do himself.

An independent contractor is hired for a project and left to perform without supervision. If you contract with a tradesman to fix your roof, you just want it done. You don't expect to get a course on roofing from the tradesman and you don't give instructions on how to drive the nails. You just want the roof fixed. If the independent contractor does the job incorrectly, causing harm, you are not necessarily in trouble.

What is your relationship with your stockbroker?

Your broker is your agent. Many people think of him as an independent contractor, the roofer described above, because they don't expect to have any control. The bad stockbroker tells very little about how the markets work and the average client knows very little about markets and investing. All the investor wants is to make money. The broker wants to make a living and he doesn't get paid for talking - he gets paid for executions.

In an agency relationship, you, the master, are in charge. You have given the broker the power to enter transactions for you, and you are therefore stuck with them, because, after all, you told him to do it. The theory continues: you know what's going on, why it's happening, but you have decided to use your broker for efficiency and access to markets of your choice. It is all, therefore, your idea!

You get a written notice after every trade, a monthly statement if you trade during that month, and, at many firms, an annualized compilation of all the activity. How could you not know what was gong on? How could you not be in charge?

The law works against you in the securities business.

In reality, the usual relationship starts with the broker telling you to trust him, that he is the professional and he will take care of things; but, if a problem develops where a bad broker harms your account, the law starts by presuming he was only your agent. Indeed, most trades by brokers on the New York Stock Exchange are considered "agency," and are booked that way in the records of the respective brokerage houses. To fix the problem, you have to get the broker to admit he made a mistake, or, you have to show that despite the presumption of the law, it was you who relied on the broker for guidance, not the broker who relied on you for instruction.

This is a very heavy burden of proof. People complain, only to be embarrassed by the stacks of confirmations and monthly statements in their possession, which they never read, or which their bad broker told them to ignore.

The Customer's Man
The Marketeer
Margin

In the old days, before the Second World War, before the 1929 Depression, a registered representative or stockbroker was known as a "Customer's Man." Despite what you may have heard from the media, everyone in the United States was not buying or selling stock on margin in the 1920's. Margin means the broker lends part of the purchase price of the stock to the customer so the customer can buy more. Unlike an auto financc company, the brokerage house is lending money against an asset that may go down in value very suddenly, leaving no security, and no insurance coverage. Theoretically, a client may own securities that are fully paid and decide to borrow money from the brokerage house to pay for a wedding or to buy a car, using the fully-paid stock as security for the loan. The brokerage house might mention this on occasion, but only as a last resort to stop a client from selling stock and taking the money altogether out of the account. The house wants margin used to buy more securities, keeping all the assets in the house. Anyone who goes on margin to raise funds to pay for a wedding is unbalanced.

Relatively few people in pre-World War Two America individually owned stock. Few people had the money or ability to get involved in New York Stock Exchange transactions, because the securities industry hadn't gotten into a universal retail mentality or capability. It wasn't easy to get business into New York City from around the US. The number of NYSE Members was always small, and they were usually local to New York City. Transactions were encumbered by paper.

The New York Stock Exchange, while powerful, was a localized affair. It had a tremendous impact on people through indirect fall-out, but individual investors didn't exist in the numbers of today.

The first ticker was used at the New York Stock Exchange on November 15, 1867. Keep in mind, General Blackjack Pershing was fighting marauding bandits under the notorious outlaw (in the US) Poncho Villa along the Texas frontier border as late as 1916-1917. The Sioux Indian Nation had been crushed only twenty years before that. It was a different era; a different world.

The electronic communications revolution has made the big retail securities market possible. That branch cage can wire orders anywhere, but if a brokerage house is a member of the New York Stock Exchange, the traffic usually comes back into New York, for NYSE listed securities.

A "Customer's Man" was an agent for wealthy investors. He had to have other income, because it was very difficult to make money as a stockbroker. Trades were few in number, requiring a lot of paper support and difficult physical delivery of certificates. Commission income didn't add up to much.

Today, professional athletes, movie stars and stockbrokers can make unlimited amounts of money, but in the past, it was different.

A customer's man could make real money trading his own account, trading as a cover for others, or working for a marketeer on the move. There was no cold calling for accounts, no hard solicitations for retail transactional business at conventions or by direct mail.

Brokerage business was done in the street, face to face, or, if the weather was bad, in bars in lower Manhattan. New York City's climate is temperate, with only 3 cold months. This doesn't mean today's subways don't get hot and steamy, but 65 years ago, the subways were above ground in Manhattan. Horses still pulled the milk and ice wagons. Many commercial markets operated outdoors until after World War Two.

Brokerage houses were small, with very little capital, prone to failure and scandal with every turn of the market.

One of the market's most tragic figures was none other than the great General and two-term President, Ulysses S. Grant, who had the misfortune to personally co-sign notes for his son's brokerage business. The business failed when one of its partners squandered all the firm's money in the market, went into horrible debt (using margin), and left town. The General had to make good on his notes to the creditors of the firm and became penniless, living for a short time on the edge of complete, personal disaster. He eventually died of painful throat cancer after heroically writing his memoirs for Mark Twain's publishing company. The book was a hit and Grant's family made a living from the royalties after his death. It's a wonderful book, still available.

Business at the New York Stock Exchange went on as usual.

The Corner

Great Financiers, or "Marketeers," as I like to call them, regularly played a game of intrigue, investing against each other and amassing fortunes, a few losing them just as fast. "Corners" was the sport of these kings.

A corner existed when a group bought enough stock to get control not only of the company, but also of the price range that the company's stock traded at. The corner was done in complete secret through purchases that looked diverse and not associated with any particular investors. Once the plan was achieved by secret accumulation of a lot of the target company's shares, the corner would be revealed, and market reactions would occur. The most devastating corner would occur where a group, which might have been just one legendary marketeer like J.P. Morgan or Jay Gould, assembled cash and picked a target.

A likely target was a company whose stock price had fallen because investors were selling shares due to poor performance of the company. Railroads were favorites. If the target company was not making profits, investors might forget that the target's railroad tracks represented valuable real estate, and their licenses were legal monopolies within given geographic areas. A railroad might not be impressive by itself, but if it were linked to another railroad it might have tremendous value because of new access not available before. If the stock had fallen out of favor, marketeers would sell the stock short hoping to cause the price to fall faster due to the increase in selling.

Short Selling

Short selling is an ancient commodities technique that works with stock, too. If you believe a stock will fall in price, you sell it. You can sell it even if you don't own it by borrowing the stock from your brokerage house. Example: suppose a stock is selling at 50. After thinking about the company, its business and the direction of the economy, you think it will eventually go to 35. If you don't own it, you can make a profit by borrowing the stock from the brokerage house.

The brokerage house charges you interest on the value of the stock while it is "borrowed." When it gets down in price to 40 you decide to "cover" the position by telling your broker to buy the stock in the market and use it to repay or "cover" the stock you borrowed.

You sold it at 50, and bought it back at 40. Congratulations! You made a profit of 10, minus any interest you had to pay the brokerage house for the use of the stock while "borrowed."

If Marketeers noticed short selling by other marketeers and thought the target company had unappreciated value, the target was prime for a corner. While the short sellers were driving the price down, the marketeers were buying, quietly getting control. As more stock was borrowed and sold short, the short seller was getting into a critical position. Situations developed where more stock in the target was sold than actually existed!

If the price went up, the short seller, who sold at 50, would be in trouble. If the price went to 55 or 60, the spread would represent a loss on the transaction because the borrowed stock would have to be replaced at a higher price: sold at 50, but covered at 55 or more.

Imagine: short sellers, like termites, are busy trying to destroy the market price of a stock by selling, selling, selling; then, suddenly, a group of other marketeers announces it has bought enough stock to gain control and will take steps that will clearly increase the value of the company. The stock price immediately takes off, up!

The short sellers scramble to buy the stock back and cover at any price, which drives the price up even more! The rapid reverse accelerates and the marketeers, who had quietly assembled the shares, now begin to quietly sell them out to the market. The short sellers end up buying back the very shares they sold, but at a higher, panic price! Shorts have always lived dangerously, accepting the potential of serious loss because there is no limit to how high a stock price can go - all for a limited profit potential because a stock can only go to 0.

The best corner ended when the shorts were ambushed by marketeers who secretly bought at low prices, then caused a buying panic, and then quietly sold out to the panicked shorts. What a vicious circle! No real value had been added to the company, but the stock price had moved violently in opposite directions, pushed by paper speculators acting in secret. Corners were typically intended to gain and keep control of the target; they could also be used for pure profit.

There were few retail investors. There were few pension funds. The impact was not immediate, but it did trickle down to the citizenry because these manipulations would cause huge losses for shorts. Since they had only borrowed the stock they sold, when the manipulated price rose, the broker would ask the shorts to cover. If the shorts could not afford to cover, the brokerage house would still have to cover, perhaps with a big loss, maybe big enough to drive the brokerage house out of business. The stock that had been loaned to the shorts belonged to the brokerage house customers. If it went out of business, the brokerage house might default on bank loans, causing banks to go of business. If the bank went, its depositors lost their money. That's how innocent people, uninvolved, were brutalized. That's why people didn't trust banks, brokerage houses or want anything to do with the New York Stock Exchange. That's why General Grant went broke, but he wasn't alone. It happened enough to cause general distrust of brokers.

The NYSE in Context

Until the 20th century, the New York Stock Exchange was a very private institution, indeed. There was no federal regulation of any kind and the public wasn't directly involved in its day to day affairs since they didn't invest. Elected officials did not have to respond to market irregularities, as much as to bank failures. The market affected only a few direct participants, but the effect on the public from bank failure was profound. Bankers regularly went to jail for failures because of frauds in record keeping or outright embezzlement.

The major market players cared quite a bit about market irregularity, but marketeers could fend for themselves. Government was not the arena for change or revenge at the NYSE; marketeers worked in constantly shifting alliances and experienced as many disasters as successes.

The average customer's man was not "in" on this action, and his small firm would not be "in." Major plays were made only by tightly controlled groups who tried to create a momentum in an up or down direction. Investors did trade on rumor of a pending corner, but they knew the danger of rumor, that it could be completely false or inaccurate.

This was the age of the legal theory of "contributory negligence," that is, if you were in an accident with a driver, even if he was 98% at fault, if you were 2% at fault, contributorily negligent at all, your tort case would lose in court. There was no Workman's Compensation for the laborers on the Transcontinental Railroad, the Brooklyn Bridge, or the Panama Canal.

Go back in time to this age of robust individualism, where individuals, not special interests ran massive organizations. You either won or lost, with attending consequences or financial glory, unlike today where taxes are the mark of the government's partnership in all enterprises, large and small, and "risk" has the ring of vulgarity.

There were no safety nets. It was all "caveat emptor," buyer beware. The individual public investor did beware the NYSE by not getting into the market, using alternatives such as real estate or small business investment as investment vehicles.

Rumors

Rumors are often completely groundless, but are occasionally grounded in a kernel of truth. Children play a school game where each gets to make up part of a story, adding it to the story created by all the children before. It's fun, and the narratives are often grandiose exploits of wild action and the eventual, triumph of right! Rumors can be like that - pure, compounded fantasy.

Others are based on a logical hypothetical that if Condition A exists and Condition B exists, it naturally follows that C will happen. This rumor spreads because it implies Condition A has occurred, Condition B is about to occur, so one must act now, without delay, to take advantage of C before it is generally known. Market rumors rely on desire, first to have private, mischievous fun, and second, to make a profit.

Another example: during the early 1980's President Reagan had weekly heart attacks - at least in the rumor mills of Wall Street. The President, thank God, was fine. In 1982, the markets would react to this nonsense, and the Securities and Exchange Commission would announce it was on the case, tracing it in reverse, getting no result. The SEC responded to press inquiry by claiming it was understaffed and that they did not comment on pending investigations. The poor President kept on "dying."

Rumors have been a plague to military intelligence, political intriguers and the investment communities for ages. Rumors of Hannibal's advance in Italy against Rome in the Second Punic War, 217 BC, caused food panics, suicides, and wild commodity price swings; rumors about advancing armies and atrocities in the American Civil War did the same. Rumors of corners by J.P. Morgan or Commodore Vanderbilt caused gyrations on the New York Stock Exchange in the 19th century. President Reagan regularly died all through the 1980's and on and on and on.

Trading on rumor was not illegal in the 19th century, but it was known to be highly risky, therefore, why bother - unless it was a sure thing! Rumors depend on the power of seduction, which is a more positive act than people realize. Investors do not sit back and become passively absorbed by rumor. They listen, attend, and often act on unrestrained impulse under the force of their own fear and greed. If an investor knows a market is dominated by devious marketeers, he proceeds at his own peril. That was the New York Stock Exchange in the 19th century, and very few investors "proceeded" at all due to logistics and common sense. People expected to be cheated by marketeers who had the real power. The best one could hope to do was ride along to a windfall success.

Investors also knew that if you owned shares and left them at a brokerage house, the house might lose them, steal them, pledge them to cover their shorts or other debits, lose or steal the dividends, or otherwise foul up. A lost stock or bond certificate was a very serious problem, because replacement was difficult. Stock certificates were transferred by hand and bonds were usually "bearer." Investors took possession of their shares and bonds, and kept them secure in vaults or in brokerage houses they trusted (General Grant trusted his brokerage house), understanding all the potential problems.

Technology

The Remington typewriter with upper and lower case first came on the market in 1878; the teletypewriter was invented in 1904, but was difficult to use. Morse's telegraph had been used in the Civil War, but it was Edison's invention of the quadruplex method in 1874 that finally allowed a single line to carry heavy, simultaneous traffic. Each of these methods requires a skilled operator, a kind of typist, who represented yet another compromise to Marketeer security or obstacle to the desired, anonymous ease of spreading rumors.

Marketeers worked through personal contact in offices in lower Manhattan, sending agents about with bags filled with cash and securities. Private clubs had private rooms for the most respectable use, the most debauched, and for clandestine business meetings. The 19th century was not a time for the least concern about trading on inside information or for the creation of rumors about inside information. It was part of life. Communication gaps were normal, even expected, therefore, the market was viewed with sober skepticism because of legitimate advantages the marketeers had on hard news. They employed the swiftest of ships, and even had picket boats offshore to get the news and mail from European Liners and Cargo vessels before ships came into New York Harbor. Marketeers had spies and obtained essential information on a timely basis unless purposefully deceived by ambushing, antagonistic marketeers. They had private telegraph codes, private runners and liberally bribed the operators and runners working for other marketeers.

In that environment, a middle class factory supervisor with spare cash living in Chicago or New Orleans wouldn't get a cold call from a broker in New York City to buy stock. There wasn't any way to "call." The nationwide network of branch offices didn't exist yet. Even in Manhattan, a Customer's Man couldn't get to his clients without special messenger.

On March 10, 1876, Alexander Bell said, "Watson, come here; I want you." The telephone was born.

That little demonstration led to the organization of the Bell Telephone Company in July, 1877. On October 9, 1876 Bell and Watson did their routine in a call from Boston to next-door Cambridge. But it took until January 15, 1915 for the Bell-Watson Team to do it again from New York to San Francisco in a publicity stunt. (They used the same words each time.) Early telephones required extensive wiring, and use of large, unstable batteries that could burn or explode. Science advanced past the problems of batteries, wires, and reliable component parts, and the telephone started to become available in major cities. After World War One, it was readily available, although expensive, with long distance interconnection among cities. The first Trans-Atlantic telephone call came on January 27, 1927, New York to London: rate: a mere $75 for the first three minutes. Few workers made $75 per week! Reliable air mail came about the same time.

While a skilled operator was required to make connections, even a child could use the telephone for direct, fairly private conversations. John Pierpont Morgan, last of the great Marketeers died in 1913, right before World War One. In 1914, Charles Merrill and Edmund Lynch formed a small partnership called Merrill, Lynch & Co. to sell investments.

Demographics indicate that the US was shifting from the farm to the cities in the War years, 1914-18. Radios passed from novelty items to reliable forms of communication and entertainment.

Charles Merrill

After serving in the Army during the "Great War," Charles Merrill came back. Merrill, Lynch & Co. went into suspended animation in 1929 because Merrill wisely cashed out of the market before the crash in October, but he returned in 1940, joined forces with E.A.Pierce and another firm, Fenner & Beane. The result was Merrill, Lynch, Pierce, Fenner & Beane, leading eventually to the modern Merrill Lynch, the giant on Wall Street. Charles Merrill was a retailing genius. He was bold, innovative and a man with vision.

If J.P. Morgan was a grand marketeer involved in major finance only with other giants, then Charles Merrill was the opposite - the man who wanted to sell securities to everyone.

The telephone made it possible. There have been plenty of imitators, but the original and still the biggest wire house remains Merrill Lynch. Most executives in the securities industry consider it the best. Other brokerage houses regularly try to recruit brokers from them especially after Merrill Lynch has gone to the trouble and expense of training.

For present perspective, the Japanese securities firm Nomura is several times the size of Merrill Lynch. The Japanese also dominate international banking. But Merrill Lynch still dominates retail securities sales in the US with a network of approximately 12,000 brokers in all fifty Sates, the Territories and the District of Columbia. Merrill Lynch has an enormous presence in trading on the floor of the New York Stock Exchange, not just in moving big blocks around, but in the sheer number of big and small trades they handle. Merrill is run under the tightest possible control out of its World Headquarters in the World Financial Center in Manhattan. The "World Financial Center" is Tokyo, not Wall Street, but brokerage public relations has never been accused of accuracy.

If Merrill Lynch closed up in one day, the effect would be cataclysmic for the NYSE.

Big Spenders

From 1870 through 1910 the average American savings rate was 20%. People saved a lot of money because a rainy day could and probably would arrive, again, without any safety net. Massive social programs didn't exist. At the same time, in Germany, the savings rate was 16%. In 1947, the reported rate of savings in the US was shattered to less than 4%, rebuilding to about 9% in subsequent years and again down to less than 4% in 1987. World War Two was a horrible experience. History is filled with temporary excesses when whole victorious populations have fun and relax after enduring wartime terror, but clearly, after the post-war return to normalcy, Americans kept on spending, incurring mounting debt in various forms and accepting inflation as a normal part of life.

This fits the Charles Merrill theory of retailing to the masses because the masses are willing to spend on anything: why not investments? Modern marketing theory is based on scientific sampling, and application of proven, successful techniques. The Charles Merrill innovation was new, unproven. It would not be approved by most of today's logic-based, expert-system, statistically choked managements.

A Change
The Retail Firms Arrive

The historic figure of the "Customer's Man" is a quaint, but outmoded image. That gentle character seems completely Victorian in the light of modern sales pressure. Selling stock today is very much like selling any other retail item, with enormous pressure on the salesman-broker to produce revenue to support the back office bureaucracy.

In large, modern brokerage houses the back office is a beast that consumes revenues with an insatiable appetite. News reports describe the occasional house that goes under while senior management plays with company yachts and condos, but that's nothing!

Every piece of paper costs money; every computer programmer minute costs more; data tubes and information services cost a lot; rents have been high in commercial centers in the 1980's and have themselves killed off firms. Advertising costs have rocketed up, up and up!

Senior managers at firms look at this avalanche of numbers in curious ways. While one firm might have a budgeting process to control expenses, another won't. One firm can think a budget important, and another doesn't know what to think. Wall Street veterans are used to firms disappearing, so the cycles of boom-and-bust are taken in stride, but the Charles Merrill theory has its dangerous side: in order to sell to the masses you have to have a large support network for the salesmen - a back room. The fixed expense of the back room kills you when revenue slows down. If you cut the back room, you cannot go after more sales to bring back the revenue. The management think tanks offer few solutions to brokerage houses, because the phenomena is new - Charles Merrill created it. He should come back to fix it!

Always remember that the biggest and the best, Merrill Lynch, is a post-World War Two institution. Forget all the Public Relations about houses tracing their roots back to 1870 or 1910 or other meaningless dates. Be concerned with what they are now!

The Merrill Lynch imitators are legion, with branches everywhere.

Can you imagine if every car dealer was able to sell you the same car, in the same condition, in the same time? Sounds pretty dumb, doesn't it? Yet, that's what retail sales on Wall Street is all about. You can buy IBM common stock at Shearson, Merrill, Prudential Bache, etc, and get about the same execution, in almost the same time. They all sell the same basic opportunity for the small investor who buys a few hundred shares of a listed New York Stock Exchange security to get dumped into the same New York Stock Exchange Super Dot computer system for execution. The big difference, when it comes to NYSE transactions at wire houses, is their business name, and office address. The unique difference worth your careful study is the individual broker who can be a great one, or a rodent. The house is not the key.

House marketing differs from place to place, and their overall profitability is different, too. One of the humorous aspects of Wall Street is the frequent cross-recruiting among firms, where senior managers go from one house to the next, without missing a beat. It works like generals going from one Army Command to the next, where the faces are unfamiliar, but the organizational layout and function, the feel of the firm, is the same. The brokers float, too.

They sound the same, dress the same, and act the same. Wire houses are controlled from a headquarters by just a few people. They know each other, regularly talk to each other, go to conferences together in places like Pebble Beach and Palm Springs, California, and Marco Island, Florida and serve on Regulatory bodies together.

Serve on what together?

Oh yes, they regulate themselves, with the SEC's blessing! For the past fifty years, the people that make the money are their own cops.

Self-Regulators
The NYSE and NASD

Didn't you know? The securities industry, under the 1934 Exchange Act is self-regulating. It is supposed to take care of its problems itself. The Securities and Exchange Commission is the watchdog to see that the industry is doing its job! The President of the New York Stock Exchange is from the Wall Street community, elected by membership vote. The New York Stock Exchange bureaucracy may be tenured, but the heads of many of the committees at the New York Stock Exchange are from active-duty, card-carrying Wall Street. The bureaucracy is well-paid and pensioned enough that it never turns on the elected leadership. In my opinion, this is the only way an NYSE Member Firm could plead guilty to serious, federal felonies related to its principal business activities and stay ACTIVE as a Member Firm.

Not all securities are listed on the New York Stock Exchange. Many are listed only at the Amex, or at other regional exchanges. The real competition comes from the Over the Counter Markets, usually referred to as the OTC. The National Association of Securities Dealers is the principal regulator of the OTC. It's a "new" creature, because it did not exist prior to the Maloney Act which amended the 1934 Exchange Act in 1938.

The National Association of Securities Dealers has its own bylaws, charter and rules. It has the power to discipline its members, even kick them out, just as the New York Stock Exchange. If a firm is an NASD Member it can split commissions and concessions only with other NASD firms, which is a major point. The National Association of Securities Dealers has a bureaucratic back room and handles most of the record keeping for registered representative licensing by agreement with the other Self Regulatory Organizations, or "SRO's," such as the New York Stock Exchange, Amex, etc. The leadership of the National Association of Securities Dealers is elected by its membership from the active roster of NASD Members.

Witness the same issue, for which I maintain the same opinion: how do you think NASD member firms can otherwise plead guilty to federal felonies related to their regular business activity and still remain as Members?

All across America, there are little firms in the securities business that are not Members of the New York Stock Exchange. There always have been. These firms are local people serving the financial needs of the proximate community, raising capital for regional projects from sources in the vicinity. They have little immediate need for Wall Street, although they share the common ultimate reliance on the New York Stock Exchange common to all parts of finance. Wall Street would like to be the only source of capital on the planet, but that's never been possible because there is just too much going on in too many places. Wall Street is content, therefore, to finance the big items around the US and leave the small projects to the little guys of the NASD. In the aggregate, because there are so many of them, the little guys count for quite a lot. Most major Members of the NASD are also Members of the New York Stock Exchange. They can be both. Every Member firm of the New York Stock Exchange must also be a member of the National Association of Securities Dealers if it wants to work in the OTC markets, and all retail firms want to be able to do that.

Think of it as being a Ford and Chevy Dealer at the same time, or an American League and National League baseball team at the same time. It doesn't compete with your principal business on the NYSE, but it starts to spread a firm thinner and thinner.

Clearing

There are many firms that are NASD members but not member firms of the New York Stock Exchange, because of the limit of seats at the New York Stock Exchange. These Non-Member firms can still get trades executed at the New York Stock Exchange by giving that business to a Member Firm. This is called a clearing arrangement, with the NASD firm known as the "Introducing" firm and the member firm titled the "Clearing" firm.

In that situation, as a customer of an NASD firm, you get confirmations from a member firm of the New York Stock Exchange that did the execution, meaning you buy IBM common stock and get a Big Firm confirmation from your Little NASD Firm. The confirmation will say "Through the courtesy of Little NASD Firm" to indicate the clearing agreement. Your NASD Firm is treated like a branch office of the Big Firm for execution, but not supervision purposes. The Big Firm does not put sales pressure on the Little Firm. They are separate in fact and law, intertwined by finances.

The big NYSE firms do clearing arrangements to make money by using their excess execution capacity, as favors to friends at smaller houses, and as a way to start acquiring the smaller firm.

The little firms look for a clearing arrangement because they want to be able to do NYSE listed business and because all the usual bookkeeping and paper flow is an expensive nuisance. The little guys also don't want to tie up their money in NYSE seats. The arrangement works on a commission split, with the big, executing firm keeping a part of the commission as a negotiated fee, and the little, introducing firm keeping the rest. Member firms can make a lot of money doing this, and they all think about it when business goes down and they need revenue to pay the rent and support the back room.

As an investor, if you do NYSE listed business through a member of the NASD who must clear through an NYSE member firm you will get the same execution as the NYSE firm's own people! Your orders will go through the same system within the clearing firm as its own employee's orders. You'll get the same response time, just as though you were a direct customer of the big firm.

Why, then, use a wire house?

If you feel confident about your abilities or if you have the humility to see and respect your shortcomings, you might join the growing ranks of investors who use discounters. Discounters are great!

You tell them what you want to do; they execute. That's it! They don't try to sell you anything, and they can give the same execution as any of the full service wire houses. The discounters are driving the securities industry to distraction, because they have increased their market share from 1% to 10% of the total business on the Street. Combine that with the radical decline in retail trading generally, and you can see why the wire houses are dinosaurs, waiting for probable extinction. A wire house sells you full service, whatever that is. Does it mean picking winners? No, a representation like that is illegal, because no one can promise you a winner. Does it mean better execution? No, because you can get that in a clearing arrangement or through a discounter.

Let's keep going. Does the full service broker give you a better monthly statement? No, the discounters give an equally good statement. Are Wire Houses more stable? Answer: EF Hutton, Thompson McKinnon, Drexel! Better selection of products? Hardly.

So, what's the difference?

Selling.

As bizarre as it sounds, if you do business at a full service firm that is a wire house, you open yourself up for a constant sales pitch. You keep going back for more. And more, and more. Why?

One reason is marketing. A bad broker needs your belief and trust. If you accept the fantasy, then you may fail to note the tragedy taking place around you.

Another reason is momentum. If you feel everyone is going in "that" direction, you will consider the attraction, too.

Think of all the dumb commercials you have seen for the brokerage industry. Do they address how the house treats your money or why you should do business with them? No. Do they say what they do better than the other houses: no! Do they tell you that they all trade for their own accounts, often with program trading techniques, and let you see what they are doing? Never! You hear syrupy rubbish about "trust us."

Word of mouth seems to be the best ad, but apparent monopoly and the security of size are the real marketing arsenal. Recall: first, you can get a trade to the floor through a discounter or a clearing firm, and, second, the mass retail securities industry is comparable in age to the baby boomers.

So, again, why are you dealing with them? Probably because the broker is your "friend." Major, major mistake. When a professional is supposed to give you advice on the market and be your teacher, it's going to take time, the real commodity a service industry sells. How much time have you spent so far on this book? Compare it to the time you have spent discussing the make-up of markets with your broker, and the time you have spent discussing an investment before committing a large chunk of your money.

Think of all the promotional garbage that has been sent your way in advertising or research from your present brokerage house. They are supposed to help you make informed decisions so that you are in charge, but instead they hope to get your trust so that they are in charge and you keep nodding whenever they show you the prompt card. If you were an ape, at least you would get a free banana in a test involving cards and conditioned reflexes when you gave the "right" answers; not in the full service brokerage business. You pay for their bananas!

Every time you say "yes" without having a full understanding of what you are doing, you look like an idiot, and the bad broker smiles. Most full service brokers, when they read this section will quietly agree with everything I've said, but not get terribly excited, because it has all been said before and people keep coming back, perhaps not in the droves of yesteryear, but if the market turns and becomes bullish, they expect them all back - in those droves, like cattle.

Remorse? No, bad brokers don't practice it. If the investment doesn't work out, the philosophical justification is that clients are never satisfied, that they are compelled to risk by their own greed and that they, the brokers are actually the victims of the clients, who never say thanks and never make enough when they do have a hit.

It is a violation of NYSE Rules for a broker to share in the losses of a client's account. Absolutely, positively illegal, and if it's done, the broker is in deep trouble. Think of it: suppose, completely above board, instead of paying celebrities to tell you who they "trust" with their investments, the brokerage house said they were so good, that if you lost money, they would refund you 10 cents on every dollar of loss! Toro, the snowblower manufacturer, guaranteed a massive rebate if you bought their machine in 1987 and it didn't snow.

Wall Street never promises you a gain. No celebrity promises you a gain in their hollow ads. The brokerage industry promises nothing. Chrysler promises things in their ads. Spaghetti sauce companies offer guarantees. Many businesses make performance promises backed up by cash! Listen to the brokerage ads very closely; read the small print at the bottom of the research. You probably HAVE spent more time reading this book than discussing investments shown to you by a bad broker, and I'm telling you to read and study these materials again!

The best reason to use a full service wire house is if you get FULL SERVICE, that is, if your broker works hard for you. The first thing he does is keep you out of the clutches of the back room. He protects you from the internal wholesalers and desk managers who want him to sell their product because of an enhanced payout - exactly the wrong reason to sell you an investment.

The next thing a good broker does is talk to you about what you really need to do to achieve your goals. Sometimes he is the messenger of realism - your dreams exceed the opportunity. He has to be frank with you, working without hype.

Goals and needs change. He should be discussing your needs, looking for those changes. He listens to you, then he looks at your present needs and those down the road. Then he makes recommendations and you select, after doing your own homework. If you can't make the decision, then you shouldn't have a securities account. If you won't do your own homework, you shouldn't have a securities account. A good broker works and works and works, reviewing opportunities, comparing them to client needs. When you have a good broker, you are blessed. Remember: you don't see a lot of the broker's best work. The next chapter discusses how brokers really work, how they get paid, and how they can harm you - for their profit. It makes the good ones shine!

Key Definitions: Control Functions

xv. The Compliance Department is the internal cop in the firm. In large NYSE firms, the department has many employees under the leadership of the Compliance Director, who has to be certified as competent by the NYSE. The department is supposed to look for trouble in all areas of the firm by use of computer surveillance, interpretation of data and personal interviews with brokers, managers and other personnel. If you have a problem with your account, don't hesitate to call this department. Ask for the director. Make a note of the person you talk to. Follow up with a letter. If you find wrongful discretion was used in your account to cause trades you didn't authorize - call the compliance department. If you get a confirmation with white-out used to cover an entry - call the compliance department. Calling can't hurt. Bad brokers can't stand the compliance department. They'll do anything, say anything to get you not to call when there is a problem with the account. Call. Follow the call with a letter to the director. Drag him into the problem. Brokerage houses are run for profit, by the sales area, but you can get action from the compliance department, even if you have to drag them, kicking and screaming, into the problem. Unfortunately, a corrupt firm will have a compliance director who keeps his job at the pleasure of his masters, chained by his paycheck to his liability. In that case, you need a lawyer -FAST!

xvi. The General Counsel is a lawyer who works for larger brokerage houses as an in-house employee. He usually has the compliance department reporting to him, and perhaps a few other departments in the firm. He may also have a staff of attorneys in a legal department handling a lot of the firm's lawsuits, advising the firm's management and figuring out what the compliance department is up to. The GC will be on the broker's board of directors and be involved in upper level discussions of firm policy. He will usually not have significant gross production: no "book." When things really go bad at a firm, the GC goes. In a smaller firm, there will be no GC; they use an outside law firm. The brokerage house may not want a lawyer around inside because they can't control one as readily as they might prefer. A lawyer can quit and go into practice elsewhere, unlike a broker who has to work for an employing firm that is a member of the NASD, or else start a new firm requiring numerous licenses and capital.

xvii. Financial and Operations Principals are specially tested and licensed by the NASD. The treasurer of a brokerage firm is usually a "finop," referred to as the chief financial officer. The head of the operations area is a finop, too. In smaller firms, the treasurer and the head of the operations area may be the same person. The first person to know what's really going on with the firm's revenues is the treasurer because he sees the income from each day and the value of the firm's accounts. He sees the expenditures, the taxes, the settlements - he knows exactly where things are going. He is usually a board member and composes the firm's financial reports and computes net capital. The head of operations has responsibility for safe keeping of all securities and for making sure that executions are reliably sent into the correct channels, that buys and sells are correctly entered in the correct accounts, and that floor personnel are working efficiently.

xviii. The Cage is located in each branch office. It contains an electronic wire system where an operator puts all data from the order tickets submitted by the brokers to get execution. It has restricted access because it may have cash, checks and securities on hand. Branches deposit cash daily to their bank, and they ship securities by secured courier to their home office each night. If you need to get a check from your account, the firm may mail it to you, or you can get it from the office. Don't let the broker deliver it. Either get it mailed from the home office or get it at the cage in the branch. The branch manager has access to the cage - the brokers can't get in. The manager will go into the cage to review order tickets, review the wire traffic to and from the home office, and review the efficiency of the wire operators. Mistakes do happen, and they can be costly. The difference between 100 shares of IBM and 1000 shares of IBM is one keystroke. With option trades the danger goes up dramatically. Understanding this, you have to examine your confirmations very closely to see that you had correct execution. A good broker watches this carefully.

CHAPTER FOUR

The Stockbroker In Action

The best way to see the environment of the broker is to follow one of his days. Let's start with a typical Monday. We'll follow "Rasputin," named after the mad monk who influenced the Russian Romanov Court before the Tsar was tossed out in 1917. I'm creating personae to offer fictional examples that will sharpen your analytical powers, using an age-old teaching technique developed in ancient Greece and continued in modern US law schools. There is no "typical" anything where human beings are involved. Keep these examples in mind! Don't be depressed, because I'm going to explain how a good broker is worth his weight in gold. Under the Socratic method, you hold an idea in the air and discuss it in all its aspects. The residue of such an examination is "wisdom."

I have never met a broker who started out to harm people, except for the bad guys that work in the illegal boiler rooms. Like any of us, most brokers start out with good intentions, hopeful enthusiasm, and a completely unfounded image of how retail brokerage sales works. That naivete fades fast.

The House

The brokerage house remakes the man, molding him of sterner stuff so that he is ready for the trenches where the broker survival rate is low. He becomes the modern Telephone Warrior, ready for battle at any place he can plug in. He's "inspired" by motivators hired by the firm, by the different levels of management inside the firm, by his own ego, and by his personal, monthly bills!

The house has a keen interest in making a profit by getting maximum performance out of the broker. If times get tough for the industry, that "maximum" may be increased!

The day kicks off with the Wall Street Journal because it really is the paper of record for finance. That doesn't mean it is the best source, only that it is the standard, and is widely read in the brokerage industry. It's a great paper. Investor's Daily is another great paper read by many brokers.

A broker zips through the financial column on the Journal's front page, flips to the third section, page C-2 to see articles "in depth" about rumors or special announcements concerning individual companies, then goes to the statistical tables to see reports of earnings, mutual funds and commodity prices.

Not all stock brokers are commodity brokers, and they may or may not know how the commodity markets work! Commodity trading requires special training, testing and a separate license. This becomes important when we consider program trading later on.

Rasputin, the broker, has stock quotes available on his video tube that change throughout the day at his choice. He can follow the same group of ten or twenty stocks or commodities with ease. The Journal takes about five, fast minutes, which is a measure of how well it's put together. It's a fast, thorough read if you know what to look for!

Rasputin the Equities Man.

Rasputin the Equities Man doesn't follow the options market because he doesn't like the frantic activity, frustrated customers and small commissions. Too much work.

He doesn't follow the commodity market beyond the price of gold, and doesn't have a commodities license. Rasputin could not read and interpret a corporate balance sheet in college, after college or for his first few years in the brokerage business. He can do the major ratios now, and finally understands what it means when the Federal Reserve conducts Open Market Activity. That's about it for his depth, because he doesn't need any more. His clients don't have a deep background in finance and he firmly believes that knowing any more than he must is a waste of effort.

He left his original firm for his present wire house five years ago, after putting in great commission years in the big bull market after 1982, arriving at his present employer through a head hunter, landing a bonus. The bonus is just about worked off, so it's time to start looking around for a new home or increased leverage in the present firm to get a bigger payout or other form of increased compensation.

His goal is to get away from being a broker and become a money manager where he can charge a fee each year based on the amount of money under management, without relying on commissions. He trades his own account on margin and loses on a regular basis. He has stopped wondering why his customers don't ask him about his own account. He has never lied about his account, because no customer has ever asked how he is personally doing!

After spending only a few minutes on the Journal, Rasputin might skim the business section of the local paper. Many locals have excellent financial sections, drawing on their own staff or the resources of the Associated Press, UPI, or Reuters. Depending on when the local paper gets "put to bed" by the publishers on the previous night, it may have late information not carried in the Wall Street Journal about a breaking story. He also knows that local clients read the local press and are more likely to ask locally oriented questions.

By this time, Rasputin is in the office. He starts the day broke!

Rasputin works on commission. If he gets a client to do a transaction, he gets paid. No transactions means no pay. If Rasputin fails to get a trade, he gets nothing. He is paid commissions at varying rates depending on the overall amount of "gross" that he does and the type of investment "product" that is sold. Rasputin has regular monthly obligations that compel him to raise cash. Since the 1987 crash, he has struggled because retail, small investors, his usual clients, don't trust the market. "It's nothing personal," they tell him, " but, I'm not sure about the market right now."

Commissions are charged to you, the customer, on a schedule that is published within the firm, but is secret, to be kept from customers and competitors; be assured, competitors know each other's commission schedule. The customers don't get to know the rates because the firm doesn't want customers demanding discounts or comparison shopping. All NYSE firms used to charge the same commission price until the mid 1970's! It was a grand example of monopoly. When Ford and General Motors advertise, they publish their prices and fight like wildcats about who has the best product, driving over or destroying each other's vehicles. A full service brokerage house will not publish its rates. If they did, customers would march off to the discounters or ask for 50% off the cost of trades. The discounters will tell you their rates, because they want you to know they are far cheaper while offering the same execution service.

If Rasputin does business, he gets paid anywhere from 25 to 50% of the gross commission generated on the transaction.

"Gross" means the gross commissions, markups and other charges that are added to the principal cost of buying and selling stocks, bonds or other investment products. You pay these charges on the way in and on the way out of most investments. It covers everything that Rasputin can sell. Almost every transaction of any kind has a charge. The total charges generated by Rasputin comprise his "gross."

If the commission on a 100 share transaction in IBM Common Stock is $175, you can see that Rasputin has to do a lot of transactions to make a living, because he will only be paid about $70 on the trade. These days, big houses expect a broker to do about $200,000 minimum gross production. If Rasputin does less than that, the house will consider laying him off.

At a major house, Rasputin would be paid out at a rate of 25-30% against gross commissions of $150,000, or, he would make $37,500, before taxes. The house wants to get Rasputin's gross production up to $300,000+, and they would like to get him up to $500,000. Rasputin would love to be there because his percentage payout goes up as his gross increases. He might get a 42% payout when he does $500,000 for a net to him of $200,000 before taxes. The variable payout to the broker is called the "grid."

Interestingly, if Rasputin goes from $150,000 to $500,000 gross, he increases production by 3.33 times; his net income, however, increases by 5.3 times, and he gets prizes and other incentives along the way.

It costs a brokerage house a minimum of 50 dollars, even more, to process each trade ticket, whether or not it leads to an execution and commission income. It costs the firm a lot to keep Rasputin in his chair: rent, heat and air conditioning, major telephone bills, secretarial support, license filings, etc.

The house needs to get the larger part of the commission to pay for the fixed expense and the cost of the ticket. The broker does not pay for his own support; it is built into the commission split. There are firms where Rasputin has to pay his own telephone bill, but those situations are exceptional, usually resulting in a larger payout to Rasputin. The big houses pay the freight, and Rasputin gets a reduced payout.

If Rasputin does $500,000 gross, he starts out the day with telephone calls, not from customers, but from recruiters. Headhunters are all over Wall Street. My experience indicates that many of the best and brightest on the Street are not working with investment clients, but are working as headhunters! It's a tough job that demands a great deal of patience leading to occasional successes.

Headhunters call in the early morning, after lunch or when the market has closed, after 4 PM EST. The headhunters have other houses as clients.

The other houses want Rasputin to come work for them. They want him to bring over his "book" of customers and deliver his gross production to the new house. The new house offers an enhanced payout for several months, say 60% versus Rasputin's present grid of 44%, and a bonus of 20 to 30% of last year's gross production. If Rasputin did $500,000 gross last year, he will discuss a bonus of $125,000 for going to a new house.

Before the 1987 crash, this was paid up front to the broker, in lump sum. Since that time, the brokers get the bonus in pieces, usually over 3 to 5 years. The payment of the bonus changes as the market changes.

In good times, brokerage houses recruit without regard to subsequent performance, throwing money to the wind, claiming they have to do it to be competitive. Brokerage managers reading this will smile, because it's been a hot topic of debate within the industry. It wasn't always that way, but since 1982, cash recruiting has been a hard fact of brokerage life.

Vulgar? Yes, but it's done!

Rasputin has little allegiance to his firm. The seduction from the headhunters outside, and the continuous antagonism from their back office makes brokers jumpy. A broker will talk with headhunters in the open if the broker has a big enough book, that is, if he does enough gross. The branch office manager, who is responsible for the care and feeding of the successful broker, may have to enter into a bidding to keep his own people.

The branch office manager gets paranoid about losing people, because his job is to steal the same people from other firms, so he knows that every office is a target of every other firm. When brokers go to another firm, the accounts often go, causing the original office "gross" to drop. Managers get paid based on the office gross, number of brokers and product mix bonuses. They suffer monetarily when brokers depart.

It costs a lot to train a broker, because the novice has to study and pass a tough, 6-hour exam, Series 7, to get his broker's "ticket." During training, an NYSE firm pays for study materials, and trains for 4 months. Then the broker tries to build his book over several years. When the broker gets to the point where he is profitable, the house knows that every other house will be after the broker.

Many houses don't train anymore. It's too expensive and too slow. They need cash contribution to the bottom line now or, more accurately, yesterday!

So they recruit! Your broker might call and tell you he is moving to service accounts better, to get better products for your selection, and so on - but too many move only for the money, carefully weighing the competing bids to the last decimal point. They get the same fundamental product mix, execution times and support from house to house. Don't be fooled, they want you to move with them to bring your gross over to the new house. I have met brokers who moved from a brokerage house because they felt their old home was becoming too insistent on selling products that were profitable to the house and potentially harmful to the customer. When this broker jumps to a new house, it's for all the right reasons. Sure, he might pull down a bonus, but he knows that his business will fall off when he moves, eating up the "bonus," as he tries to explain why he moved to his customers. The old house will fight to keep the customers.

Rasputin is only concerned about the money. It didn't happen overnight, but at one point, Rasputin became consumed by the money. That's all that matters. The customers are just a key to the treasure chest. He has no moral quandary any longer - only immediate greed. If he moves, he will do anything, tell you anything to drag you along. Your account may get transferred out without your even knowing it!

You are supposed to OK the transfer IN WRITING by signing a form at the new firm. Rasputin will sign your name in a second!

Moving an account can cost you money if you are invested in proprietary house products such as a house mutual fund that cannot move on the electronic network from one house to another. Investment products can be designed to make transfer difficult. There is nothing special about the fund, except for this feature, which is meant to make you stay at the firm or get out only if you decide to sell. Your moving broker will try to offset this burden by offering discounts on other trades at the new house. Just when it makes sense, the old house offers you discounts to stay with them. Everyone wants you! IRA accounts may have a hidden transfer fee approaching or exceeding $50! If you are going to move the IRA account to follow your broker, find out if there is a charge.

If you are going to move your account to follow your broker, see if the old house will compete with the new house to get your business. They often do. Ask!

Rasputin talks with the headhunters, meeting them for lunch or dinner. They tell him how great he is and how the other house is so much better than his present house. They feed his ego. If Rasputin's branch office manager feels Rasputin is going to move, he, the manager will start to work on Rasputin more than usual, flattering Rasputin, passing him good accounts of departing brokers, maybe upping his expense account.

Morning recruiting happens at about 8:15 to 8:45 AM. Rasputin has skimmed the papers, and is on the phone. If he is a big producer doing $650,000 gross per year, he'll have his own office; if he does less gross, he will share an office, or, if he does under $250,000, he will be out in the bullpen with no office. Rasputin shares a secretary. If he was a big producer, he would have his own, but a mid-sized producer will share a secretary with 3 or 4 brokers. A registered sales assistant is far more valuable than a normal secretary.

After he talks with the headhunters, Rasputin calls his pals to see what they like. These other brokers are with other firms in the area and Rasputin knows them from business and recruiting efforts. If Rasputin can get one of them into his house, he can get a small piece of their gross production credited to him as the recruiter. Rasputin tells his friends what's going on at his firm, and they return the favor. This is the way rumors start, with brokers chatting, occasionally with malice, often with boredom in a quiet market. This can go on for 20 minutes, through several calls.

While on the phone, Rasputin is looking at his cash reports, that is, a daily list of all his accounts that shows how much cash is available for investment, which, for him, really means "available for Rasputin to trade." This list arrives on a computer printout or is on Rasputin's video tube. It is that brief: the account name and number and the amount of money available for investment. Rasputin studies the list as he talks, marking a few accounts that have potential. It shows cash and margin buying power.

While he is reading and talking, because he works in a big house, a "squawk" telephone speaker box or ceiling mounted speaker is carrying a telephone roundup from the product managers of the firm, who are letting Rasputin know what they have got in their inventory and how they are ready to serve him. Regular morning speakers with a short time allotment might be his OTC Desk, Fixed Income Desk, Governments Desk, Insurance Department, Direct Investment Department, Commodity and Option Desk, and so forth.

Each speaker gets a few minutes to round up the advantage of using their respective products that day. The desk managers get paid on the basis of their own unit profitability, making them wholesalers within their own firm, and they want the brokers to sell their product over that of the other desk managers. The brokers try to get an advantage or price break from the different desks, or at least get favors in return for their business. Tremendous, lasting friction can develop in one day between brokers and a desk.

The firm's research department gets on the box for a few seconds to give an overview of what they feel the day will bring, and they'll mention a few issues worth following. Part of the department's job is to get the sales force feeling positive, ready for action, raring to go. Brokers always look for a story, one they can tell clients to get their interest. They don't want the old news - they want fresh ideas from any quarter.

From this telephone roundup, a bad, lazy broker picks up sufficient information to sound like an expert to his clients, often implying that he, the broker, has followed a company or an industry and has come to conclusions on his own.

Many firms have rules telling Rasputin he can recommend only the firm's research picks and can sell only the approved list of firm products. The firm's back office is terrified of maverick brokers who do their own research. After all, the broker isn't at the firm to come to conclusions! He's there to sell!

New York Stock Exchange Rules require the firm to approve every piece of research, whether from the firm's official department or from the broker, before it goes out. A Supervisory Analyst must personally sign off on the research quality and the manner of presentation.

The firms often provide scripts to the brokers with bright ideas to quote to clients. In big firms, it comes over the wire network to the branch office, and has fill-in-the-blank format for the broker's use throughout the day.

The research department will also jump onto the squawk box during the day with breaking news or information in capsulized form for use in soliciting orders. The New York Stock Exchange and the other Exchanges have marketing departments that put information together and send it to houses concerning sophisticated products like options. Rasputin's video tube provides access to pre-written, canned letters for solicitations to clients. All he needs to do is fill in the blanks in the form letter with the individual name of the client, and it's all set. If he decides to write and send his own solicitations, he has to send them to the Compliance Department, who then sends it on to the Legal Department, who will invariably say, "no!"

Rasputin has this formidable array at his disposal at the start of the day! Put another way, the only thing Rasputin has to do is make the call and sell - everything else has been done for him by the back office! He doesn't have to think, analyze or engage in long discussions - he's there to sell, move to the next client, and sell again.

This leads to the constant battle of who needs who? The brokers feel they carry the firm. The firm feels they have to nurture the brokers.

Firms tinker with ways to control the broker, but the broker, always thinking to the day he might move and get a bonus, is looking for ways to remain independent, and squeeze more money and benefits out of the firm. The poor fellow caught in the middle is the branch manager.

The brokers yell at the branch manager, blaming him for the back office. The back office berates the manager for not keeping better control and squeezing more gross out of his brokers.

Pity the poor branch managers who get Knute Rockne (legendary Notre Dame Football Coach) half-time football lectures from regional superiors, who have just gotten similar lectures from their superiors, which is supposed to make the firm's gross production rise. It's easier to levitate! Noise does not cause success.

If the manager does get enthusiastic and start to push his brokers around, a big producer might be offended, call the head of sales, and complain about the manager. Then the head of sales will call the manager and tell him to calm down and let people alone! What a circle!

In my opinion, branch managers are too often hired to be kicked around, blamed for failures on all sides, then fired, or fed to the regulators if there is any problem. You'd be better off to have a job as a crash dummy than be a branch manager in the securities business. It is one of the few, true "no win" jobs. I never understand why people work as branch managers when the exposure is so great and the rewards so few. Good ones are grossly, grossly underpaid.

Houses don't like the brokers to waste time researching or studying. They want brokers to get on the telephone with clients and sell, sell, sell. The house doesn't need clients in the office, asking for special services. Clients exist to buy, then sell, then buy again. Big houses, like a lot of big companies, hire "consultants" to review trivial aspects of their business, as though these corporate druids might be able to stave off the cycles of bull and then bear markets.

The house provides the research and product chatter. The house even provides lists of leads for Rasputin to cold call for business. Rasputin can buy his own directories from list brokers covering everything from a list of all local attorneys and accountants to lists of all owners of pre-1965 Buicks. The house gives Rasputin an expense account for this purpose, but if the manager wants, he can buy a list for Rasputin and charge the branch. If Rasputin is a big producer he will expect free lists from the branch manager.

If Rasputin does solid, regular business, he won't like to cold call for new accounts. He's not alone in that because a lot of successful brokers hate it, considering it demeaning and a waste of their talent. They prefer instead to get referrals from friends and clients. Referrals come easy to a good broker, because he does reliable, productive work, and satisfied clients are happy to pass his name to friends and business associates. But, I have met excellent brokers, with reliable business who make it a discipline to cold call almost every day. They might not like it, but they do it. Managers want brokers to cold call because the home office insists it's an effective system. The home office wants YOU!

In big firms, the home office has a sales motivation staff, usually made of former brokers, whose now-salaried job is to get transactions going. In my opinion, they are like cheerleaders who are held responsible for how the team plays. They second guess the local efforts of branch managers, which agitates the managers, and then, after hard effort, the poor motivation staff may be fired to cut costs when sales slip in a bear market. Volumes of traditional sales literature recommend cold calling. When you receive this kind of solicitation, be very careful. It can be an innocent inquiry looking for regular business. It can be the last resort of a slipping broker; it can be the first resort of a new hungry broker, or worse - it can be a boiler room, that is, a house that uses high pressure sales techniques to sell garbage stock. Remember, a stock sale does not have to be in writing. It usually IS done on the telephone.

When that telephone rings and it's a stockbroker cold calling, don't take a chance - hang up. You have no idea who is on the line or what his real motivations are. They can be honest or criminal - you can't tell from the telephone, and no one has the right to put you on the spot. You have the right to hang up. It's not rude - it's prudent!

Brokers, on occasion, use computer dialers, devices that call and call until you pick up the telephone to answer. You've gotten this kind of call - a computer message telling you to hold on for Mr. Rasputin if you are interested in investing in exciting areas that will be the center of activity in the 1990's.

Rasputin is thinking about his mortgage payments, luxury sedan and country club payments and the losses he has taken on his own account. He needs money. Having studied the cash report, having been groomed by the day's squawk box discussion, Rasputin is ready to go! But he has to wait; the manager wants to have a sales meeting at 9 AM for 10 minutes.

The manager has to have sales meetings because the home office says so. Topics covered include the same materials as the squawk box, but with a bit of intensity. The manager also cracks the whip. If the OTC desk manager tells the sales force that he has a lot of Big Doggie stock in inventory, it is the branch manager who has to tell brokers, in person, that he expects them to get rid of a chunk that day, per broker. If a house use a silent sales quota, how would you know? You should be suspect. Ask your broker if the house uses quotas.

The big producers come to the meeting or not, as they please. They can't be forced either way because managers must be concerned they will leave for another house. The manager has no forceful control over these brokers and they know it. Some take pleasure in telling the branch manager what they think of him on a regular basis as a form of manager-baiting. Other big producers will lead the sales meetings because they love their work. A good, big producer is the most valuable teaching asset in the firm, because he shows younger producers how to build a successful book without problems by daily, honest example.

The manager can insist the smaller producers come to the meeting and meet his demands, because he knows they must be concerned about being told to leave for lack of production. The subtle, office dynamics are intense. Small producers are easily replaced. They are, therefore, the most logically prone to accept pressure to sell whatever they are told, without question in houses that employ sales pressure. It's a matter of individual integrity and will to resist this pressure.

If he is a nice guy, the manager may offer a small prize to the broker who gets rid of the most Big Doggie stock that day - baseball tickets, dinner or another token. In large firms, the home office runs contests all the time and tries to get outside vendors to pay. Branches try it, too.

Here's how it works: assume a mutual fund company wants to sell its Fund through the brokerage house. The Fund will offer to pay the regular sales commission to the house and broker, but to seduce the interest of the brokers even more, the wholesaler from the outside Fund will offer to take brokers to dinner - in Washington, DC, in April when the cherry blossoms come out, as part of a weekend of information seminars about the Fund!

All a broker has to do is sell a lot of the Fund, then he will qualify to go to Washington, DC and learn about the Fund he has just sold. It's nothing more than a prize. The "contest"may be run by the firm, and the Fund may quietly pay the firm for its cash outlay. Firms constantly try to get Funds to pay for contests.

The mutual fund pays for this with your investment money, dumping it into the general area of "sales promotion." They fly in the "winners," wine and dine them, and make an after dinner speech for a few minutes to tell the brokers how great they are. The brokers love it and many now expect prizes to be offered.

The practice has conditioned greedy brokers to demand it, so that a fund without a promotion will not be sold by the brokers, just as General Motors and Ford have conditioned savvy auto buyers to wait until a rebate campaign starts to buy cars. The difference: when you buy a car, YOU spend YOUR money, but when you buy a mutual fund, THEY spend YOUR money.

Did you notice that the merits of the investment can fade while the sales machine whirs along? If the OTC manager got on the box and tried to tell his sales force that he had a lot of Big Doggie stock but it was a poor investment and they should avoid it, he'd be cut off!

By 9:30 AM Rasputin is ready for action, waiting for the opening rotations of the New York Stock Exchange. His video tube displays selected stocks throughout the day, with automatic changes as they are reported on the tape. There is no ticker tape - it is all video supplied by services such as Bunker-Ramo and Quotron. Their service is great! Reuters does it, too. It can be expensive because they bill per level of service on the tube. It's like cable TV - you pay for each "channel."

Want commodity prices? That's $20 more per month for just that tube service. Want more; pay more. It adds up and the branch manager has to be careful about which "bells and whistles" are on his office billing. The regional managers watch this very closely. Every one in management at big houses watches how much is being spent on tubes, paper clips and coffee these days, because expenses are not being supported by revenues. Houses are tottering. With all this financial worry in the back room it's easy to forget that they are also supposed to be watching the brokers!

Rasputin calls around through his book, especially to clients who show up prominently on the cash line. The squawk box keeps on going, with commentary on the way prices are opening. He turns down the volume on the box, operating on his own, with his own clients. As he gets them on the phone, Rasputin makes the day's pitch for trades. If he gets a few, he writes out the order ticket, jumps up and rushes to the cage to put them in. When the trade is executed, he gets a payroll entry!

A lot of pros will make a few calls around to their broker friends if anything strange has happened in the market, or if it's an unsuccessful morning. The easy day is over at 11:15 AM; either he has fast, easy trades or he doesn't.

After that, Rasputin has to work on cementing relationships and presentation of more complex products that take time. These are the big ticket sales that may require personal visits or multiple telephone calls with follow-up mailings. The payoff is larger than a fast stock transaction. An example: Rasputin is working on a client who has inherited $100,000. Rasputin wants to sell him $50,000 worth of his house's mutual funds because Rasputin would get a payout of about $2,000 on that part, and he wants to sell him an insurance annuity to capture the other $50,000 for another $2,000 net to Rasputin. This is a patient stalk, requiring time over many days. The client is steadfastly nervous about the stock market; Rasputin agrees as he does with any client position. Don't argue - keep talking and find what the client does agree with, then get a sale.

The client knows he has to put the funds to work, but isn't sure how. Rasputin brings up five or six choices, but adroitly moves the selections around so that Rasputin's favored, big tickets appear the best. The client feels he has made the choice himself! By putting commission before the welfare of the client, Rasputin has crossed the line. He didn't have to, but he did. He's a bad broker. Other brokers, faced with the same environment and the same opportunistic temptation will still do the right thing, trying to educate the client and help THE CLIENT select the best product without regard for the attractive commission.

It also happens that if Rasputin sells this particular insurance annuity, this month only, the insurance department will give a 75% payout to generate more business, so that Rasputin might take down $3,000, net to him, on that annuity sale. The client's money will thereafter be locked up for years in the annuity, which Rasputin is not thrilled about because it hinders his ability to move to another firm. Still, it will pay this month's rent, and, if the mutual fund investment loses money, Rasputin can always point to the insurance annuity as a kind of winner, which may keep the client happy. Do you see what has happened to this broker? He's given up his integrity in pursuit of his own benefit at the expense of the client. The client no longer matters as an individual, but does matter as the way to get at the real target: a big payout.

Don't get me wrong: there is nothing inherently wrong with commission based sales in general, but in the securities business, it can motivate a weak broker to cross the line and start pushing you into investments you shouldn't touch and probably don't understand.

Rasputin doesn't like to do municipal bonds because he once was embarrassed by a redemption from a municipality within two months after he had convinced a client to buy $125,000 worth of a particular issue at 105 per bond. The recall was at par, 100 per bond, so the client lost $5 per 100 value or $6,250. The client wasn't happy, but Rasputin was able to convince him to take that redemption money and buy a variety of other bonds that later went up in value. He lucked out. On the other hand, if he had explained the possibility of the redemption up front to the client, he wouldn't have been burned and might still offer municipals. Rasputin's position is unreasonable - it is his personal preference and can short-change his clients.

Since that time, Rasputin will not talk to the manager of the muni desk, and regularly tells clients that the municipal market is not very fair. He's lying. "Better to go to the NYSE or do mutual funds," he says. If the muni desk manager would buy Rasputin dinner, all that feuding would stop and his clients would be able to consider Municipals again.

Another scenario is that at 9:35 AM, as the market opens, Rasputin calls his New York Listed Desk and tells them to get a 5,000 share block of XYZ common stock. He tells the desk he will send down the order tickets in a little while, but he wants to make sure the block is done as he is filling them out. Rasputin isn't supposed to do this, and the desk knows that he may be playing a game, but they pick up the block at the price Rasputin gave and call him to say it's done.

Rasputin scrambles to get people to buy little pieces. He should have had the orders before getting the block. If the price goes up during the day, he'll call and tell you he has 500 shares at 35, that the market is now 35 1/2, and that you can have them because you are such a good client. You think it's great because he is offering a 1/2 point advantage. It might be at 35 1/2 - or it might be at 34! How would you know if you're at work? It might be bouncing around, and you cannot tell if his story is true or not. It might have been 35 1/2 ten minutes ago, but when he called it was down to 34. Suppose he just dumps it into your account - how would you know? You take his word about the price, but do you know how to look it up next day?

You might first hear about the trade when you get the confirmation. One thing is sure: if Rasputin takes a block, he has to get rid of it. If he doesn't, it will be sold out, and if there is any loss, Rasputin will be personally charged for the full amount. Any loss to the firm will come out of his paycheck that month, to the exact cent. He might also get into serious trouble with the manager, because it is illegal to take down a block without a customer order in advance; it happens. If Rasputin is caught, the manager has to take action or he will look like he is part of it. Rasputin probably wouldn't be fired for the first offense. If there is any loss, Rasputin must pay it off, or be fired.

Even worse, if Rasputin does this a few times and can't get rid of the stock, the one time he calls with a bona-fide big order his own desk will not deal with him, just as he does not deal with the municipal desk. He will be internally blacklisted at that desk. That is another reason bad brokers move to another firm: they have so botched things, that the desk managers will not deal with them any more. Time to get new managers at a new firm.

Over time, personal feuds and friendships develop between the brokers and their favorite desks. It can seriously affect you.

Many brokers pass on lunch. They work on calls throughout the day, looking for trades, seeking clients who might be interested.

By 3 PM, many are worn by the constant grind, the cold, constant rejection - it's difficult to accept. Brokerage is not for the thin-skinned. Forget all that video cliche about people holding three telephones and yelling back and forth. That's a trading desk. Retail isn't that wild, but it wears as much, because it is a one-on-one," full court press." Trading desks can become a free-for-all, but direct retail sales is harder work. Unless Rasputin has a customer who likes to follow positions through the market close, it's hard to get business at the end of the day. The firm research department will come on the squawk box in the late afternoon with a review and projection of the close, giving brokers a chance to call clients and try to get a last ticket. Late afternoon is a good time to send out the canned, pre-printed research pieces that all the wire houses put out each week.

New York Stock Exchange Rules forbid re-publication of individual research reports from the past for the purpose of selectively claiming victories with the implication that the house's research always wins. The house must publish the results of a full universe of its recommendations over at least the prior twelve month period. It makes very good sense. Bad brokers get around this by saving research reports as they come out, and if one is a winner, the broker will send it out for a while to show that the house and the individual analyst are "hot." The implication is that if you invest with that house, you will get a good recommendation, just like the one in your hands from the past. If that one went up, then the next will, too. Rasputin knows he could get into trouble if he does this, but he has crossed the line and feels it's nothing more than a little, white lie. It's a full-blown fraud.

Analysts develop followings among brokers. The afternoon is a good time to chat. Astute brokers call the analyst trying to get a line on bona-fide information. Others call to see if they can get anything beyond the published report, or maybe get the analyst to speak directly to a big account the broker is trying to impress.

Slow afternoons with no trades allow brokers to call around the back room, straightening out their insurance policies, payroll accounts, and politicking to the extreme. As salesmen, trained to work on the telephone, it's hard to get away from it.

The Book

If Rasputin has been lucky enough to get a few trades, he posts his "book." Each broker keeps a record of every trade he has made for each account. Traditionally, it is a small, loose leaf binder, with pre-printed insert pages, listing each account. If Rasputin does a trade for me, he notes the details on my page in his book that day or the next. This is the most valuable thing he owns because it displays all his business and is highly portable - to another house.

"The book," is his stock in trade. He treats it with the greatest confidentiality, because recruiters will want to eventually to see it as proof of gross production. Houses occasionally claim the book belongs to them, but when one firm recruits from another, they routinely tell the target broker to bring his book over when he comes. Many big producers have their secretary post the book, but they can do it themselves. Small producers have to do it themselves. The book is supposed to stay in the office at all times.

The branch manager will occasionally look at the book, because it shows what the broker has been up to with individual clients and with clients as a whole. Most big houses require the branch manager to review the book once a year and initial off. Managers avoid initialling unless they absolutely have to because it means they have seen the book, reviewed it and think Rasputin is OK.

The broker's book is the most accurate way to get a fast impression of the type of business Rasputin does, how often he does it, and if he does IT to all his customers at the same time. Have you ever tried to call 15 or 20 people when they are at work? It's hard to get them, especially for a discussion on investing. Rasputin's book will tell the story of trades in time sequence. If Joe's account, my account, Frank's, Mary's, Donna's, Al's and others traded in the same security on the same day, either Rasputin was very lucky to contact all the accounts BEFORE he did the trades or he did the trades and scrambled to get the client's to agree. Do you want to see your page? Ask!

The Firm's Disclosures

If you want to find out about a brokerage house and the individual broker, you can ask to see a copy of the firm's BD filing, that is, their Broker Dealer license filing that is sent to the SEC and to the various states. It's a public document and shows all the bad things that the firm has been found by regulators to have committed. The broker has a file, too, because he has a license in your state. If you want an easier, armchair way to get this kind of information, you can write to:

Manager, Special Services
National Association of Securities Dealers
9513 Key West Avenue
Rockville, MD 20850
(301) 590-6500

The NASD will send you a form. Fill it out, send it in, and they will tell you what the data bank shows for final adjudications. It will not show you there are 2,000 pending lawsuits against the firm, or that there are 15 against Rasputin. It only shows adjudications: final disciplinary actions and criminal convictions. The NASD lets the broker and firm know you have inquired. Do it! Don't use a broker without having this report! Feel free to ask if your broker is being sued by any clients.

If you ask for the complaint file against Rasputin at the NASD or at the SEC, they won't give it to you. If you ask for the complaint file against the firm, they won't give it to you. All you get is the NASD list which is already on the Broker Dealer license form, so the NASD is not giving anything new.

By 5 PM Rasputin has had it, but the day goes on because it's "sales night." The branch manager is buying pizza for the office and wants everyone to stay late - sell at night. The desk managers are staying late to run "specials" for that night only, giving the sales force a break on markups and a higher payout for transactions.

Rasputin remains at the office because it pays him more to make a trade at night then it does during the day, so he saves a few up from the day and puts them in at night.

Nuclear Rasputin
An Options Man

This fellow lives on the edge. Most options customers are retail, that is, human beings, not institutions. They lose, by industry tradition, about 90% of the time.

Oddly, even though they have increased risk of loss, listed options and commodities departments have done as well, if not better than ever, in commission revenues for major houses since the 1987 crash. It is as though investors had given up on long term stock positions in the environment of violent stock upheavals. If equity prices can go wild any time, why not use options? How much wilder can things get?

Plenty!

A speculator who follows stock has to put up a lot of cash to carry positions, even when he goes on margin. A trader doesn't intend to keep a stock over years. He wants several fast points, then he's out. He's a trader, not an investor. He'll buy on rumors or what appear to be informed guesses - he looks for a fast advantage.

A professional speculator uses discipline that eludes retail investors. He can take a loss and get out. He doesn't "marry" a stock. There is no time. He has to recognize an opportunity, take the position, and look for the next opportunity. The stock speculator has just as hard a time as the retail investor in trying to deal with wild price fluctuations caused by program trading. If he is on margin, he can get hurt, maybe wiped out.

When the option speculator buys or sells contracts, there is no intent to keep the position for more than six or seven days, unless the option "runs," that is, takes off the way he had hoped. They don't often "run." Nuclear Rasputin loves to day trade, that is, open a position and close it in the same day. Like a banker, he feels better when the books are closed each day. He doesn't have to take overnight positions. He can, but it isn't essential.

Simple Option Theory
The Wild Side

If a stock sells for 50 per share, it will cost $5,000 to control just 100 shares while hoping to get a 4 or 5 point gain before getting out. On margin, the same $5,000 can control 200 shares. But with options, that same $5,000 can control a far greater number of shares. By buying a "call," the right to buy the stock at a price of 50 for the next 3 months, Rasputin may be able to control each share for $3, not $50 cash for the outright share or $25 for the share on margin. If that right to buy the share for $50 for three months costs $3 per share, or $300 for each 100 share option contract, Rasputin can control over 1,600 shares for the same $5,000. He never has to buy the stock.

If the stock moves up three points, to 53, Rasputin can sell the option in the market, take out his appreciation per share from the option and probably get $2.50 profit per share on the 16 call option contracts or 1600 shares controlled thereunder. He didn't have to buy the stock to make a profit.

Nuclear Rasputin almost has to be a "rocket scientist," a term that will constantly appear in brokerage discussions, because he has to work with a discipline of small numbers to either grab a profit or minimize losses. Mathematical discipline contradicts imperfect human execution.

Nuclear Rasputin uses discretion, which means he trades first and tells his customers second. This is legal because he has gotten the customers' written permission on a special discretionary power form used by his brokerage house. He couldn't operate any other way, because the options market operates too fast to get in touch with people. His customers have to trust him, believing he will use his best judgment as to what to get into and when to get out.

Now that the evil genie is slightly out of the bottle, let's go over options a bit more. There will be further discussion on options later.

Options Explained Again

You are familiar with options from real estate or car deals. If you want to buy, but aren't sure about the particular property, you might decide to make a deal with the owner: for a few dollars down, he'll hold it for you at a set price for a short time. If you pay the rest of the purchase price, you get the property or car. If you don't pay, you lose the money you put down. You bought an option on the property for a set price, for a set time, with specifics about how and where payment would be made.

In the mid-1970's the exchanges developed listed options as a way to further the liquidity of investments and offer alternatives to investors who owned stock and wanted other than simple buy/sell strategies with the straight equity.

If you buy a March call option on Exxon common stock at 45, you now have the right to buy 100 shares of Exxon common at 45 per share through the third Friday in March. When you buy the option, you do not own the stock. You never have to buy the stock. Options expire on a set date. They die. Options lose some value to time each day.

If the price of Exxon goes to 80 per share, the price of your option should rise, too, and you might decide to sell the option and keep that profit. How much will that profit be? If your option allows you to buy the stock at 45 and the stock has run to 80, your option has intrinsic value of 35 times the 100 shares it covers, or $3,500. This is an extreme example, but it is the way options players work. They look for home runs, not singles. In the age of sudden takeovers, stocks do go from 35 to 80, and lucky individuals do make that $3,500 on 1 option contract.

The Research Department Chapter discusses "short" option tactics.

Dink-a-Dink Triumphant

This is exactly how Nuclear Rasputin explains it to his customers, emphasizing the possibility based on the "what if," scenario of a few recent takeovers. "Patrick," he says in an enthusiastic voice, "what if you had bought 40 or 50 "calls" of Dink-a-Dink? You'd have made hundreds of thousands of dollars on 20 grand down!" It's a fraudulent pitch; don't go for it. A good options broker has to spend a lot of time to educate you on the way the product works, then has to see if it can fit into your financial picture FAIRLY. Options are not suitable for most investors. By LAW, they are not suitable for many financial institutions like Unions, Credit Unions and others. Does that tell you something?

When Rasputin tries to drag me into options, he shows the true colors of the monster he has become, quite different from the good broker who patiently works with the client and may, in the end, tell the client, "No," that options just aren't for him.

Ah, but a major league, fence clearing, mammoth home run of hundreds of thousands of dollars - it does have a seductive ring! Rasputin wants to pull me into his mental maelstrom!

Rasputin likes to keep his attention riveted on the markets during the trading day so he tries to avoid wasting time with people whether it be customers, fellow workers, or anyone else, because he has to clear the decks for action that may come at any time. This isn't required conduct. It's quite possible for an options broker to be a normal fellow, to be able to sit back and objectively review and discuss markets, but my Rasputin cannot. He has also crossed the line of legality, putting his own interest first, preying on customers who don't understand how options work, how the markets move, and how leverage works for and against the derivative-product investor. He doesn't bother to waste time educating customers about the product any longer because it takes too long.

No Promises

Nuclear Rasputin can get into trouble by promising results, or seeming to promise results. He can mislead customers about his ability to spot opportunities, when all he sees is the same video pricing you could get in your home on a PC. If he wants to trade the rumor company options, he is making an inherently dangerous decision, because his trading your account on rumor is illegal.

Could it be worse? Yes. Nuclear Rasputin may have to trade all day long to move in and out of positions. Every time he does a trade, he generates a commission. While options commissions are not large PER TRADE, they can be frightening in the AGGREGATE for the entire account over time. A sophisticated customer understands this.

Nuclear Rasputin knows that no system has ever been invented to consistently beat the market, except the adage, "Buy low, sell high!"

He knows he doesn't have a system, but he claims he does to his retail investors. Does that sound odd? This Nuclear Rasputin approaches investment intensely, seriously. He can come to believe it is possible to develop a system because of faith in mathematics. Like an ancient alchemist or numerologist, he searches for this "truth" even as legions of program traders determine the market's momentum. The innocence of a hobby is long past, however, when he tries to convince me that he really does have a "system" that must sooner or later "work."

This is no exaggeration. Charles Dow built the famous "Dow" theory of market forecasting on mathematical analysis. It does not claim to predict individual prices; it only demonstrates market movements as a whole. The innovation and application of mathematics made him famous. Graham and Dodd, other theoreticians, had their statistical model, and they're famous, too, not because they promised any result, but because they rationally said their formulae could be an aid for investors. Notice I used the word, "aid," and not "THE ANSWER."

Genius and mathematical investment theory go hand in hand, right into the garbage! Every few years a new theory arises, rockets to prominence, and then, abruptly, crashes. The Street veterans snicker and look for the next, passing "truth,", providing the three elements of drama: a rising and curious beginning, a dynamic interplay of events leading to a crisis, and then the resolution. It's the beginning, middle and end. The end is usually a bear market.

The Street is filled with technical analysts who approach investing based on trends and activity of stock prices. They don't review the merits of a company's product or management plans. In fairness, a rational, technical analyst doesn't claim to have the "truth" or any scientific system, but he does interpret factual, mathematical occurrences in the context of discovering possible repetition.

If the analyst sees that every Tuesday, at 2:16 PM, IBM moves 1/4 point, he will extrapolate and predict that this will happen next Tuesday. Coincidence becomes a forecast. Don't laugh - this is serious stuff. Investors follow different stars in the search for profits; a few DO invest based on star charts! Why not?

Intent

Rasputin means well. He does. How can he think he will be fast enough to get in and out when he isn't on the floor, and is competing with program traders? Because on top of being greedy, looking for sport and commissions, he isn't very knowledgeable about options. How would you know if he were? If you knew how options really worked, you could sniff out the Rasputins in a few minutes for the bad brokers they are, and get a good one.

While he has your account, you will trade often. You'll be on margin. You will go from the pursuit of great profits to the defeat of controlling losses. Limiting losses can show a great performance by a broker, but that isn't why you put money in the markets. It is also embarrassing to Nuclear Rasputin, because he can blow the account in one day or over time. If it happens over time, the commissions will make the account look like it was churned. True, options must trade frequently, but the danger to his scheme is the mathematical relationship between the account value at the start, the value at the end, and the amount of gross commissions generated by the number of trades. The numbers are all there.

The underlying danger is the suitability of the client. How many people are suitable for this kind of an account? Not many. How many people could really understand what was going on with their cash? Very few. If you ask Nuclear Rasputin to explain what he has been doing, he'll get in trouble if he says he played the takeover stocks on the basis of rumors. He'll get in trouble if he says he played the hot options on the basis of inside tips.

Now you can see why there aren't many options brokers - there are not that many customers who can handle this kind of action. I have seen sophisticated customers use options intelligently. They had excellent brokers. I have looked. There has never been a consistently successful options system in the history of United States finance, else we would all be doing it, which is how the system would lose its special nature and become the norm against which other systems would arise. People can be obsessed by the allure of options. Even as you read this, there is some poor soul working on overdrive in a small office in lower Manhattan, searching for "the system." When he cracks, there will be another. After him - another. The individual carnage is very sad. It is swept aside by the tide of events. In mid June, 1990, there will have been an auction of Drexel property at its old building, 60 Broad Street. Over 1,000 computers are on the list. Big ones. Useless ones.

The Manager

The branch manager who recruited Rasputin is concerned. Managers are concerned about a lot of pressures, but option brokers require the most delicate handling. The branch manager is worried that if any of Nuclear Rasputin's customers accuse Rasputin of churning, or violating suitability standards and misleading them about the potential of their investments, there can be massive damage, serious lawsuits and a fired manager. Good managers work with their options brokers closely, and if they find a Rasputin, they fire him fast, before he can do any damage.

The Conflict

Nuclear Rasputin produces a lot of gross commissions. He trades all day long. The manager needs the gross to keep the office production up. If he makes Nuclear Rasputin slow down, the gross goes down. This is an intense, daily conflict of interest. What to do: help the good ones and fire the bad ones. The manager can tell which is which.

Options were originally developed to hedge, to provide alternatives to investors who owned stock. Naturally, retail brokers realized the speculation possibilities of options early on, so today, options are not used as a conservative hedge; they are independent, used alone for leveraged speculation.

Not Me!

As far as the house goes, supervision starts with the manager, runs up to the options department and across to the compliance department. By NYSE rule, special officials have to be appointed to maintain supervision. They are called the Senior Registered Options Principal (SROP) and the Compliance Registered Options Principal (CROP). In brief, they have to put together a program of training and surveillance that is supposed to make it hard for you to get beat by a bad options broker, yet options remain one of the most dangerous products the firms offer.

With all these supervisory layers, the top management has a defensive barrier to any charge of a failure to supervise the broker, because they can point at the branch manager, the CROP and the SROP as the ones who failed, not them!

Discretion

Options brokers often use written discretion. All options brokers have to consider using discretion, whether they have it in writing or not, and the house knows it. Markets move too fast and customers are not available by telephone. Even if they were reasonably available, which of ten customers do you call first? By the time you get to number 10, the price position may have shifted for the worst. If you get customer one, do you put in the ticket for him right away or do you wait to get all the customers and put in the tickets together?

Why would you ever be so trusting as to give control over your funds to a stockbroker? Stop here, and let's debate: give me a reason why and I will counter with several reasons why not. Tell me it's like giving a power to a relative to run your affairs, and I will counter that as well. Your broker is not your friend. It's business. He makes a living off trading. Giving discretion is dangerous in the extreme, and worse, its evil can linger long after the account has suffered, because it may strip away your right to recourse. Would you give city hall the right to assess AND pay your taxes by taking it out of your accounts? Would you let the grocer select your diet? Do you think second surgical opinions are a waste of time? Discretion is serious - don't give it out to a broker as a matter of convenience. Give it only when absolutely required.

The worst reason to give discretion is that the product area is too sophisticated and you don't understand it, so you leave it up to the broker. If that's the case, you should definitely not invest. Most people I have met have no business being in the securities markets. The risk is too great, the detail too absorbing. Most people can't afford to lose, yet every stock market investment has risk.

Boom! It Explodes!

How does a firm supervise brokers like this?

If they blow up, the firm feigns surprise, claiming it never knew the broker was so bad. The branch manager gets fired, the Compliance Department says they warned the branch manager and the Regional Sales Manager about the problem, and the Head of Sales says he wasn't told it was all that serious. The Regional Manager goes on an extended road trip, and the Legal Department mops up like the Environmental Protection Agency -EPA- discovering asbestos. Ugh, how did this get here? The SRO's censure the manager and bar the broker for a few years, after which he'll be back. Next case, please!

A Few "Don'ts."

Don't do options unless you are willing to lose everything very fast, maybe more than you had in the account! Yes, be prepared to go into the red!

Don't expect to find a "system" or a broker who really knows any more about breaking news than you could if you had the time.

Don't do options unless you have read <u>Characteristics and Risks of Standardized Options</u>, put out by the Options Clearing Corporation. It is 73 pages of small print. Your broker is supposed to give it to you for free when you open your options account. It will take hours to study. You are better off at the race track. In a race with 10 horses, one will win. That's guaranteed. One horse will win each race. There will be several races each day. It's fun, the horses are magnificent, the jockeys daring, and the entertainment is refreshing. Why trade options?

There are many stocks that have corresponding, listed options. They trade all day in an international market that has no real beginning or end. On top of all that, option trading is not fun. If you are hedging a large position, you don't mind if you lose on the option.

Hedging

What is a hedge? Imagine you are a farmer who grows wheat. You are having a mild season and the crop is growing nicely. Prices seem pretty good just now, but they may drop because a lot of farmers are doing well. You would be happy to get today's price for your crop. You hedge your crop by selling a few commodity futures contracts, promising that for a small payment now, you will deliver your wheat to a certain place, on a certain day, in a certain condition, at today's agreed price.

Reversing the position a little, imagine you make cakes by the millions for sale all over America. You need wheat. Lots of wheat.

You can't sit and wait to buy on the day that you need wheat because prices could be out of balance due to unique weather or because the Russians are buying. You see the prices today and they look good. You need the wheat in two months, not today. You'd be happy to pay today's price in two months. What do you do?

You hedge. You buy a commodity futures contract for the delivery of the wheat to a certain place, at two months from today, in a certain grade or condition. You are all set to make cakes within your budget. If prices do run up and away, you will have your wheat at today's price. If they drop, you can let the contract go and buy at the lower market price. In that event, when you hedge, you don't really care if the contract price falls to zero because it would only fall if wheat prices were dropping. The wheat would cost you less. The "hedge" worked.

The same is true of securities. If you own stock at 50 per share, but you think the price will drop to 40, you can sell a call at 50. If you were a short seller, and you wanted protection against the price of the stock running away and forcing you to cover at higher prices, you would buy a call and keep it in your back pocket. If the stock ran up in price, you could get stock at the call option contract price.

If you are willing to lose everything, and you feel like playing with hot money, then do a little studying, and go ahead and trade options for pure speculation. Hedgers are balancing the money invested in the cost of the option against another position which will react the opposite to any change in the option price. A hedger tries to lock in the status quo NOW; an option speculator tries to guess what is going to happen and bet on that guess with no hedge. Why not spend the money on your kids, or spouse, or donate it to a charity? If, in the end, you still feel you have to do it - recognize and adjust to a compulsive disorder. You're hooked!

Rasputin can become addicted to options. Managers have to watch that Rasputin is not the moth circling a flame. Managers have to help him contact his customers on a regular basis to make sure all information is clear, correct and understood.

A Challenge

Go back and read this chapter. How much time have you spent thinking about options? Even now, do you understand them enough to put up real cash? The firm won't let you trade options until you sign a form saying you understand what's going on and that you want to go ahead and do the trades; and further, that you have read and understood that 73 page booklet that explains how options are listed, exercised, traded, and reported.

Let me offer you a little wisdom from the Report of the Presidential Task Force on Market Mechanisms, (The Brady Report) from January, 1988, at page 111-21, concerning the October, 1987 crash:

" In many options markets, retail investors are the major component. When the broker places emergency margin calls, the retail investor with exposed option positions is the first to be called. In the absence of additional margin, these positions are liquidated. Discussions with many brokers revealed forced liquidations contributed to the enormous downward pressure in the market throughout the day."

Stay away from options. .

Boiler Room Rasputin

This slug is dangerous. He works for dangerous people. Organized crime plays this game more often than you'd imagine.

It is legal to register a worthless company. That's right, you can put together a completely worthless shell, file the papers with the SEC and go public. It's expensive, but it is legal. The filing has to follow the SEC format requirements. The US Congress is considering a law to make SEC approval a requirement for a "blank check" or "blind pool" company as these entities are known. The SEC, as of May 1990, opposed such responsibility on their part. Bureaucrats hate to "sign off."

The SEC doesn't approve the filings of public companies. It accepts the filings and makes them available for public scrutiny. The SEC can object to the filing if they can show fraud or substantial defects in the filing format, but filing a worthless shell is not in itself a fraud.

The fraud comes later.

A good example of an exploitable entity is a "blank check" company.

A blank check corporation is legal. They can be successful. Investors put money together and a guru decides how to invest it once the money is gathered. The guru doesn't have a definite plan as the money is being gathered. He says, "Trust me! Invest, stand back, and let me do my thing!" Successful blank check promoters with proven, reliable records of honest performance can gather funds faster than you might think logically possible. These are real, substantial people known to the investment community. A "blind pool" is the same, except that the guru will invest in one sector of the economy, such as the oil, banking or health care industries.

But let's assume I am a scammer. I put a filing together and say that the object is to raise money which I will later invest in areas that I haven't decided on yet. Even if I have no background in handling such investing, I can go forward with the filing. I state, clearly, that I don't know what I will invest in, but I want to sell stock in my project to the public so they can fund my undecided efforts. I will sell Common Stock. Once funded I will pay myself a fat salary. I own a lot of the Common Stock and will sell a little more to the public at the initial offering.

Who would be dumb enough to buy this stock?

That's not the question! The real message is not to look at the buyer's foolishness - look at the expertise of the evil promoters. They know how to sell. This scam works on raw selling power.

In criminal law, a conviction may not stand if the defendant was entrapped into the conduct, that is, if the police so enticed a person to commit a crime that an otherwise law abiding person would be unfairly enticed to engage in the wrongful conduct. The classic case: an undercover cop offers to pay $500 for one marijuana cigarette when the normal street price is $2. The opportunity for windfall profit might be so attractive as to be irresistible. That's entrapment. People who never handle narcotics might be tempted to fill that kind of ultra-profitable order.

Boiler rooms work on human frailty. They use a telephone to reach right into your house and capture your attention with entrapment.

With my little "blank check" all registered and ready to go, I engage a few people to sell. And sell, and sell, and sell. I mean hard sell!

I hire Boiler Room Rasputin.

I put him in a room filled with similar rodents, armed with headsets and telephone lists for potential victims all over the country, even the world! I give him a script.

Rasputin calls you after dinner and asks: " Would you like to get in on the ground floor of a guaranteed, 100% profit deal! It will only cost you $2 per share and there are only 10,000 shares left, because the price was at $1 yesterday, and it's being gobbled up."

He continues, " Yes, the only reason it's being offered to the public is because of SEC rules that require it be offered to investors in all the states, and you were referred by another investor in your own town! I can't tell you who that is because of investment confidentiality, but they said you could use the profit. We are not allowed to buy the stock ourselves because of those same SEC rules, so this is a great chance for you to cash in before the crowd eats up the whole opportunity. I can only put you down for 5,000 shares, because we have to spread it out to other ground floor investors. You have to send the check today! We cannot hold the stock more than 3 days. It will probably be at $6 per share by then, so you could sell it, and make $20,000."

It's all lies. Dreadful, harmful lies.

The SEC has nothing to do with it, hasn't told anyone to spread anything out and hasn't approved of the investment in any way.

It's hype and it's illegal, but it happens. People send in their cash and get shares in the company. I get the capital, pay myself a salary and play around in the market with what's left over after these "expenses."

The stock does begin to establish a price base of $2, then it moves to 3, then 4, then 5. It's all pressure selling by telephone.

I own a lot of the Common Stock. Yesterday it had no value. It still has no real value, but I'm one of the few people who knows it.

Today it has a lot of MARKET value. Boiler Room Rasputin is selling the daylights out of the Common to victims all over the US, but they don't know each other, and there is nothing in writing about the false promises. They can't pin it on me. They see the price inching up, just as promised. No one is reading any of the information I have filed.

The best part comes when the quote systems pick up the action on the target stock. How did it get there? I openly applied for listing on the "NASDAQ" system - after all, it's a registered, public company and there are real shareholders! Well, there are now! The "National Association of Securities Dealers Automated Quote" System gets me on the video tubes. I can apply for listing at regional exchanges, too. Once I get the stock "listed," I obtain an apparent legitimacy. Until I can get the stock listed on the NASDAQ or on a regional exchange, the price will be quoted in the "pink sheets."

Next, I pay a few analysts-for-hire to send out glowing reports about my company to brokers around the country, because I know too many brokers go for the "story" behind a stock, forgetting the balance sheet. My analysts send materials to the brokers right in their offices. If I am successful, my need for Boiler Room Rasputin will decrease as the real brokers get hooked! I need Boiler Room Rasputin to get the wheel turning, but once it's going, I can silence him and ride the interest that the real brokers will cause.

It's a better mousetrap. I get the broker's clients' money for my intrinsically worthless stock. The brokers haven't heard Rasputin's fraudulent story. If they did, they would have known it was a scam. They fall for the price movement and the bought analysts.

They can have my stock.

There are about 8 million compulsive, pathological gamblers in the United States. How many more can be had by a combination of hard sell and seductive entrapment based on fast profit?

Once the brokers move in and create the frenzy, all eyes are on the movement of the price, not on the merits of the investment. Remember the Danish fairy tale about the Emperor's new clothes?

In that story, Hans Christian Anderson recounted how two tailors went to a king and convinced him that he should engage them because they could produce the finest garments. The king deserved the best, they told him. The tailors cleverly played on the human nature of the king and his respectful subjects. The subjects did not want to get the king mad by saying that the tailors were not making garments. The tailors convinced the confused king that the people approved of the tailors' work because the people applauded the fine clothes each time they saw the king. The implication was that the king would be insane not to see the clothes that everyone else "saw." The bizarre situation fell apart when a young child laughed out loud to see the king publicly strolling with no clothes! The child's laughter was the undeniable voice of truth. Respect and visible fact had been manipulated by the tailors to their gain: they got paid for doing nothing. They were liars.

Boiler room scams depend on momentum.

Trading in the stock can be started and increased by the most desperate and illegal of methods. Like a forest fire with humble origins, the activity grows and becomes a comprehensive spectacle.

People believe because they want to believe.

Do you get junk mail from real estate developers who promise prizes if you show up and tour their buildings? Do you get prize offerings from sweepstakes you never entered? You are naturally suspicious of this activity, which can be perfectly legitimate. The heavy-duty marketing makes you suspect a scam.

I've gotten cold calls from brokers around the country offering me the "opportunity" to buy stock at under $5. Many are probably legitimate hard sells, but I've listened to illegal offers. When I sense the latter, and ask for precise information such as the address of the salesman and his name, they hang up. Time for another call to another potential victim.

I don't know where they got my name, but we are all on mail and telephone lists.

Another way for this illegal promotion to operate is for a scammer to buy a registered company that is dormant, broke - a lifeless shell. I don't know why, but a lot of this takes place way out west.

Several investment magazines carry ads for the purchase of these shells. It's legitimate. Genuine promoters can use the old shell for a number of valid purposes.

A criminal scammer buys one of these shells and goes to illegal work. The shell has been registered for years, so no new registration has to be filed. The old one has to be updated, but that is a lot simpler than doing a new one. Once updated, by sending in current information to the SEC, it's alive!

It vibrantly comes to life when the same technique as before is used: Rasputin starts selling the Common with fraudulent promises and gets the price to move up. The brokers notice the price movement in good old Big Doggie, Inc. By "coincidence" they get news releases and analysis in the mail about the "new" Big Doggie, Inc., the company that has found a new polymer coating that is invisible and can extend the useful life of nuclear wristwatch engines. AH! A technology stock! Quick, get shares! The pitch implies General Electric will buy the company; maybe Ford, or IBM! The real brokers, always hungry for a story, call through their book and announce the great opportunity they have discovered after their hard work pouring over reams of market data. These are bad brokers caught in a crowd frenzy.

Of course, Ford, IBM and GE are not going to touch this kind of monster and have nothing to do with it. Their names are used illegally by the scammer. The story takes an acceptable, plausible concept - scientific breakthrough - and runs up the momentum of price. The real criminal act is my sale of my common stock to the enticed, defrauded public. I make money by selling my stock, which cost me nothing.

What! Did I do anything wrong? No way? I didn't call anyone, or write the research? Not me! Go ahead, prove it! Of course, I did do it, plain as could be, but now try and catch me! That's the problem for the enforcers: catch and punish this bad guy.

All I did was send in current information to the SEC about how worthless the company was and how it was tinkering with nuclear watch engines. I can't help it if dumb brokers hyped the stock. I have every right to sell the public my Common Stock if they want to pay for it. Go ahead - show me what I did wrong! Sue me!

It breaks when a "child" says the king has no clothes, or more likely, a State Attorney General announces that the product has no basis in known science. A humorous article will next appear in the financial press and fade from the memory of man until the next scam, next week.

When Penny Rasputin calls you after dinner to pitch a stock for under $10, just say NO! Hang up before he gets the pitch going. The bad guys make it dangerous to even think of buying from the honest ones. It's easy. Hang up. Put the telephone down, back on the receiver. It's not rude. Penny Rasputin is a rodent, a slug, a vampire; you're the target. He thinks you're dumb, greedy, and inherently passive. You are a sheep, awaiting slaughter.

Hang up! The SEC has a rule that a broker is supposed to send you a written permission slip to do trades for securities under $5 per share, unless the shares are "listed." That's why, as a scammer, I wanted to get on the NASDAQ or onto a regional exchange - to be "listed!" You are supposed to sign the form and send it back in. A legitimate broker will comply with the rule, but a bad one will forge your name or just bang out the trade because they don't intend to be around for an SEC audit. Bad brokers will forge margin and options papers; this new form is no obstacle to a bad broker. They will also explain the form as a bureaucratic necessity, like the warning on cigarettes, that doesn't apply to this hot stock, but you have to fill it in and return it. A lie!

Remember this: a criminal sits around and thinks of ways to get at you, often using legitimate artifacts as the tools of his trade. If a bank robber uses a GM car, that doesn't mean GM is evil. If a scammer uses the penny stock market, that doesn't mean that stocks under 5 or 10 dollars in value are all evil. It's the use the scammer puts them to that makes the projects evil. A lot of legitimate companies start out small, then grow to be giants. US Steel did start out as a billion dollar corporation, but most companies start very small and grow thereafter.

This is what the scammer uses on you. He wants to convince you that he has the "one" that you should try to get. He lures you to it. Prestigious media have carried phoney stories planted by criminals who intended to take advantage of the media's reputation.

Don't buy stock on the basis of a cold call telephone solicitation. If the idea interests you, look up information about the company; call the state securities regulator as mentioned in our later chapter about NASAA and the state regulators.

If it sounds too good to be true...

Daylight
An Honest Man

I have met a lot of brokers I respect and admire. If there are thieves, liars and psychos in the business, there are also honest men and women who plug away, often without any acclaim or gratitude, doing the best they can for their clients. The trouble is trying to sort the good from the bad.

The good brokers should start a union.

Forget the SRO's handling punishments for the wrongdoers. Let the "peers" judge. A good broker hates the bad ones, and is mad as hell that bad ones are allowed to run around and harm people by frauds, lies and evil schemes. The blot of a bad broker spreads like a foul oil slick, covering the whole industry at times, so that public opinion polls routinely report low esteem for brokers. Good brokers suffer unfairly!

I've said several times that the business works on handshakes. Very few, if any, documents have to be signed before you can trade in a cash account. Once the account is open, the trades are not signed by the customer. If most brokers were evil, the markets would be filled with unauthorized trades. The fact is, most trades are authorized in the normal course of business, in regular transactions between brokers and their clients. If clients want an investment, they can order it.

If the good brokers could pass the sentence for the bad ones, more wrongdoers would be tossed for life. A few of the bad ones might be lynched! Why won't it happen?

Because senior managers would be tossed with the broker trash when real discipline was handed out by the people who know the score.

The Soft Touch

The SRO's are too soft. The brokers would be tougher. The brokers can also go right through the fog and tell who the top management flunkies are who should be made pay. The disciplinary reports are filled with little people put in the deep fryer - not the big ones.

I like brokers.

I like talking with them, learning from them, marvelling at their resourcefulness and their resilience. Some of the most gracious and intelligent men and women I have known are brokers. I can smell a bad one fast, using my sensitized experience. It's not intuitive.

How do YOU tell if you've got a good one or a bad one?

The first step is to study your accounts using the questions in Appendix C. A good broker educates you. You aren't surprised by events, because you understand and approve them as they occur. A good broker tells you the truth, doesn't make wild promises, or use mind-games on you.

A Good Broker

A good broker will say "no," when you bring up bad ideas. He may tell you a trade is not for you, because it ISN'T. I've seen brokers spend time reviewing and rejecting ideas brought up by their own house as inappropriate for their clients, and I have seen brokers leave houses because they took objection to the intense marketing efforts of the back room which attempted to get the clients into questionable, but revenue-producing transactions. In effect, a good broker may pass up the opportunity to make a commission because the investment isn't right for you.

These brokers are like gold. They shine. They don't tarnish. They get better and better, surviving up and down markets, doing business with generations in the same family. They work like a small service business with a principal product - integrity.

No Prisoners

Here's my recommendation for flushing out the bad brokers. Forget the SEC and the SRO's; they have had their chance for over 50 years and have failed to make the business any safer for investors than it ever was. Let the brokers decide.

Use a grand and petit jury system where the SRO's present the case, but a panel of licensed brokers drawn by lot from the brokerage community makes the decision on guilt, and then determines the sentence. Tear down the old boy exchange and SEC network. That won't happen because the top managers don't want to give any control to the brokers. Here's an alternative. Under the 1988 amendments to the 1934 Exchange Act, there is a bounty provision for turning in wrongdoers.

Turn in the Boss

The good ones should turn in the bad ones; then, if cause exists, they should turn in the management who covered up for the bad broker to keep the gross production going.

"Turning people in," has an awful sound. It goes against the American grain, sounding more like a communist or fascist tactic. But, which of us would harbor a robber by our silence? Which of us would protect a pickpocket? Which of us would silently allow the conning of a retiree's nest egg by a criminal? Who is so shamefully disposed? Then why do good brokers not speak out about the bad ones in their midst?

This tolerance is a miasma. What has happened is that the brokers have such distaste and fear of the SEC and the SRO's that silence is inherently defensive. The regulators have long lost the trust and confidence of the brokers because of the regulators' ignorant, brazen attitude and constant rhetorical posturing that they know everything and that the brokers are ALL the enemy. It's time for dialogue. Not the SEC and the top management in the usual intimate dance step, but one with the SEC direct to the brokers. It is time for the SEC to come down from the heights and go into the offices to LEARN how the business works and how a broker can help a client. If the brokers would only talk to the SEC, the bad brokers could be bounced in a short while. Trading mutual insults achieves nothing.

Therefore, the key is to get long term, professional employees at the SEC. Raise their salaries. Give them whatever it takes to keep them in place. Remove the animosity by instilling experience in the staff, and the regulatory system will work better. Invite brokers to speak to the SEC. Get the SEC to speak to the brokers, not just lawyers. Isn't it apparent that brokerage management has failed to self-regulate while pursuing the all-glittering bottom line?

Get management either in or out of the picture. If the top management is finally held responsible for bad brokers, guess what: the bad ones will be kicked out! Fast! Make firm presidents sign the Form U-4, the hiring form for all brokers. Brokers, if you have the goods on your top management coddling a rodent, turn them all in! Every day the bad one is loose, every shot he fires into the public body harms your profession! How can you be so neglectful of your own welfare? How can you tolerate such humiliation!

The good broker's worst enemies don't trod the ground as would mere mortals; rather, they drift in the shapeless clouds of senior management throughout the securities industry.

Key Definitions: Selling, Selling, Selling

xix. A Registered Representative is what we commonly call a stockbroker. They go by many different titles for marketing purposes. In the past, a stockbroker was known as a "customer's man," but today they are "account executives," "financial consultants," "investment executives," and other exotic, meaningless titles. The RR has to pass the Series 7 exam, a 6 hour test, given by the NASD, and he has to work for a firm that is responsible for what he does. In firms that specialize, the registered representative may not handle the full range of investment products, therefore he may have taken another, less extensive examination to cover only the product he is selling. Some brokers only sell variable annuities - they don't have to take the full Series 7. In the business, the registered representative is referred to as the "broker," or "rep," or "RR." Forget the titles and use the industry terms. He has to be licensed by the states he does business in. You can ask the NASD for an information sheet about the broker.

xx. A Sales Script is literally a script, in writing, down to the last word and blank space for the target's name, that is used by brokers to make fast sales calls. Professional motivators put these together to get the maximum marketing bang for the least time. A good script leaves you hanging, asking for more, and works in 30 telephone seconds. The brokerage houses put these together, the product wholesalers make them available to the house, and brokers invent them on their own. When your telephone rings and you get a sales pitch from a broker, he is probably reading it for the 100th time that day or week, and he's fishing. HANG UP. Don't bother with a telephone dialer. I get calls at home and the office because I am on mailing and telephone lists (unfortunately) all over the country. The typical entry: "How would you like to have some great information about the exciting possibilities for terrific investment returns now available to investors who take fast action and take advantage of the 1992 European economic shakeup?"

You can substitute anything in the press for the European economic part. The caller will make it seem that if you don't act NOW, the opportunity will pass. Don't fall for it. Let "it" pass. Telephone pressure sales are bad for your financial health.

xxi. Cold Calls are made by hungry brokers or their assistants to random numbers or to numbers from lists that they or their brokerage house have bought from list brokers. Did you buy a car last year? If so, you're on lists. Are you a homeowner - you're on lists. There is nothing sinister about being on lists, just be aware that you are on lists somewhere. When you get cold calls from brokers you don't know, don't be polite - hang up. Learning to hang up is difficult. Here's a practice technique for people with brokerage accounts: call up your brokerage house, get your broker on the telephone, and hang up in the middle of a conversation about the weather. Need something easier: call a local, FREE info number about sports, weather - anything. Call them up and when the tape starts, wait ten seconds, then hang up. Telephone manners don't apply to cold callers - learn to hang up. Don't let them "into" your house on the telephone. Cold calls are supported by interesting statistics about the success percentage per so many calls, so when you hang up, the caller is already onto the next potential victim. Hang up. Hang up. Hang up. Hang up. Hang up. Hang up. Hang up. Hang up. Hang up. Hang up.

xxii. Sales Assistants work for brokers. A big producer, that is, a broker that does a lot of gross production, may have several sales assistants to help him post his book, keep track of order tickets and take calls from customers. Once the big broker has you as a client, you may end up dealing with the sales assistant more than the broker. That may be fine. Some sales assistants are great! The broker usually gives them a small split on his commissions - otherwise they are on salary as employees of the branch office. A good sales assistant working for a good broker will move with the broker when he changes firms. It's an informal partnership. The sales assistant can get you research pieces from the firm, discuss activity in your account, get you copies of monthly statements, explain how to read your statements, and, if he is registered as a broker, take your orders. Get comfortable about dealing with a sales assistant. Because they work for salary from the firm and a derivative split on gross commissions, they are not as hungry. They don't make a lot more if they take you to the cleaners, and they can always get work in the securities business, in banking, or with the government. Try dealing with a sales assistant for a while - they won't recommend hot items, because there is no pressure on them to use the hard sell. If you work with them, you're on the way to using a discounter! A discounter does the same thing, except they don't make any recommendations. They just give service. Some sales assistants go on to be brokers, but many are quite content to remain as sales assistants where they don't have the pressure to sell, where they can get jobs in many industries at their pleasure making about the same salary, and where they can go in and out of business to suit their family needs. Small producers don't have sales assistants. Some brokers don't like to use them preferring to deal with all their clients direct, but big producers who handle a lot of small accounts for "human being" customers have to have them because they can't take all the calls or fill in all the forms. Even with computers, the need for sales assistants to do mailings and post accounts has remained. Increased reliance on cold calling telephone sales techniques has absorbed the brokers' time which has given more emphasis to the sales assistant. They still post the books and handle routine client inquiries. Every broker wishes he had a sales assistant!

Chapter Five

The Research Department

Origins of the Research Man

Larger firms have Research Departments, wherein great ideas are forged and given to the brokers for use with investors. In January, 1990, Merrill Lynch was reported to have 130 employees in just its Equity Research Department, which doesn't address bonds, options or commodities.

The first, real financial newspaper in the United States was the Wall Street Journal, which was founded in 1889 by Charles Dow. There had been and continue to be financial newsletter writers, but the Wall Street Journal was the first regular newspaper dedicated to the activity of the financial markets in lower Manhattan.

Dow? Yes, the name should ring a bell. He developed the Dow Industrial Index, Railroad Index, etc. at the turn of the century, and kept tinkering until he felt he had it "right." Dow died in 1903, but his theories have become the banner of market theoreticians, waved about to imply credentialed "truth," in the face of any question. Every day, people get news about how the Dow Jones Average did on the New York Stock Exchange from radio, T.V. and newspapers, perpetuating the Icon's hold on our collective attention.

There is nothing sacred about the Dow Industrial Index. It wasn't dug up in a great archaeological expedition. It does not represent anything more than Charles Dow's collection of numbers. Over in Tokyo, they use the Nikkei Average, a similar method for issues listed on the Tokyo Exchange.

Unfortunately, it has come to be regarded as a Gospel according to Dow, which is a major mistake. All Dow wanted to do was create a mathematical model. Each day he would take the closing prices of certain stocks on the NYSE, add them up and divide by a constant number. The result would change from day to day as prices changed. It is useful as an indicator of what generally happened that day on the NYSE, but that's it - nothing more!

Under modern usage, The Dow Industrial Average is made up of 30 of the largest companies listed on the NYSE. Take all their closing prices, add them up and divide by the "constant," which "changes." You have the Index for the day. The stocks used in the Dow change, and the "constant" changes slightly from time to time as "experts" tinker with the underlying theory to adjust for stock splits and company substitutions. It's called "fine tuning."

You can own NYSE Listed Stock and watch the Dow go through a gyration up or down, only to find your stock hasn't moved at all. In reverse, the Dow Industrial Index can be moving in a slight range, and your NYSE Listed securities can be getting killed!

Go back to the '87 Crash. IBM dropped on crash day from approximately 150+ to about 105 per share on a day where real prices were unreliable. Logical, you say, because the Dow Industrial Index dropped by 500+ points to under the 2,000 mark. In January, 1990, the Dow Index was over 2700 and IBM was selling under 100 per share!

Beware the use of the Dow as an investment tool. Be cautious of it, don't be overwhelmed by it, don't give it any more credence than a passing curiosity. The Dow has nothing to do with the OTC markets, the cost of bonds or what's coming next, except that it is one of dozens of indicators. Serious financial types just hit the ceiling. "Not related?" What? I believe thusly - everything is related. The Dow is a strictly defined average. It does not use OTC stocks. It does not contain bonds. Are there people who look at the Dow Average and see inferences of effect on the bond and OTC markets? Sure. In 225 BC an Egyptian named Bolus authored a serious treatise about the stars and human beings that had a major effect all through the Mediterranean. It was a best seller in its day.

You laugh? We have recently learned that the appointment schedule of former President Reagan was influenced by the stars as well!

There are other, more broadly based indexes that use the same kind of average-divided-by-a-constant method, by using a "basket" of 500 stocks, such as the Standard and Poors Index. The Dow has a de facto media monopoly, but is not as broad as many others. Charles Dow could have made it more broad - his theory considered and rejected that. His whole point was to take the big 30; nothing else mattered as much.

The Shakespearean evil that lingers after Charles Dow is the development of technical analysis. He used mathematical, logical models that absorbed the measurement of past performance as an indicator of future trends, and let it loose in a nation that loves to play with idiosyncratic data. If you go back to old newspapers of the 1900 era, while enjoying their charm, take a look at the sports pages, especially horse racing and baseball: they are filled with statistics. So are the periodic reviews of boxing. The trivia of past sports performances was often reduced to math models, supporting predictions for the next season, or used in trades to get players with certain strengths. Number crunching has been used in breeding horses, racing boats, track and field, marksmanship contests and other endeavors.

Technical research was no use to a marketeer: he knew what he wanted to do, how it could be done, and just did it! Ultimately, that's true for sports. At some point, the talk stops and the action starts.

The American Civil War was a milestone in military history. It was a conflict of modern logistics involving mass movement of troops over great distances, for either quick engagements or unending battles of attrition. The courage and heroics of commanders in the field were matched by the abilities of anonymous staff officers who could bring firepower and troops to bear in tremendous, overpowering quantities, thereby reducing many of the critical components of battle to questions of numbers - whoever consistently had the most troops, cannon, ships and replacements would win provided the will to win remained dedicated and forceful. Battles could be lost, but the war would be won by industrial might supporting military adventure. The comparison would be this: the world's best mile runner can be defeated by an average 4-man mile-relay team in a one mile race.

Logistics is a mathematical "art." It will not ensure victory, but it helps categorize reality. The lessons of the American Civil War were employed by the Great Powers of Europe, especially Prussia. The Franco-Prussian War of 1870 was a logistical exercise of movement executed according to a master plan based on mathematical averages.

When Charles Dow was at work, the world was under the spell of numbers. Marxists proclaimed that Socialism was a true "science" and that past efforts at democratic reform were sentimental, corrupt attempts to subdue the natural integrity of man under a leash of economic restraint called "charity." Charles Dow "invented" market research as we know it today. The 1920's saw the Wall Street gang preaching Dow theory as Red Square was preaching centralized five-year plans. Both relied on mathematical models.

Numbers could be used to predict or justify almost anything. This was not dehumanizing in intent. The turn of the century was also an age of invention. The Wizard of Menlo Park, Thomas Edison, and his pal, Henry Ford, were men who championed scientific innovation and made life generally better, or at least different. They worked in the realm of ideas, but their lasting genius is shown in their ability to organize massive execution of their dreams. They invented systems of production, not just novel products. The assembly line, however, makes you a number. Your work is quantified, part of a number picture, a part of the grand entirety. You, individually, are nothing.

When you hear of the Dow or of any Logistical average, think of World War One. Highly educated, experienced military leaders repeatedly wasted the flower of European Youth in mindless, massive engagements of flesh against metal to gain mere yards of useless earth. Models that were supposed to predict outcomes based on quantification of activity didn't work, with tragic consequences. In sports, such embarrassments are funny; in real life, they are not.

Yet, people want to rely on numbers. Logical support makes people feel more secure that they are acting correctly, reducing the risk they will go wrong. No Generals were shot after World War One because their theories were proven wrong; the explanation was that the theories had to be "fine tuned." If you travel in Europe, stop at one the cemeteries for our Soldiers who fought and died in the Great War to End All Wars. They are maintained by grateful governments as monuments to our fallen brothers. When you see rows of crosses stretch gracefully within the tranquil boundaries of honored, holy ground, you are looking at brutal reality, the real quantification of plans undone by events. Chapter 8 discusses this in further detail.

Never trust a mathematical model with anything that matters. Formulate the best plan possible, give your execution 110%, and be prepared to change, without hesitation, when reality dictates change!

The World War One debacle for finance came in 1929. I have heard many, many theories of what really caused the crash. I know it happened. I have my own theories about why, but I do not claim to know to a certainty why it happened.

Number-mania is addictive to many people. Look for it; be careful of it! When you see anxious advisors telling you what to risk based on their models, examine their sincerity based on their personal co-investment in the adventure. The question is: where are their dollars at risk?

Technical vs. Fundamental

Technical analysts use past occurrences in mathematical models to predict the future trend and, therefore, the probability of future actions. A technical analyst is never without his chart book, which shows the stock performance of a target company over time in relation to certain averages, such as the Dow. It will show price, volume and other, exotic charts of past activity.

Fundamentalists are concerned about what a company is doing. What are its chief products, what is management like, what are its plans for the future? Past market performance is interesting, but not the main point of interest.

A short distinction: when discussing a company, a fundamentalist writes prose, a technical analyst draws a graph.

Which is more reliable? It's your call. Review both kinds, make your own decisions. Would that the world were as simple as the technical side implies! Look around you: do you live and breathe ideas, do you have plans to do things, to achieve, to grow? Is the past truly a prologue to all the future, or merely one aspect of the puzzle?

Research in an NYSE Member Firm

In a New York Stock Exchange Member Firm, there must be a Supervisory Analyst serving as one of the required approval authorities for any research intended for distribution. As stated earlier, the SA must personally sign off on individual research reports to ensure that the piece is grounded in fact, fairly presented, and published in accord with NYSE Rule 472, "Communications with the Public."

The NYSE gives a special examination to test the qualifications of a Supervisory Analyst to document his knowledge of accepted financial research techniques and legal-compliance issues as well. This is a very important position because of the special expertise involved. There are very few Supervisory Analysts.

In good times, a 1,000 broker firm can support 8 to 20 people in a Research Department, depending on commission revenues. If a firm has five thousand selling brokers, it can support 50 to 85. The Department has a simple mission: come up with ideas for sales.

The Research Department will have a sprinkling of Ph.D.'s, and a majority of MBA veterans working in an isolated think tank. The mission is not to probe into intellectually interesting areas - they are supposed to come up with information that the brokers can use to call accounts and get business. Business means selling.

An analyst is supposed to look around in his area of specialty and come up with reports on a frequent basis. Each analyst follows a defined group, such as the auto, chemical or auto industries. What if he doesn't see a good prospect in his group for a three month period? He's in trouble. He is supposed to find them. He is supposed to find them to support the sales machine which devours ideas.

Analysts are not trained inside the house. They are brought in and let loose on day "one." The only training in a house is for the selling brokers. The analyst is usually recruited by the Research Department in a casual way, except for the occasional superstar who comes out of government or is a darling of the media.

Superstars rise and disappear. Wall Street doesn't pay much for a regular analyst because there are so many of them around. The supply/demand curve favors the house.

Making Money on the Way Down
Shorts and Options

Research should not be concerned with market direction, so much as the likelihood of change, because, theoretically, an investor can make money in an up or down market. The direction of the market is interesting, but it is the actual movement of a security that is critical. Let's explore this at some length, relating it to research editorial policy.

If a stock moves up three points and you own it, you make three paper points. If you sell, you realize those three points, but you have given up your ability to get any further gain.

You can make money when a stock goes down.

You can sell short. This was discussed earlier.

If you want to do this, you tell the broker to sell short. He goes to his Operations Department and makes sure they have the stock. The broker puts in a sell ticket, specially marked "Short."

The trade goes through a normal execution, except that the stock isn't taken from your account - you don't have it - the stock is, instead, taken from the firm, delivered to the buyer, and your account is put on margin for the value of the stock you have just borrowed.

If the stock goes down, you call your broker and tell him to buy it back in. Once bought, your broker's books are in balance. Your account is no longer borrowing the stock. If you originally sold the stock at 50, and it dropped three points to 47, where you bought it back, you made three points, minus the interest charged by your broker while you were on margin and commissions (of course).

Want a better example? Suppose you sell wheat for bulk delivery to a bread baker a week ahead. Today's price is 5 cents a pound. You believe next week the price will be 4 cents and you will be able to get all you want. You will sell all you can today at 5 cents, then go get it at 4 cents and deliver it next week. The price dropped. You made money, one cent per pound. When you sold the wheat, you didn't have it. You were "short." When you got the wheat, you "covered."

Commodity traders are comfortable with the primacy of price change over the direction of change as the opportunity for profit.

Short selling is very risky, because the stock can go up! It can go right through the roof, and you can lose your shirt. Remember the

Marketeers of the 19th and early 20th century? Sharp Marketeers looked to trap short sellers whenever possible. On a lesser scale the same happens today.

Because the trade ticket is marked "Short," the NYSE can issue data on how many shares have been sold short for a listed stock. It's called "the short interest." It is published regularly by the NYSE and reported by the financial press such as the Wall Street Journal. The NASD publishes similar statistics for the OTC market.

A lot of short interest can mean investors believe a company is going to do poorly in the future, or it can mean modern marketeers are playing a game, trying to drive the price down. It is hard to figure the price target of the short interest. It could be one point, two or twenty!

There is another, less risky way to make money when a stock goes down. You buy a "Put."

A Put is an option. You don't buy the actual stock.

Let's do one. Finegan Motors Corporation isn't doing too well against the Japanese Auto Industry, and its dealers have cars sitting in sales lots for months. The forecast is for poor auto sales.

You decide Finegan Motors Corporation will drop in price.

Finegan Motors Corporation is listed on the NYSE. It has listed options. When you look in the paper, there are prices for Puts and Calls.

A Call is the right to buy 100 shares of Finegan Motors Corporation at a set price for a set period of time, typically at three month intervals, ending on the third Friday of each third month interval.

You can buy a Call Option if you think the price of Finegan Motors Corporation Stock is going up. If it doesn't go up, the most you lose is the money you paid for the Call. You don't have to buy the stock to make money.

A Put is the right to make an investor or speculator buy 100 shares of stock from you at a set price for a set period of time. An example: Finegan Motors Corporation is selling today, January 2, at 55. If you buy a June 50 Put, you now own the right to force a party to buy 100 shares of Finegan Motors Corporation from you at a price of 50 through the third Friday in June. You can "Put" the stock to them.

What's so good about that if the price today is 55 and you can force someone to buy it for 50? ANYONE would love to buy it for 50 and get the five points!

Notice - the right to force the buyer to pay 50 lasted through June, six months forward. Suppose in March, the price drops to 40, because all those Finegan Motors Corporation cars are still sitting on the same lots. Finegan Motors Corporation stock is selling on the NYSE at 40 and you can force people to buy it at 50! Now you see the value of owning a Put! You can make 10 points. The Put may have cost you only a few points. The percentage profit leverage is terrific! Sounds great!

Do you go and buy the 100 shares of Finegan Motors Corporation at 40 and force a party to literally buy the shares for the full price of 50? If you wanted to, you could actually exercise the option. In practice, you will sell the option in the options market, and make your profit without ever owning the Finegan Motors Corporation stock!

Options are very, very interesting, and my examples are not meant to get you ready to use them. I oppose retail investors using options, because retail investors seem to constantly lose. Options are tough to understand and hard to correctly time for execution. Brokers have to either get discretion in writing or sweat out being able to contact you for permission to sell the position when the time is right. Brokers don't make much on option commissions, so they must do a lot of options trades to make it economically worth their while. For most brokers - too much work!

But, you can see that it is possible to make money when Finegan Motors Corporation is headed down by either going short or buying a

Put. There are other ways that get more complex, using options strategies where you have bought and sold options on the same security, straddling both sides of the price fence.

Getting back to Research, if you can make money on Finegan Motors Corporation's way down, why is the market so traditionally reliant on an upward direction?. Why aren't investors trading and making money without regard to market direction? If Finegan Motors Corporation goes up 10 or down 10 you can make the same money! A big movement in the Dow, either way, should cause joy! Savvy players have to be happy. Direction is theoretically irrelevant to a sophisticated trader.

Starting a Research Collection
Finegan Motors Corporation Fights Back

The Sunday papers are filled with advertisements offering free packages of recommendations for the price of a stamp or toll-free telephone call. Get it. The worst that will happen is a hungry broker from the responding firm will call you as a follow up to your inquiry. Hang up on him.

But examine the research piece. Get a lot from different firms. Forget the color and texture of the page, the flashing logos and other hype - look at the guts of the report. It will usually say you should buy a stock. A good piece will be one full page or two pages, front and back, of the same flyer. You'll notice a similar format in the presentation, including hedge clauses on the bottom telling you that this is just an opinion and is not guaranteed.

Once they have told you to buy the stock with their essay, what next? Do they tell you to sell it at the appropriate time? Maybe.

Sell recommendations are not highlighted as much as the buys. A little art comes into play. Sells are negative and negative news is not well received in the sales area. A Research Department may put out a special buy recommendation and later issue a sell for the same security within a group of recommended actions. Yet, a sell should have the same opportunity for profit.

Everything is relative, and the world is small. Suppose an analyst decides that a big company like Finegan Motors Corporation is a screaming sell, opining that Finegan Motors Corporation should be sold right away, either short or long, or by options strategies, and that it might be good for 10 or 15 points. To support that, the analyst will have to have his facts lined up. A Supervisory Analyst will have to sign off. The firm can put it out to thousands of customers, and beyond through newspaper and radio ads. How do you think Finegan Motors Corporation will feel?

Finegan Motors Corporation will be irate! "So what," you ask? They can do things about it. Finegan Motors Corporation employs a lot of people who have a lot of brokerage and bank accounts. Finegan Motors Corporation deals with a lot of banks that lend money to the brokerage industry. Finegan Motors Corporation is one of the biggest listings on the NYSE, and when they talk, the NYSE listens! Finegan Motors Corporation sells occasional new issues of bonds or stock and can approve or disapprove members of the selling syndicate. They can tell their people not to talk to any callers from the brokerage firm. They can bad-mouth the brokerage house. They can threaten to sue! They can threaten to buy the house and fire the management!

I have seen little newspapers take on giant corporations with only the resolve of integrity as the paper's arsenal. We expect this from the press - why not analysts? If an analyst wants to act with purity of intellect, the businessmen that run the firm have to be concerned about the reality of a relative universe with the possibility of revenge. On top of that, what if the analyst is wrong? What if Finegan Motors Corporation goes up and a bunch of brokers have boldly convinced people to go short or use options? How will brokers who just bought Finegan Motors feel when their firm research contradicts their recommendation? The fallout could be serious. While Supervisory Analysts take an exam, regular analysts don't.

The brokerage firm wants to get business from Finegan Motors Corporation, not get Finegan Motors Corporation mad at them. They want the brokers selling the easiest trades possible, because they aren't up to complex strategies. They don't want a lawsuit, either.

The Research Department is more likely to downplay the event. While they may issue a half-hearted sell recommendation, it will be most often buried, really aimed at getting people who presently own the stock after having bought it earlier through the brokerage house to consider selling. The client sells, frees up cash and the broker can get the client to buy another investment. It won't be a hard sell recommendation if a major company is involved. It will not attempt to bring up anything that could seriously embarrass the company.

If the Research Department has a "sell" recommendation, they better have a spectrum of "buys" ready to absorb all the suddenly-free cash. Customer cash is useless to the house unless it trades.

If the Department analysts feel it is best to generally sell off and go to cash, they will have a hard time telling that to the public. These days, when public investors hear negative news, they sell and sit on cash proceeds. The house doesn't get business.

Brokers don't make money on investors that sit on cash. They need transactions. A broadly negative analyst is, therefore, a liability to a brokerage house. The analyst doesn't have to be consistently negative, just seriously negative, to cause significant damage to transactional revenues.

The house loves to get an analyst who can come up with a stream of stock picks that go up. Let's recall: flip a coin and you are right 50% of the time. Take out a coin right now. Let's experiment. Flip it five times. Did it come out 3 to 2, 4 to 1 or 5 to 0? I just did it and got 4 to 1! I know that if I do it 10,000 times, I will get close to 50-50, but in a small sample, statistics can be meaningless. Any analyst can be red hot for a year; all he needs to do is take positions! Lady Luck may take care of the rest.

Suppose the analyst puts out a buy recommendation, and the stock rises. He then puts out a sell, but it is a "soft" sell that really says the rise is over and it is time to take the profit and buy something else that is due to go up. The broker gets a client who buys, then sells, then buys again with the same cash. A happy client keeps on trading and offers referrals to new clients. It's all positive, up, up, up!

None of this firm research existed before 1900. No one needed it. Marketeers did their own maneuvering, and the public wasn't involved directly. Research, therefore, is used to get you into the action as a retail customer.

How did the Wall Street Research Machine miss the Crash in October, 1987? Why didn't they have alarm bells going out to the public? Firms were hammered in their own accounts.

They don't want to see it. They can't see it for fear of customers going to cash and sitting on the sideline, which is exactly what has happened since 1987, and is the reason brokerage houses are laying off in droves. Wall Street, collectively, hasn't got a clue about where the market is going. Worst of all, they may be losing you, the consumer!

They want investors to feel secure that all is well, that prices will continue to rise, because Wall Street believes negative news and forecasts will make investors pull their money out of securities and put it in those dastardly banks.

Back to the Sunday Paper - take a look at the education section where universities put their ads. How many business schools have commercials in your paper for MBA degrees? Where do all these degree holders go to work when they get out of school?

The top 20 MBA Schools in the nation place their graduates in the old boy networks of industrial America where they convince banks to lend to Latin America and to accept overvalued land in the US as security for other loans. Others go to insurance companies, where they convince the company boards to buy brokerage houses and invest in "safe" real estate to compete with the banks. What about the hundreds of universities with no old-boy networks that have the degree pump going: where are they sending thousands and thousands of MBA's?

A Ph.D. in Economics is not a hot ticket. There are plenty of them around - trying to get jobs teaching in business schools!

According to the US Department of Labor, the hot occupation for the future is the paralegal!

An analyst in a brokerage house doesn't earn much and is easily replaced if he gets on a cold streak. They go cold all the time. Wall Street has a few media "names." You see the same individuals being interviewed regularly, as though there was a bull pen with 10 pitchers always ready to come out and throw a few innings.

They throw the same tired, hedged pitches, hide behind diversity as though it were proven truth, and make sure that their introduction prominently states what brokerage house they are from. They must get the name of the firm out - that's their function. I'm not talking here about small Investment Advisory firms that go out of business when they are publicly wrong, nor am I including the publishers of market newsletters who, when they are wrong, are instantly, viciously ridiculed in the press. These professionals take positions and incur risk. It's their livelihood. They are good or gone. They earn their audience.

Have you ever seen the celebrity analysts' track record? Have you ever seen the entire track record of the Research Department of the brokerage house you use? Have you asked?

Life can be embarrassing when faced with facts. Alan Greenspan, the present Chairman of the Federal Reserve, gave a favorable report about real estate investment in 1984 on behalf of Lincoln Savings as a paid economic consultant. Lincoln has emerged as a lightening rod of comment about the Savings and Loan problem, and the estimate of the taxpayers cost to carry Lincoln is approximately 2 billion. Not millions - billions! Mr. Greenspan now says he was wrong. OK, we all make mistakes. His happened to make the newspapers because of who he is and the coverage given to the Lincoln Savings case.

Show me the brokerage house Research Department that has ever issued a piece to say that their prior analysis was wrong for the listed reasons! I have never seen it.

Research Performance Statistics
Complete List, Please!

The NYSE has interesting rules about how a firm can plug its research. They cannot reach in and pull out the winners, leaving the losers floating in the barrel. If a NYSE Member Firm wants to talk about their research performance, they have to give a universe of ALL the picks for at least a one year period, showing all the recommendations with the specific buy - sell price recommendations. To make it worse, the firm has to describe the general market conditions, which means they have to compare themselves to how the Dow Jones Average did.

So, you might ask to see the brokerage house's research track record and be told that they can't show it to you because of NYSE Rules. They can show it, but it has to be complete. They may not want to show it!

What if the best the Research Department can say is that it matched the performance of the Dow Jones Average? So what? That's not superior. If you follow Charles Dow's theory, then all you need do is buy the 30 equities that make up the Average. Sit on the investment, don't trade. You will match the Dow every time.

The firm has to stand behind its recommendations, not that they must guarantee things they recommend will go up, but the firm has to offer supporting information to you, the client, upon your request.

Let's take that again. If a NYSE Member Firm makes a recommendation to you, they must offer to provide you with supporting information.

Has your broker ever called you in the morning at home or work and told you that the Research Department has just been on the internal squawk box recommending Finegan Motors Corporation, and that it is time to act?

Don't do anything!

Get the Research piece and ask for the documentation supporting the recommendation. The broker probably won't send it, because he knows the momentum of the sale has passed. He can't get you to move on his telephone pitch, and sending information will take time and effort. For what? One trade? It's not worth the broker's time. Besides, if you want to knit pick, you will probably be a pain in the future, and the next thing you'll do is ask for a discount on commissions!

Suppose you have a really good broker and he is happy to send the report. Do you know how to read a balance sheet? Do you understand and use the same information that analysts use? Previously, I referred to Finegan Motors Corporation lots filled with cars going nowhere. That's a fair indicator of surplus inventory that most people can understand. Can most people understand a balance sheet? My experience has taught me that only a few people can interpret and use "hard" financial information. Brokers know this, and they use it as part of the sale. The full service NYSE Member Firm Wire House prints thousands of copies of its research pieces, scatters them about, and knows that you probably cannot understand the underlying financial mechanisms of balance sheets. Many financial statements are great works of camoufl-age. The fog gets quite thick at times.

The research piece is a sales tool meant to impress you, catch your interest, and induce you to do business. If there was a better way to get you, the research would be tossed out the window. The discounters don't bother with research, having elected for that window.

Did you know that analysts can work on a bonus basis? Houses figure out ways to quantify the results of the analyst's publications, not based on whether they go up as predicted, but rather, based on whether they generate trades, and therefore income, from the reports. If the analyst is right every time, but doesn't generate transactions from the brokers, what good is he? If he is wrong every time, but generates gross commissions, he's great!

Realistically, if he is right a lot, he will develop a following among the brokers. While on a hot streak, analysts become almost cult figures. Because he has been right in the past, the brokers follow his every recommendation and will buy a stock without hesitation or investigation because the guru has spoken.

The analyst gets into the self-fulfilling prophesy business. He can make a stock go up by just mentioning it! The firm cannot legally separate his recommendations from the rest of the department to give you only his track record, but the brokers will do it on the telephone.

This creates another kind of problem.

If the analyst is really good, who gets his information first, the firm or the customer? Firms trade for their own accounts all the time and they take it very serious. Is the firm using the information first? Is the analyst using it himself first? Do certain brokers get it before the other brokers in the same firm? If it comes out in printed flyers, who sees the drafts?

Where do analysts get their information?

The next question might well be, "Is there a Santa Claus?"

No, there is no real Santa, only the good intentions of humble mortals at Yuletide. Perhaps that's far better than a real Santa could ever be. If brokerage research was all that good you would never see it - the houses would use it exclusively, secretly for their own accounts, to trade the house's money.

If the Chairman of the Federal Reserve can admit to a mistake about Lincoln Savings, we should all pause to question what the reliability of research is? It isn't great. Every research piece comes with a hedge clause that says it is based on a lot of information, BUT IS NOT GUARANTEED. It's just an opinion.

The analyst usually covers a group of stocks in a similar industry. Suppose he follows the drug industry. He will call around to the major companies to make sure he gets on the mailing list of the company shareholder relations and public relations offices. The analyst wants to have names he can call at the company to get follow-up information on any breaking news.

The analyst has no way to get "inside" information from the company; inside information is illegal. What is it? Material, non-public information that an ordinary investor would probably consider relevant, if he could get it, in his investment decisions. There is no statutory definition in the 1934 Exchange Act on purpose, because the law in this area has only evolved in the past twenty years.

Another view: information is either public or "inside." If it is public, it has been reported by the company to the news wire services and often put out in direct publicity releases to select analysts representing major securities industry brokerage houses. If the information has not been put out to the public, it is still "inside" and may not be used for trading.

Analysts have no greater resources than you do. They use the library, they study the subject area, the products, the technology, and they call the company - you could, too!

You can call Pfizer, the pharmaceutical giant, and they will be happy to send you a copy of the annual report and tell you where to find periodic financial reports made to the press and the SEC. If you ask them for late news on what the next major drug announcement will be, or how their profits for the quarter are shaping up, they will politely demur and tell you that such information is not for publication until final results are in and the public is informed in the routine manner.

That is how an analyst gets his information, and it is the limit of what he can get. He can't get "inside" any more than you. A good analyst will tell you that.

The analyst takes all the public information he can get on the company, studies it, extrapolates toward future results, guesses at future business conditions and comes up with a research report. If you had the time, you could do the same.

It doesn't take a genius. It takes a good "researcher." The predictive element is pure luck. It is not a science. The analyst does not probe too hard, doesn't badger a company's executives with detailed questions about curious events or allegations about wrongdoing and doesn't follow leads that might lead to a real "story."

The analyst has a very difficult job, a very unfair one. Fundamental Research is hard work, but the best it does is take you up to the present financial status of a company. A historian takes you on a journey through the past, but stops at the present, because no one can predict the future. Future trends are fascinating; we all enjoy the fun of making informed guesses at the future. Predictions are dangerous!

Every Spring, baseball analysts predict who will be in the October World Series, who will win the American and National League Batting Championships with what averages, who will hit the most home runs, and on and on. Baseball is made of statistics and is therefore prone to "sporting" guesses, but we enjoy the art of these predictions and smile when, after the season, the actual occurrences vary from the predictions.

Similarly, we accept analysts reports on the Stock Market. Unfortunately, if we reject an individual report, we accept the concept.

Don't! The analyst is a new invention of the 20th century. The retail brokerage industry is a post World War Two invention. You are the target, and research is but one tool. Armed with that healthy skepticism, let's use a report.

The Public Library

Here's how to use a report. Understanding that a skilled researcher has gathered data and published a condensed report, accept the shortcut on your own research. You don't have to look as far or as long as he did. He did a lot of your legwork, but not all your homework. Go to the library!

Take a look at the "usual sources" to see what commentary the press has entertained about the company. Public libraries are great institutions! We should have a National Holiday to praise the selfless dedication that goes into your local public library! It may be 50 miles away, but the staff could help you out on the telephone or in the mail, and no matter where you are, if you are in the stock market, you should make a regular habit of using the library.

Go to the reference desk and ask how you can look up information on Pfizer. The librarian can steer you to standard references and computer listings of articles on Pfizer and the drug industry. Your branch library may have Standard and Poors Reports or Value Line's loose-leaf reviews, and it may have microfilmed issues of the New York Times and the Wall Street Journal. It may have boxed inventories and current issues of Money Magazine, Inc., Fortune, Forbes, Barrons, Investor's Daily, and so forth. If they don't have it there, they can help you find citations for articles on Pfizer. They can get the articles for you through other libraries on inter-library networks.

The problem may be they have too much! Let's say that Pfizer is selling at $50 per share. One hundred shares will cost you $5,000. That's a lot of cash to invest, especially when a 10% drop translates into a $500 bite! Don't buy a stock without taking a look at it yourself BEFORE you invest!

This doesn't mean that you become an expert, but you might read a brokerage house research report and find that the same company was panned in an article in a major magazine last month where the concentration was not on the past profits of the company but on the legislative uncertainty concerning their main product. The combination of a Wall Street Journal profile of the management of a company, and the Value Line statistics on past performance might give you a different view than the brokerage house analyst. Maybe the brokerage house was the underwriter a few years ago for the public issue of the stock under review!

It's your money, and you should take your own look. You don't have to subscribe to the Wall Street Journal, but you should read it. It's a great paper, filled with statistics and discussion that has gotten more readable over the past five years than ever before. Forbes is a terrific, chatty magazine aimed at many levels of readers, filled with timely information about a lot of companies, with a comprehensive style that makes reading it a pleasure. If you can read and understand Sports Illustrated, Readers Digest or Consumer Reports, you can read and understand Forbes. Try it - you'll enjoy it. You'll also come away from the experience with knowledge.

All these publications take great pains to produce clear, reliable and topical articles. It's not just for wealthy coupon clippers.

If you make a pleasant habit out of going to a library reading room and browsing through a week of the Wall Street Journal at one time, you'll find it educational, fun - and practical. The Journal is the principal research source used in the brokerage industry. Second Place might be argued as a tie among several sources, including all the major papers such as the New York Times, Washington Post and Los Angeles Times. My own usage is that the New York Times is the primary source, the Wall Street Journal is the next, Money Magazine follows, then there is a tie for Fortune and Forbes. I read a lot of other magazines at the library covering specialized industries and finance in general. I am amazed at the number of excellent free-lance writers who cover the money beat and the variety of insight they command.

Take your kids or spouse along on library trips. Get the Dow Jones-Irwin book that tells you how to read the Wall Street Journal, which will help you understand the statistical tables. Can you understand baseball statistics? Can you keep score in tennis or bowling - you can understand the Journal's statistical sections.

What's holding you back? I go into reading rooms or reference sections and see them empty! Where are you? Get up! Go! It's all there for you!

Consider this: suppose your broker calls and tells you to buy Big Doggie Stock, now, right away, before the crowds find out! Find out what? Go to the library, and see what's available on Big Doggie and on its industry group. If Big Doggie doesn't show up in any articles, but the industry does receive coverage, you've just discovered an anomaly.

An anomaly is an inconsistency. If a broker is telling you about a stock worth buying, but you can't find any information about the company through the library system, where has your broker done his research? What depth does it have? Where is his supporting information? The answer is that the broker is using imaginary research, the word of mouth rumors that are intended for suckers and market addicts.

Are you one of those? Drop the broker. Analysts don't create their reports from a void; they use reliable, historical information gleaned from many data sources, and then they make a guess. Bad brokers test the wind or the rumor circuit and start calling their book.

A good broker will give you his thoughts and refer you to the articles he relies on. A bad broker tells you he just got a "call," and you get the impression he is giving you a "hot tip" that requires immediate action! Don't fall for one of the classic rumor scams! Don't!

Whenever you get a recommendation, take your own look. Do it a few times, and you will be hooked on your public library! Take a look around and see if you ever, that's right, ever, run into brokers in the same library doing what you are doing. Well, you reason, they get all that material, all those magazines in the office. Right?

Wrong!

You might think that markets in flux create a greater requirement to have Research people around - no. Analysts represent fixed cost. In business, fixed cost is a beast. It eats you up when there are falling revenues.

Fixed cost includes the entire back room, rent, light etc. When revenues fall, fixed costs have to fall or the house goes under.

Since 1987, brokerage houses have put great effort into cutting down on fixed cost, from major rent obligations through the cost of magazine subscriptions. If your broker wants to get Fortune Magazine, he has to pay for it himself. Branch managers spend a lot of time cutting services from the video tubes and dutifully reporting these achievements to their superiors up the line. Only big producers are exempt because they carry their own load, and they can walk.

Jettisoning the Ballast

The first to get laid off in a Wall Street slow down are research people. They come and go. I don't know what an analyst aspires to in the brokerage house. A few achieve notoriety, but most analysts are academics and have no place in management. While they may be tapped for ideas, they generally don't get their hands on real, firm trading money. They usually work in tiny, plain offices, away from the public-image luxury of the Sales Office and senior management area. In early 1990, they are being laid off in heartbreaking droves. Where do they go?

Why do analysts do what they do? I have met many around the Street that wouldn't do anything else! They love it. They know companies like fans know their favorite teams, keeping in mind that the word "fan" is derived from "fanatic."

Occasionally, they become brokers. Others become money managers. Funny thing: some ex-researchers become very, very good brokers and Investment Advisors because they always had the talent and their frustration as an analyst was often due to their integrity. It wasn't that they did not have a string of hits - they go because they cannot generate sales. It always comes back to selling.

House Analyzing House

Why don't brokerage house analysts review each other's firms?

It's a de facto truce. They hold off.

Consumer activists tell us to check out the track record of roofing contractors before we sign and give over money. Where do you check out a brokerage house? Recall again Ford commercials where a Ford truck will be directly compared to a Chevy, then a Plymouth; then come the revenge commercials from Chevy and Plymouth. Aspirin commercials take on hard competition by brand name. Popcorn does it. Even Burger King does it. Why not full service wire houses and why not on the basis of the other guy's research? Why doesn't one house tell you that the other guys have lousy research and you should avoid that firm, just like airlines do with time of arrival-departure percentages? When did the brokerage industry get a statutory exemption from the Federal Anti-Trust Laws? Basically, they got it in the 1934 Act. The statutory control structure makes the industry a club.

Competitive marketing would be easy because the frequent turnover of employees in the industry, from one house to the next, means there should be no shortage of sources of house secrets.

You'll be able to find articles in the press that describe brokerage achievements, personality changes, lawsuits, earnings, and industry trends, but you won't be able to get research reports by one house that are critical of another house. New York Stock Exchange Rules come into play. If one house was critical of another, it could suffer formal disciplinary proceedings within the NYSE. A house doesn't have to be 100% certain about its other, regular research, but we have looked at the ways in which Finegan Motors Corporation can defend itself from over zealous analysts. Brokerage management can be pressured to fire an analyst or gag him. The analyst doesn't publish the report - the house does. The house can refuse to publish it. If the analyst publishes on his own, he can be fired.

Road Shows

Senior officers of public companies have to get used to talking to analysts at road shows which are staged news conferences where the company official gives a canned speech with visual aids, and takes a few questions.

A good road show will be held over a free lunch, take as little time as practical and leave as good an impression of the company as possible. Nothing new comes out, because the company's lawyers have briefed the speaking official on what is "public" information and what is "inside." The road show is meant to sell an image of the company.

Road shows are used for brokers when a new issue of stock comes to the market and a house sales machine is trying to get excitement going. The key ingredients of a road show are the quality of the food and the club the meeting is held in. It helps if the show ends with the distribution of colorful selling material, especially if it works well on the copy machine en route to investors.

An effective road show can make a big difference for a company's stock price, especially if the analysts come away impressed with the list of other guests at the meeting. Analysts should be able to work without a show. It helps to get a heavyweight from the local financial community to show up as a guest, to beam approval when the show is over. There are even rent-a-celebrity companies that will have people from the theater and cinema drop by at birthday and cocktail parties - why not road shows? One of the reasons analysts enjoy this diversion is they get a free meal away from the office. They will not ask difficult questions about products, activities, policies or internal politics. If they do, they won't get an answer. The subsequent report will not comment on canned answers or refusals to comment because the analyst is not allowed to pick a fight with anyone and his ability to follow up is limited.

Don't mistake an analyst for a journalist. Let's repeat that so there is no mistake: DON'T MISTAKE AN ANALYST FOR A JOURNALIST. A journalist follows and reports the facts as a professional. An analyst supports a sales effort.

Company leaders remember: road shows that travel to the analyst may be the only way the analyst gets to see the company. He may have no budget to go to the company's operations, home office or annual meeting. The analyst may have a boss who tries to skimp on telephone time and won't let him charge back expenses for library trips. Don't laugh!

If you own stock, call up the investor relations department of the your issuer and ask if they do road shows, and where you can get a schedule. Try to go. If your company doesn't do road shows, find out why. Are they hiding? Get on the publicity list. Go to annual meetings!

Alternatives to the Library
Information Services in your Home

Too busy to go to the library? Can't get invited to road shows? Over the past few months I have gotten several mailers from different information services that bring the market into your home. I don't know if this is good or bad, but it has technologically arrived in 1990, marketed to the masses. The easiest is to use the Wall Street Journal's pay-per-use "900" telephone line that will give you news and stock quotes anywhere you can use a touch tone telephone. Why call your broker and give him another opportunity to SELL to you. The broker has been trained to get an order from every caller. He usually has to work at calling you. He loves it when you call him.

Another - a service that uses the T.V. cable and hooks up to my computer, allowing me to buy two levels of service to obtain quotes and news. Their upper service is about equivalent to what brokers have on their office videos, except that the quotes are delayed 20 minutes behind the floor. On a busy day, the brokers can get the same delay. With this one, you don't need a telephone line or modem. Call your cable company and see what they have to offer. The NYSE sells the live quote information to distributors who provide it to brokers and other sophisticated users. The public gets the LATE quotes for free.

I can buy services that work on directed microwaves. Some use telephone modem hookups to my computer. Various cable T.V. companies run the Financial News Network in the daytime, where a tape runs across the bottom of the screen. If you haven't seen it, look for FNN on cable T.V.. It is very educational.

It's all there!

There is nothing the broker has that you can't get, except the latest flow of rumors, which is of no value in investing.

Guru-based Price Jumps

Let's have another view of the Research Department. If an analyst is on a hot streak, he can develop a following of brokers who have buying power and are ready to employ it as soon as the Guru speaks. The brokers call their hero all the time. If one broker finds out what is going to come out, he can get the jump on his friends, buy stock that is about to be recommended, then sell it as the price goes up when the regular publication of the piece comes out. It's illegal.

You have watched the half-hour programs on PBS and CNN that follow the market, haven't you? If so, you have heard discussion of how Finegan Motors was up this week because of a buy recommendation issued Wednesday by Big Brokerage House. When the buy comes out, the action will start right away. A buy recommendation from the right Guru at the right house can be worth 2 or 3 points all on its own. This precludes the time required to do a little homework before jumping in. This kind of instant rise is great for the House because customers who blindly follow the recommendations get a quick paper profit! If it falls later on, so what - that's later. Stay away from stocks that jump as soon as a research report gets out. The report is only re-hashing public information. What you are seeing when this phenomenon occurs is a frenzy of mindless, retail activity. The institutions don't work that way. You shouldn't. No investment has to be made right now - another will always come along. Take your time and make your decision when you are in control, not when your broker tells you to jump.

Controlling the analyst

Brokerage houses take steps to watch what the analyst is up to, especially since the 1934 Exchange Act was amended in 1988 to include harsh penalties for firms that don't create internal systems to control this kind of activity. Remember, we are now talking about only a house recommendation.

The recommendation can be a kind of inside information, and its misuse may be a Federal Crime. A recent SEC action involved misappropriation of Business Week Magazine materials. Several civil cases and a few criminal prosecutions were commenced based on the wrongful dissemination and use of Business Week Articles before the official publication time. The case involved cash payments for copies of articles. Business Week Magazine had nothing to do with it, and was a victim of the activity of a few investors and stockbrokers.

Brokerage houses have to watch out that analysts don't trade on their work before it is published, and that they do not hand out information to brokers in anything but the most controlled circumstances. Publication of their work has to be closely watched and the timing has to be carefully coordinated so that the New York City brokers do not always get the jump on their broker colleagues in the same firm in California, Texas or Montana. How do you give 5,000 brokers the news at the same time so they have the same opportunity?

By wire. They put the information on the internal wire in short form and then send the full length version around in the house mail to each of the offices. They can also put it in their video system. It is possible to control the publication of the material so that it is universally available electronically across a full system at one time.

Make no mistake - the public does not have to get all the research product of the firm. Because the firm wants to get institutional clients and money managers to send in transactional business, the firm may have special reports made available to these clients that you as a retail client don't get. It can be very general, based on trends, or it can be a rifle shot, one company recommendation. The Hartford Courant, the largest circulation newspaper in Hartford, Connecticut, and the longest-running, regularly published newspaper in the US, has an interesting product. If you pay a special fee, you get a fax version of the paper before the regular, printed one is available. It's a great idea! If you need late breaking stories, they can provide them, in fax print! You don't have to wait for news with the radio or T.V. on, and you get a chance to re-read the text. Does your brokerage house do that for you?

Free research is worth, well, what? It is legal for a brokerage house to compose and sell research publications, just as publishers sell their newsletters. The newsletter business is very different. If you can get free research from the wire houses, why would anyone bother to pay for a newsletter with subscription prices from the hundreds to the thousands of dollars. One reason is the newsletters may include a promise that they will call you when any flash opportunity/disaster shows up. Another is that their business is information, not transactions. If they are not successful, they lose clients. It's do or die.

Would you buy research pieces from a brokerage house? You do. Your commissions pay for the department! Compare the discounters' commission schedules with the wire houses. One of the reasons for the marked difference is the cost of carrying a research department. When the research department is gutted with layoffs in a brokerage slowdown, does your house reduce your commissions? Of course not. The house may raise the commissions!

Whether research makes a hit is irrelevant. Commentators have been waiting to see Wall Street start selling its research for the past twenty years. The theory is that if Wall Street can't get your transactional business, maybe they can get you to buy information. It hasn't happened. It won't. What they put out is not worth buying.

True, when the Guru speaks there may be a sharp rise in the price of a recommended security, but that's because the brokers go to work selling. The rise happens before the report could possibly be mailed outside the house. The reason the racing sheets sell is that they get you ready for the race next Wednesday at 2 PM. Most securities research is old as soon as it is published. Would you buy it if you knew the brokers already had it electronically and had played it out before you got your mail delivery?

This does not mean that old research has no value. It is useful to someone who wants to make an investment and plans to hold on for a while. Old research can be quite useful in the endless search for fundamental value. It has no use to traders, who move from one investment to the next with the ease of breathing and a single motive: fast profit. So, why don't houses try to sell their research product and compete with the newsletters and investment managers? They don't want you to invest; they want you to trade. If you invest and sit back for a while, they don't make any money.

The firm uses a "Chinese Wall" to take care of this and a few other wrinkles. In theory a research analyst at a major house does not know what the investment bankers over in corporate finance are doing. It is debateable, based on Wall Street's track record, that the investment bankers know what they are doing either. If the investment bankers are getting ready to sell stock for Finegan Motors Corporation, they don't want Analyst Guru putting out any research that might technically interfere in the timing of the deal or knock the company. The analyst doesn't know what the investment bankers are up to, and the investment bankers don't know what the analyst is getting ready to publish. I have a later chapter on Chinese Walls.

Your brokerage firm - how do you tell if their research department is any good? It depends on what you mean by "good?" Flip a coin. Show me the research department that probes, that pursues leads about the competence of management, about the nuances of how management treats shareholders. Show me the wire house research department that ever "broke" a story about corporate misdeeds in all its study of the target entity, interviews with executives and data sorting. Show me the one, brief, shining moment in Wall Street research where an effort by a technical analyst who watches the charts and tiniest movements of a security was the undoing of an inside trader, exposed by his numerical footprints to the keen eye of the trained and honest observer who turned in the wrongdoer!

If you buy stock based on their recommendations alone, prepare to lose. If you succumb to the pressure sale of "buy it now," or "sell it now," while your broker is on the telephone with the latest research piece in his hot hands, you are, in the axiom of my predecessor-philosophers, a "chump." Get thee to a library!

An Editorial Polemic
A Call to Arms!

A special note to analysts or would be analysts: quit!

It takes a moment to walk through your cubicle door, pass along the hallways of your captivity, and enter back into the currents of life's ocean. Leave now! Academics need to breathe, create and find practical, real applications of their theories - you need to recognize a dead end erected before you. The securities industry only uses you as bait, as sales support for the brokers. You are better educated, more intelligent and harder working than the management wizards.

Forget the chatter of "how will you pay the bills?" You live in a nation built by immigrants, surrounded by a legacy of legendary adventure in pursuit of individual liberty and achievement. George Washington walked the same streets in lower Manhattan you daily trod. Alexander Hamilton is buried in the yard at Trinity Church. The glory of man is the ability to act, to choose, not just talk. Can you feel your pulse quicken in the face of this challenge?

How did you reach this end? Now that you are in it, what is its possible appeal? Is a paycheck such a fearful manacle when you have education and hard experience at your command.

Analyst, if you are any good, sell your wares in the marketplace of ideas - pick up the pen and write! Publish a newsletter; become an investment adviser! Take risks based on your ideas. If you are good you will succeed; if not, you tried! Take a lesson from the press, as often MORE underpaid than you! Investigate, look, think, accept the reality of your findings and publish! Answer to the master of the public good, not a broker hunting you on the telephone! Smash the barrier of your insecurity! In the next few years, more of you will be terminated.

Students - absorb the fervor of my challenge and when recruited by the wire houses from the warm comfort of your university nest, just say "no!" Work in business on your own, or for a real, competing business or in league with consulting partners. Start a newsletter. Take a risk based on confidence in your own research. Don't be impressed by the large, hollow brokerage firms. Don't sign on unless you believe the house will at least productively survive. Many won't.

Second Polemic:
A Call for Aid!

What good is research when the markets move on rumor? It seems that columnists and broadcasters tell us about rumors all the time, not to stir the pot, but to explain why particular stocks moved that day. It's not research. Research takes too long.

Speaking of rumors, where is the SEC? I see reporters on the television finance shows openly talking about rumors involving buyouts and the like. That's inside trading being discussed. It is the journalist's obligation to note the rumor and report. I'm not criticizing them in the least; quite the contrary, in reporting rumors they are letting the public know what is playing on the Street, levelling out the field by showing the muck remains. If financial journalists were not digging and letting the public know the action, who would? Where is the SEC, though? I thought they claimed to have dented all this insider trading and rumor mongering. If you don't already - please - watch the financial press in action, and be thankful they care.

Prove it to me, please - ANYONE! Show me that rumors are dead, that insiders do not move the prices of specific targets on a regular basis. Alleviate my misgivings - show me all these journalists are lying - there are no rumors of any effect!

Or foreswear this jaundiced mockery intended to embezzle the public's confidence for an unworthy end of regulatory self-aggrandizement. Enforcers - bring us the criminal's head, not his tennis racquet! Bring us the baron, not the serfs!

Wall Street brokerage research is intended to support the sales area by providing new ideas, just as writers keep a soap opera going on television by convolutions of plot.

Meanwhile, all around Wall Street, programmers and block traders, who could care less, shake the markets. Analysts don't.

Enough said. Well, maybe one more item.

Guess who the great originator of free research was? That's right, Charles Merrill! His marketing brilliance keeps popping up because he was the one who created the mold - the rest remain imitators.

Key Definitions: The Law

xxiii. The <u>Securities and Exchange Commission Annual Report</u> is composed each year and sent over to the President of the Senate and the Speaker of the House of Representatives to explain what the SEC has been up to for the preceding year. The report has general discussions about policy matters and how the SEC has performed for the prior year. It also has great statistics about what the SEC really does. What is their budget, how many employees, how many exams do they conduct? Get it from the Superintendent of Documents, US Government Printing Office, Washington, DC 20402. The 1988 report cost $5.00. It's a great bargain.

xxiv. The <u>SEC Department of Enforcement</u> gets all the news headlines, but is only a small part of the SEC. It is located in Washington, DC at the main SEC Office. If you have a complaint, you can send them a letter, but their mission is not to handle consumer issues. They run the cases where the SEC has decided something very bad has happened and requires a halt and some penalties. They don't have the manpower to handle a lot of cases, therefore they selectively handle the bigger ones. The new chief of enforcement is William McLucas. If you have a problem and want to bring it to the SEC's attention, contact the SEC Consumer Affairs and Information Services Office in Washington, DC. The complaints go into a database to observe trends. In fiscal 1988, they got 49,000 complaints! Some trend!

xxv. A <u>Broker-Dealer</u> is a licensed entity under the 1934 Exchange Act. Because it has a license, it can buy and sell securities in transactions with the public. It can lose its license if it violates the law or various regulations concerning how it does its business, how much capital it maintains or if it fails to keep the correct books and records. A "BD" is licensed by filing with the SEC. It must also be a member of the NASD if it does public business, and it may be a member of the NYSE, but does not have to be an NYSE member. Most securities firms, or "BD's" are not members of the NYSE. The firm also has to be BD licensed in the state where it is doing business. Additional licenses are required by each broker at the BD. The broker files a form "BD" with the SEC and most states to get its license. The form is public information, so you can get it. Before a bank lends to a house, the bank gets a copy of the Form BD. So should you. Ask the house for it, or get it from your state securities examiners. The SEC has it, and it is available from them.

xxvi. An <u>Investment Company</u> has a separate license under the 1940 Investment Company Act. It is not a BD license. Sometimes the same company may have a series of licenses, such as a BD, Investment Adviser, etc. This should not impress you. You can become confused as to which hat the entity is wearing when you deal with it. You are most familiar with mutual funds as licensed Investment Companies. Some BD's have their own mutual funds, or captive Investment Companies. A lot of Investment Companies are set up as Massachusetts Trusts for administration purposes.

xxvii. The <u>1933 Securities Act</u> is a federal law that requires a series of public disclosures from issuers of securities. The whole idea is to have as much information as possible out in the public area before allowing companies to go to the public to get funds. Various registrations apply before securities can be distributed in an underwriting. This law mandates the "prospectus" when new stock comes out. Most investors and brokers have never read the law, which is, unfortunately, quite complex. Many investors don't understand that an incredible amount of information is made available to them under this marvelous statute. It's all there for the asking: registrations, applications, prospecti, amendments, etc. This law is referred to as the "Truth in Securities Act."

xxviii. The <u>1934 Exchange Act</u> is a companion to the 1933 Act. It provides for the licensing of the various Self Regulatory Organizations or "SRO's" such as the NYSE, and has all the licensing provisions for BD's and individual stockbrokers. It discusses margin, net capital, books and records and includes the various anti-fraud provisions that the SEC relies on for enforcement work. It's a highly technical piece of work that is amended from time to time. Most recently, the Congress amended it to provide for tougher anti-fraud provisions including bounties or rewards for people who turn in fraudulent bad guys. If you want more information on the bounty provision, contact the SEC for particulars on their program, which is still evolving.

xxix. "<u>Full Disclosure</u>" is a term which generally describes the whole thrust of all the forms and licenses required for public filing by the 1933 and 1934 Acts. There are reams of paper available about brokerage houses and the brokers. It is available to you, but, you have to make the effort to go and get it. Research people use this material all the time, and your broker can get it for you if he's serious about offering "full service." The SEC has regional reading rooms for your use. You can use the Freedom of Information Act to get information. The Congress has put a great deal of thought into shaping Full Disclosure. Don't be bashful! It's yours. Use it!

Special Note:

Roulette is a gambling game that has slightly different rules in Europe and in the US. Get an oblong table. Put a roulette wheel in the center. The European wheel has 37 subdivisions, cut like pieces of pie, from the center out; the American wheel has 38. Each slice of the pie is numbered and is alternately red or black in color. The European wheel has one "0." The American wheel has an additional, "00." You can bet that the little ball will fall into a space on the spinning wheel by selecting the exact number, or betting in blocks. You can bet the ball will fall somewhere between 1 and 18, or between 19 and 36, that the ball will fall into an even or odd slice, or a red or black slice. The "O" and the American "00" change the odds to the house's favor. In roulette, you bet against the house, not the other players. The odds are never 50-50, even if you bet colors or odd-even because of the "0" and the "00." Roulette is a statistical delight for the data freak.

If you are considering options transactions, consider roulette: simple to describe, it is illegal unless you have a casino license. Roulette would appear to give you better odds than options. Roulette and the NYSE were devised at about the same time, the dynamic late 18th century.

Chapter Six

The Fire Drill-
Who's in Charge?

Bureaucracy

We have thus far gone into uncharted waters by looking at exactly how an order gets filled and whose fingerprints are on the paper trail of executions and confirmations. It may sound like a bureaucracy - it is. Brokerage houses, though, are like any other high pressure sales organization, in that the real work is done in the trenches, beyond the immediate control or expertise of the people running the organization.

The higher up the chain of command you go, the less the people know what's really going on in the organization. There is no great need for top leadership to know the details. Their job is not to look at the individual trades, but to look at the big picture, the overall commitments to rent and other fixed costs in real relation to the actual and projected revenues. If a brokerage house acquires a big, new headquarters, it should figure out what to do with the old space so as not to pay rents on two locations. According to press reports of its demise, Thompson McKinnon, among other failures, didn't. It's gone.

As the Eastern Bloc - Warsaw Pact crumbles into pieces, the only bureaucracy still holding onto Stalinesque management methods may be the brokerage industry. The Soviets have so far decided to face the music and adjust. The brokerage industry will suffer the fate of reactionaries through history - cyclical upheaval, pain, and common lessons relearned every 5 or 10 years. The leadership are self-proclaimed heroes when the market is going up; they have a list of scapegoats when it goes down. There is an old saying - "A rising tide lifts all boats." When the stock market is going up, the brokerage leaders are carried by the industry tide. The good ones are highlighted when they make money in a falling market.

Who Runs the House?

There is no question about this one - the big producers run the place, Street wide.

Brokerage houses make a lot of money in good times, but they put very little aside for a rainy day. Large bonuses are paid, vain crusades are commenced at great expense to create "systems" to harness the market, offices are expanded, new investments are created - all the usual items of large bureaucracies that have their moment in the sun.

Experience is supposed to teach us how to adapt and avoid the pitfalls of the past. Anyone knows that if you touch a hot stove, you can get burned. We learn as children, and are thereafter safe, inoculated by our own experience.

Not so in the brokerage business. There is no prologue to the present. When the market is good, there is no long way down, only up. Houses run strong, then falter in a bad market and disappear. They hire by the thousands when times are good, then fire by the thousands when the market stalls and their plans collapse. Therefore, people that generate revenue can walk all over the leadership at a brokerage house, insulting managers, throwing tantrums, negotiating with the competition within the full view of managers, and generally raising hell. Why not? They pay the bills. They do what the senior management can't do - sell. Why not, therefore, enjoy the spoils of daily war? This is especially important in flat or down markets.

Providing support for cults of personality within a firm is how the "beast" consumes the entity. Because history has little meaning to Wall Street, when they make money, they spend it with great liberality, effectively disregarding tomorrow. They spend it on trips, expensive leases, expensive furniture, bonuses and product fantasies.

Your broker is enticed to sell certain products and services with rewards dangled in his face in addition to his net commission income from the grid. He can get prizes, cash awards and honoraria for hitting the firm's mark. It costs the firm a lot of cash to pay for the contest prize and administration. Sadly, the brokers have come to expect it, and like a wise old horse, they won't leave the stall in good times without the morning's promised carrot.

If the big producers didn't come in to work, it would be noticed immediately and painfully. Revenue would stop; how would the beast be fed? If the top three or four managers of a firm disappear, so what? What do they gross?

There is a lot of merit to this view. The cash flow comes from the big producers who do one million and up in gross each year. The profitability margin on this kind of employee is wonderful! They compulsively work like slaves, cultivate big customers who bring in other forms of big ticket business and tend to diversify their activity into insurance, direct participation products, and managed money. The big producers develop the connections that bring in large transactions for the investment bankers. Big producers keep the municipal finance department hopping and they buy Unit Trusts from that desk. Long term big producers cause the least amount of problems and end up more selective about who they keep as clients. Some short term big producers are dangerous - they are more likely to be predatory.

Don't take my word for it. On December 2, 1987 the SEC issued the Advanced News Release Text for Chairman David Ruder's speech to the Securities Industry Association at Boca Raton, Florida.

Ruder was concerned about the October crash, but to his credit he promulgated what I will call the Ruder Manifesto:

"...In recent months, the need for individual securities firms and the securities industry as a whole to preserve standards of integrity has become particularly acute. The events of October, coupled with the recent insider trading scandals, appear to have cast a shadow on the public perception of the industry's commitment to the small investor. Complaints to the Commission regarding securities firms have doubled following the events of the past months. In this crucial time it is important for the public to know that the industry is committed to maintaining high ethical standards and to protecting the public from securities law violators.

To achieve investor confidence and reduce abusive sales practices, firms must be particularly sensitive to their supervisory and compliance responsibilities. The securities firm is the first line of defense against dishonest or illegal conduct by the securities professionals it employs. I cannot emphasize too strongly that supervision cannot simply be delegated to your legal and compliance staffs. There must be an ongoing commitment by each of the senior managers of the firm. Until compliance receives the same kind of attention as your profit centers, you will continue to face the likelihood of breakdowns that can lead to undesirable publicity, with incalculable losses in customer confidence.

Firm supervisory systems depend on the presence of knowledgeable, trustworthy supervisors watching over the activities of securities firms employees in the home office and in the field. They require safeguards to avoid predictable and recurring problems, and defined procedures to ensure that securities activities are carried out under the eye of qualified supervisors. They also require regular audits of all securities activities to assess the effectiveness of established procedures and to detect instances of illegal or dishonest activity. While these procedures may be costly to maintain, they increase customer confidence and reduce costs resulting from customer arbitrations and SRO and SEC disciplinary actions.

The front line in any supervisory program is the branch manager. In an uncertain market, branch managers will be facing economic pressures that create a strong temptation to overlook problems with their registered representatives, particularly top producers of revenues. Securities firms must remain attuned to these pressures. They must train and supervise branch managers as well as give special attention to complaints against top producers.

Speaking of top producers, careful selection of employees is also an important supervisory function. Care must be taken both in the hiring of sales personnel, and in providing them with supervision appropriate to their background. A particularly noteworthy problem is that of the dishonest, but high-producing registered representative who roams from firm to firm. If you hire an account executive who has a record of customer complaints, you must realize that you are accepting the obligation to develop and maintain special supervision of that person."

Chairman Ruder hit it right on the head - big producers that roam around from firm to firm in search of bonuses can bring heavy baggage: complaints! They were hired on Wall Street in the 1980's because they brought revenues in to feed the beast. The problem became so severe that Ruder had to take it into the open.

Unfortunately, having made the appropriate comment, there was no follow-up except deal making with bad guys by the SEC. I am not aware of any major firm CEO, President or Chairman who has been disciplined by the SEC for failing to supervise these predators.

The predator big producer can't be supervised.

Firms can fire them, but the predators are beyond control. If they are controlled, their gross production will shrink because they can't beat up their customers any more. Then they are small producers. These producers do a lot of gross because they do tremendous numbers of trades for retail customers, mostly on wrongful discretion in securities that are not suitable for the client. As a client you don't know what the broker is up to. You don't see the rest of his activity, his product mix and gross production. If a house hires and then fires the predator, the broker's bonus (the house's money) goes down the drain, and litigation between the broker and the house will follow which is expensive and useless. The predator big producer spends his bonus as fast as he gets it, becoming judgment proof.

It's odd. Some big producers are like a gift from heaven. They may drive the back room crazy with demands for support for their clients, but they never have a customer problem. These are long term brokers who have built a business over years - they really are small businessmen within a larger entity, acting with autonomy as though in a loose confederacy. Branch managers just have to live with their weak control position. Then there are other big producers that are animals. This is what Ruder was referring to: the horror documented in the press and the SRO disciplinary releases.

The further oddity is that the firm can sense it before they hire the animal. In recruiting, they examine the customer book of the big producer. They ask if he has customer complaints. They inquire about the number of places he has worked over the past ten years. Firms get the information and even if a few lies are used to ease the trail of destruction, the hiring house has a sense of problems to come. Ruder and the SEC knew that. He challenged the industry leaders on that issue, because it was getting out of hand.

In the Final Report of the Regulatory Task Force of the NASD issued in March, 1988, the members of the Task Force recommended that all hiring firms take a look at the disciplinary history of the hiring candidate. They described an interesting mechanism.

When a broker is hired, he fills out a Form U-4, which gives his employment and educational history and asks if the broker has ever been arrested or investigated for a serious complaint. It does ask for convictions - but it also requires arrests and complaints. If a firm is going to hire an animal, how do they learn the track record before bringing him on board?

The Task Force recommended that a copy of the U-5 Termination Form be given to the departing broker. The U-5 is filled out by the firm, not the broker. It is supposed to reflect the reason for the termination and whether the broker is under investigation for anything at the time of termination. If you have the U-5, you can get a sense of what the broker is all about. The Task Force did not say YOU should get a copy of the U-5, just the new firm. Naturally, if the broker had it, the new firm could demand to see it. If they see the U-5, they "know."

The Task Force also recommended that a hiring firm be able to access the Central Records Depository (the CRD) directly to review the full history of the broker. This would include all the information on the U-4, and all subsequent complaints, settlements and judgments against the broker. They were very concerned about the right of privacy of the broker, so they further recommended that the broker candidate sign a waiver of such rights. If he refused, the hiring firm was to deny employment.

This is right out of Ruder's recommendation, but it was tailored down by clearly declining to impose any strict liability standard. A brokerage house could hire an animal, knowing he was an animal, but the NASD will not automatically take action against the firm just because they knowingly hired him.

Recruiting gross production like purchasing bulk meat was bad enough, but Ruder was precise and erudite: if the Street was going to recruit bad brokers, then the Street had to take responsibility.

Ruder is gone. What does the SEC intend to do about it? As a measure, look to see when the top man in a firm is disciplined by the SEC or a Self Regulatory Organization - not just a branch manager. The branch manager often has no control. In the end, a lot of people could exercise control, but pass on responsibility.

Recruiting

Recruiting is done primarily by the branch manager. He follows leads and develops contacts in the local area and tries to steal brokers from the local competition. He may land a big one.

Really big producers are courted by headhunters and they don't deal with the branch manager so much as the regional or headquarters sales managers. Meetings are held without care for geography. People are flown to the home office from wherever they sit. Recruiting becomes competitive and a candidate who is marginal because of complaints can become courted because he is the biggest grossing candidate on the plate right now and the house urgently needs revenue.

So, recruiters can hire a rodent, knowing exactly what they have done, reasoning the firm will be able to control the bad broker and stop any wrongdoing. The firm CAN control its brokers, not just theoretically, but practically.

Brokers can be controlled, at a cost of their production. The recruiters, however, walk away from supervision before the ink is dry on the bonus check, which is why Ruder was saying firms could not just delegate the supervision role to their Legal and Compliance Departments. He wanted the senior management to stay responsible.

There is an old legal theory that holds true under most jurisdictions in the United States: if you bring a <u>dangerous animal</u> onto your property, you are strictly responsible for any damage it does if it gets loose. A dangerous animal is a specie that everyone knows is prone to doing damage, such as a lion or tiger. The topic is headline news in tragic cases where Pit Bull dogs kill children.

What is wrong with holding the senior officers of the firm personally liable when they bring in a broker who is a dangerous animal? They know the danger when they bring in the wolf. They don't even fence him in - they hand him a telephone and tell him to do gross! What is a branch manager to do?

If the branch manager catches the bad broker, will the manager fire him? The odds are the manager will be perplexed, because he has stumbled onto a big producer, not just an average guy. Will the head of sales back the manager up, or will they fire the manager if he takes action? Will the home office agree that an action must be taken, but hold it against the manager and fire him later? Ruder seemed to allude to each of those circumstances when he said the manager must be trained and supported. Ruder knew the big producers are recruited by the home office, not the branch, and yet the branch manager takes the brunt of the blame if a disaster occurs. The case reports from the NASD and NYSE are filled with manager carnage, but the senior managers in the back office escape.

If the big producer blows up and gets caught with all the usual monetary damage, there is no question that the branch manager will be fired; the only question is: will the compliance director be fired?

A favorite excuse for senior managers is that brokers cannot really be controlled until the firm has received complaints in writing. That's not true.

Bad brokers can be stopped by watching the mix of their business, the frequency of their trading, the financial assets of their average clients, and comparing it to common sense. Managers have the tools and the experience. The question is whether they have the courage to take action.

If a firm has any sense, it must reject the temptation to hire a bad broker because he can bring instant gross production if they know he's an animal. They can tell. They should act.

There's another maxim of the business you should be aware of: only a fool gives up his book.

What this means is that a successful broker should resist giving up his clients, even if that means he cannot move up in the organization. If a broker decides he wants to be a branch manager, a firm may demand he give up his book. This doesn't mean he keeps the accounts but stops doing active business; it means he gives the accounts away to other brokers in the firm, who WILL continue to get them to trade. If you give up your book, you give away your clients.

Once the manager does that, he depends on the firm for his paycheck. He is now a captive. If he quits, he has nowhere to go. He has no book.

If he has maintained his book, he has mobility because he can always go to a new firm and bring his old clients along. Think of it as a safety valve which the firms want to close off. If anyone with a book can walk, then enforced loyalty depends on stripping away the book.

Senior officers in a firm rarely have a book, perhaps doing a few trades for old friends, but that's it. They are captives within their towers. Think for a moment: when have you heard of the senior leadership of a brokerage house going on to positions of leadership in business? How about elected leadership in government? Donald Regan, formerly of Merrill Lynch, was a rare exception.

They are shadow men, with little legacy.

No One Wants the Job

In many reviews of business, we expect to hear tales of ambitious young men and women who start in the mail room and go on to become the president of their company, taking it on to new achievements, dispensing wisdom with the certainty of their success. If that's too extreme, we do hear of ambitious individuals who work their way up from lower level management to the top of the company.

The last thing a successful broker wants to do is leave his clients, give his book away and go off to the starry ether of top management. Lately, as the SEC has begun making warlike noises again, the top job has become especially interesting.

I am calling for enhanced personal responsibility for the boards of directors and senior management of houses as a way to get to the root of effective self-control. How do you take that if you are in a position of power in a brokerage house? If the brokers do bad things, I call for penalties on the president, the heads of sales, the board of directors and others. It's time to take responsibility into the board room. Why not? Haven't they brought the dangerous animal inside? Haven't they offered assurances of "trust" and "safety" in their advertising? NASD Principals, not mere soldiers, approve all the advertising.

At this point, however, I must add another reason for brokers to stay in production: they can make more money doing gross than the president of the firm makes through salary and bonuses.

Not only can they make more money, good brokers do it with less hassle, less annoyance, more pure fun and personal success. They can pass on their business, the book, to relatives whom they train in the brokerage business. In the retail sections of a brokerage house, the highest paid individuals will generally be brokers, not back-room types, which is as it should be. It drives insurance company owners of brokerage firms to distraction.

Individuals who work on product desks are usually paid on a mix of salary and bonus, depending on the performance of their product. They can also, in a good year, get more income than the president - if they are good. One of the sporting techniques used to decrease the appetite of the "beast" is to reduce the product managers deal, bit by bit, thereby reducing his income, when times are bad. Where is he going to go? Appreciate the humor of irony, however, for as soon as the market heats up, the product manager becomes a profit center. Figures make him look "good." He can now waltz off to a competitor under the banner of "See what I can do!" The dynamics of house compensation are worthy of farce theater.

Therefore, big producers don't want to be the president. Product people don't want it - anyone with a piece of the action, compensation based on revenues, doesn't want it. The real power lies at the bottom of the management triangle, among the producers. The nature of their business makes them antagonistic to joint action. They work alone or in pairs. If they united, threatened to walk en masse, management could not hope to remain productive. That's why the real assets of the firm go home every night after the market closes and the firms have no real value, only a "book" value.

Investment bankers work the same way. They are paid on the basis of revenue they bring in, as displayed in the way Michael Milken was paid at Drexel. He starts the year at a minimal salary, then works for a piece of what he brings in. That is sales tradition, and no matter what they say, investment bankers are salesman, too.

An Aside-
On Titles

What is wrong with being a salesman? If I go to a shop, I expect to see a salesman or saleswoman. If I buy a car I expect to see a car salesman. I deal with real estate and other brokers. What's so terrible about being a "salesman" or a "broker?"

I like salespeople.

They work hard and perform the vital link in production: they sell the goods and get the cash. To be fair, while company presidents are interesting, there are far more potential company presidents floating about than good salespeople. Good salespeople have to have talent.

It's almost unheard of to find a salesperson who wrecked a firm, yet presidents and derelict corporate boards do it all the time. As America is rethinking the direction of its business energy, as we see small business blooming, maybe the "call" to high office in large bureaucratic companies will become a mark of failure more than achievement, as though one rose as a "party functionary" as opposed to being able to do anything else.

Why is it so terrible for a broker to call himself, "Stockbroker?" It's what they are. Why are they called such mushy names as financial consultants, account representatives or other Madison Avenue creations? It has always struck me as demeaning. I feel the term "Customer's Man" has a certain charm about it.

To make matters worse, and perhaps more embarrassing, almost all the brokers you run into will be called Vice Presidents of the firm. A firm with Five Thousand selling brokers may have a total of seven thousand vice presidents when you count the back room! This is supposed to impress you - you are dealing with a Vice-President. It means nothing. Everybody is a chief!

The United States has a President and a Vice-President; the Vice President is also the President - of the Senate. There is a bit of difference between the "Presidents."

When placing investments, deal with people; reject titles. The banking industry, which has a lot of "Vice Presidents" is nothing compared to the "Vice Presidentified" securities industry. Don't, repeat - don't think your broker is important because he is a "Super-Duper-Senior-Exalted-Anointed and Appointed Vice President for Life of Big Doggie Brokerage." It has nothing to do with whether he is any good, what licenses he holds, what his specialty is or how he is going to treat you.

I call on brokers to act like mature business people - if you are good, you don't need the camouflage of advertising rhetoric that has been heaped on you by people that have no experience in your area of sales. A thoroughbred shouldn't pull a milk wagon. Forget the "Vice President" nonsense. Be the best STOCKBROKER in your firm! Let the senior back room barnacles worry about the order of their own, multi-syllabic, meaningless titles.

Key Definitions: Research Reviewed

xxx. A Supervisory Analyst is a person registered with the NYSE who has demonstrated knowledge of financial analysis and compliance matters who is able to act as the supervisor of a research department. He must sign off on all research matter that is intended for distribution to the public under NYSE Rule 472. This means he has to approve research pieces done at the department level AND put out by the brokers. Some brokers like to do mass mailings to all their clients of their own "research." The "SA" has to sign off on this in an NYSE firm.

xxxi. Published Research Recommendations are usually done by retail firms as newsletters intended for your consideration to get your business. There is a "hedge clause" at the bottom that tells you there are no guarantees. This is intended for you, the customer. The research department may also be doing other research for sale to other firms, to Investment Advisers and to special customers. Research is also done for the firm's own trading account and the corporate finance department. Don't think that a research department publishes all its work.

xxxii. Individualized Research is something your broker might do just for you. It's legal and might be very good. It might be junk. Be very careful about this kind of literature. Professionals who manage big mutual funds or pension funds use this private material all the time. They understand its limitations. They know how to reject it or to use it in a context of other information. It will not appear as printed, newsletter-style material. Be very careful about using it unless you understand how to do your own research.

xxxiii. NYSE Rule 472 covers "Communications With the Public." It is an excellent idea, intended to limit NOT the amount of information, but the manner of control and therefore quality of information that gets out to you for use in selecting investments. It does not apply to NASD firms. There are no guarantees in investing. Research can give a recommendation, but it can "guess" wrong. Rule 472 requires the house to have a good reason from the recommendation, that is, a file full of data and work notes. Read the hedge clause at the bottom of recommendations. Further information is usually available. Ask for it! See what you get as the additional material, if anything.

xxxiv. Fraud is the deceptive practice of intentional dishonesty where someone takes advantage of you to get your money or goods. The most sophisticated business people and firms are the VICTIMS of fraud at times as evidenced by the number of recent lawsuits by banks against their real estate developer customers who pledged property to the banks as security for loans, but gave false information about the property or their business assets in their applications. Fraud isn't an accident. It doesn't happen by the position of the stars or the moon. People do it. To you!

xxxv. Churning is an abuse of your account, a fraudulent practice, wherein a broker causes trades to occur for the purpose of generating commissions. Profit or loss on the trades doesn't matter, just that the transactions generate commissions. You can end up with a profit and still be a victim of churning. It is one of the traditional forms of abuse in the securities industry.

xxxvi. In-house Research is the free material you get from your broker, published under the house masthead as a newsletter.

xxxvii. Outside Research is done by firms that are independent and usually don't sell stock. Some is excellent; some is junk. Some of this so-called research is actually paid for by the company being "researched," which should cause you to have misgivings about the independence of the report. A research firm does not have to be licensed as a broker or dealer, and does not have to be a member of the NASD or the NYSE. An in-house research staff is expensive to maintain in slow markets, so Wall Street lays off analysts in droves when the market slows. Firms then use materials prepared by some of the independent houses. Firms can also buy the research of another firm and distribute it to their clients. Watch out for that - while it is "independent" of the house handing it out, it is "in-house" for the firm that composed it.

CHAPTER SEVEN

THE SECURITIES AND EXCHANGE COMMISSION

Problems

The public suffered severely in the Great Depression, which is often thought to have begun with the October, 1929 New York Stock Exchange Crash. There are various theories about when the depression began, one group claiming long before 1929 in the midwest farming regions, others claiming not until 1932, but the point is moot. By 1932, the economy was in very bad shape and the American People had elected Franklin Roosevelt to the White House with a platform of radical change. Roosevelt's first 100 days in office were highlighted by spectacular attempts to change the course of the depression by governmental leadership.

Politicians still argue whether big government helped or hurt the eventual recovery that was delivered by World War Two.

The 1929-32 securities industry, however, was a prominent whipping boy in the halls of Congress, because the aggressive forms of marketeer activity had not escaped Congressional notice. The damage, having tricked down to the masses because of widespread bank failures, became a concern for all. Wall Street knew change and regulation was coming, but the question was, "how?"

One extreme was that nothing would happen, just as in the past, but that hope faded as the depression got worse.

Another extreme was that the Federal Government would take over the securities business completely. This wasn't likely since it would have meant the end of creative capital because the Government regularly proves it cannot run anything effectively. The Red Scare was washing over the West following the establishment of the Soviet Union. Anarchy in Germany after the First World War was a recent memory. Government confiscation was, therefore, out of the question.

That left a compromise in between.

In 1933, Congress passed the first part of the statutory coverage, by putting together a Truth-in-Securities disclosure law. Its objective was to put all the information reasonably available about a public company out in the open so that investors could make up their own minds based on their own analysis. In theory, it's a pretty good idea.

The 1933 Securities Act defines what a security is, and what you have to say about it when you want to sell it to the public. It also tells you what documents must be controlled, and how registration of a security works. It makes selling stock to the public a bit harder than it used to be because of the way information has to be set out, but all it mandates is disclosure, disclosure and more disclosure. The Act defines the term "prospectus," which is the most important document that must be published when a new issue of stock is set to go out to the public. That's where all the information is printed. If you get the information you can make up your own mind. The Government won't tell you how or where to invest. The choice is yours. The problem is that you have to get accurate information AND study it.

Next, in 1933-34, Congress decided how to control the mechanics of the securities industry leading to the 1934 Exchange Act. This was the mechanism intended to put controls in place over how securities were traded. It could have changed the way business was done. It changed the system of licensing and formal protocols of authority, but the securities business didn't change markedly.

The 1934 Act made the New York Stock Exchange quasi-monopoly legally secure, and discouraged competitors by creating licensing requirements that very few groups could ever meet.

Consider: if you want to start most businesses, you do it by gathering the right capital and the right people. A few businesses such as bars and taxi cabs have numerical license limits in various jurisdictions, but setting up a securities exchange under the 1934 Act is like setting up a nuclear power plant: difficult in the extreme.

So, the grandfather status of the NYSE was basically preserved and promoted by the new law.

Most importantly, the first Chairman of the five-commissioner secretariat at the SEC was none other than Joseph Kennedy, a smuggler and marketeer who was a critical supporter of then New York Governor Franklin Roosevelt in the 1932 drive for the Democratic Nomination for President.

Joseph Kennedy was a salty individual, perhaps a rogue, and could never have been given a prominent cabinet position because of his background. Imagine the humor of Joseph Kennedy being given the job as the financial industry's chief regulator! He was never convicted of a crime, but historians agree that he was a daring, brilliant individual who enjoyed risk and was a ruthless marketeer.

After creating the SEC, and after the President had appointed the roster of Commissioners, no one was quite sure what the Commission was supposed to do. There was no model or set of instructions that came with the law. At this time the FBI was just a child; big government was gearing up, but hadn't matured as it would during World War Two. The SEC, once created, had to create its mission.

The SEC was supposed to take applications or filings for distributions of stock to the public. That was a librarian's function. The Library of Congress accepts even more filings under the Copyright Law. Was the SEC supposed to enforce law and formulate policy, or just enforce the law? The Congress did not make policy mandates for the Roosevelt Administration in 1933, so the SEC was left in a confused paradox. It had an uncertain mission with an unlikely missionary, Kennedy, as its leader.

So, the SEC did nothing. Kennedy did nothing. That was his job. No SEC actions followed the usual surveys, investigations and discussions that were held to determine if illegal actions had caused or contributed to the '29 crash or the aberrations of the current marketplace. Kennedy looked like the head of an organization that was supposed to be doing things to restore the faith of the American investor in the American finance markets, but it turned out to be a Department of Motor Vehicles for public securities. Peculiar filings were required. That was all.

Next came James Landis, who did nothing as Chairman of the SEC.

William Douglas, who was later to become famous as a Justice of the US Supreme Court, came next as Chairman with only theoretical finance qualifications, but he robustly engaged in battle with Wall Street, raising the idea of Street self-regulation as a compromise.

Under this agreement, the SEC would sit back and watch the Exchanges. The Exchanges would run enforcement against their own members in the tradition of the Dutch Guilds and Hanseatic League which did monitor and discipline their membership. Douglas made enough noise to make people believe he was serious.

There wasn't a complaint volume to deal with in 1938, once the agreement was struck, because the financial community was dying, firms were closing and resurrection was far off. The Douglas-Wall Street deal looked forward and tried to prevent embezzlement, fraud and practices that endangered the financial life of brokerage houses with the ripple effect danger to the banking industry seen in the early years of the Crash. Brokerage firms were troubled by capital problems, paper crunches when trading did occur, and by lax controls that made malfeasance, including theft, easy. When houses went under, they took banks with them and therefore harmed the public.

Roosevelt had enjoyed support from Wall Street in 1932, even though he was a reformer. Kennedy was from the Wall Street Community. Douglas was from the other side of the US - Washington State, but was considered an Easterner because of his teaching tenure at Columbia and then Yale Law Schools.

Politics does make for interesting bedfellows. There is nothing strange in seeing conservative businessmen contributing to liberal politicians when it appears the liberal will win.

Compromise reigns over political existence, and Douglas, who seemed ready to fight with the Street, was soon gone - to the Supreme Court! Insider trading didn't exist before, during or right after the Douglas Chairmanship. From 1934 to 1940, the SEC had FOUR Chairmen! They continue to turn over too frequently. Why?

Charm School

The SEC has been criticized as an initiation for securities lawyers before they go off to Wall Street to be practicing attorneys, a kind of school with a revolving door led by political appointees. It's been said for over 50 years!

This isn't intended to insult anyone, but to address the reality of the 1934 Exchange Act.

Thc 1934 Exchange Act was passed in a politically unique time because the nation was changing, big government had arrived and the depression had hit bottom. The Act calls for political recognition of the Commissioners with Senate approval of any appointments. That continues to this day. The political balance leads to a revolving door at the top of the SEC.

Section 4 of the 1934 Exchange Act read:

(a) There is hereby established a Securities and Exchange Commission (hereinafter referred to as the "Commission") to be composed of five commissioners to be appointed by the President by and with the advice and consent of the Senate. Not more than three of such commissioners shall be members of the same political party, and in making appointments members of different political parties shall be appointed alternately as nearly as may be practicable. No commissioner shall engage in any other business, vocation or employment than that of serving as commissioner, nor shall any commissioner participate, directly or indirectly, in any stock market operations or transactions of a character subject to regulation by the Commission pursuant to this title. Each Commissioner shall hold office for a term of five years...

(b) The Commission is authorized to appoint and fix the compensation of such officers, attorneys, examiners and other experts as may be necessary for carrying out its function under this Act, without regard to the provisions of other laws applicable to the employment and compensation of officers and employees of the United States and the Commission may, subject to the civil-service laws, appoint such other officers and employees as are necessary in the execution of its functions and fix their salaries in accordance with the Classification Act of 1923, as amended.

The Commissioners must have certain political qualifications, but there are no experience qualifications. There is no testing requirement, no need to demonstrate proficiency in finance or any related art. Senate approval is required.

The way the Senate works, that approval is first passed on by a Committee within the Senate, then recommended by that Committee to the full Senate for approval or disapproval.

Wall Streeters, being no fools, can muster sufficient monetary and political clout to influence the vote in the Senate, which is how a republic works - compromise.

How does the President decide whom to appoint? Politics! There can be a thousand reasons, but foremost is the need to satisfy a constituency. A sponsor must propose and then support the candidate Commissioner to get the President to appoint. Once appointed, the Commissioner can't work <u>except</u> as a Commissioner, which is a hardship for 5 years in Washington, DC. Why would anyone want to be a Commissioner under those terms? Because it has to pay off later, somehow. There is nothing new about recruiting regulators.

The staff has no requirement to pass any tests or show proficiency in finance. The practice has been to hire attorneys right out of law school, when they don't have a background in securities.

Unfortunately for the staff, to rise to the level of Commissioner, one has to be identified with a political party. When hired and working within the staff, politics are illegal on the job. When an individual works hard and rises to the top of the staff, that's it! They can't rise to be a Commissioner until they become political. So, if one rises to the top of the staff, the next step is out. Why stick around on the staff for more than a few years of indoctrination? Hence the criticism of political Commissioners and revolving door staff.

The SEC has different Divisions with different, respective missions. The 1933 Act required mountains of paper be filed before stock could be sold to the public. It gets filed with the SEC. In 1989, about 40 million pages of documents were sent into the SEC, causing the Commission to look into computer scanning devices for document storage.

They don't approve corporate filings, but the staff read them and if they have serious objections they can take steps to stop an issue of securities from going public. It's an interesting system, because Congress, in its wisdom, saw that having to wait for the SEC to <u>approve</u> a new issue might end Western Capital Formation. They don't approve, but they do get a chance to fire a torpedo upon sufficient reason.

The SEC is spread out around the country in geographical divisions, each with a Regional Administrator whose job is to perform several functions centering around examinations of broker-dealers, investment advisers, mutual funds and helping out the local US Attorneys in criminal prosecutions. The Regional Administrators have staffs that are considered expert in a few places, luke warm in others. The regional offices bring their own enforcement cases for fairly simple violations, but they are capable of doing major cases. Unfortunately, many of the major cases are passed on to the Washington Headquarters where the SEC has more theoretical staff for investigation, but it requires more travel time. If the financial industry is headquartered in New York City, Los Angeles and Chicago, why is the SEC Enforcement Division headquartered in Washington? Taking one deposition in New York City requires too much time. Imagine if the Department of Justice had to send all the big cases back to Washington, out of the hands of local US Attorneys!

Headquarters enforcement seems to get all the news coverage, which is why senior attorneys inside the SEC were seeking the December 1989 appointment as Chief of the Enforcement Division.

The present Chairman of the SEC is Charles Breeden whose principal credential is that he served on the Bush Presidential Campaign; otherwise, he is a Harvard educated lawyer who worked in a Wall Street Law firm for a few years. He may turn out to be the best of them all. Time will tell. His most important qualification under the 1934 Act is his political party. He could create a great precedent if he said he would not work for the securities industry after he left the SEC.

What are "they" supposed to do at the SEC? This still isn't clear.

The old agreement between Commissioner Douglas and the New York Stock Exchange may still be in place, that is, the SEC will not get involved in day-to-day affairs, and the exchanges or Self Regulatory

Organizations, as they are known, will handle the intricate details of daily events. The New York Stock Exchange Enforcement Department has hired a new chief, and is staffing up to terrorize the branch managers in the Member Firm network, but it remains to be seen whether any Members or senior officers of Member Firms will be disciplined.

Chairman Breeden, in his news conference of December 27, 1989 surrounding the appointment of William McLucas as the New Chief of the Enforcement Division, indicated that the staffing problem was serious, that it was hard to bring cases when lawyers were hired and then left after 18 months, clearly implying that part of McLucas' job will be to stop that exodus. Poor McLucas, for reasons beyond his control, will almost certainly fail in this mission, because the SEC has always been a finishing school for lawyers, a place to go, get a credential, then leave and hopefully make a lot of money working directly for brokerage houses or for hire on Wall Street. If Wall Street hits really hard times, it will be easier to keep SEC staff in the government.

McLucas can't get the money to keep the mandate even though the original 1934 Act implied that the SEC might be exempt from pay restrictions applied through the rest of the Federal Government. It is unfair to McLucas to recognize the problem of staffing as the key and not raise the alarm about the SEC budget and the reality of the revolving door. It implies that McLucas is supposed to solve a problem that the Commissioners should tackle head on with Congress.

But, remember politics, if McLucas really wants to gear up for enforcement activity against the Street, the Street will oppose the logistical key - money. No money, no enforcement, no matter what the intentions. His hands are tied before he gets going, despite the best of intentions.

My experience with the SEC was that the junior attorneys were there to get a credential and get out, going to work for Wall Street, either inside a house or within a large Wall Street law firm, trading off the SEC years as time off the drudgery of a law firm associate's life. The Commission recruits bright attorneys, then loses them to Wall Street.

Wall Street law firms offer excellent compensation in good times, but the workload for young associates is comparable to serfdom. The associates pay a great price in personal sacrifice. It is not a glamorous job. New lawyers in these firms work for about 70 hours a week, doing research in the back room. Undergraduate law school does not attempt to teach finance to the students. An honors graduate may not be able to interpret a financial statement, unless he learned elsewhere.

Associates learn on the job. Many walk out. They leave after a few years for a mixture of personal and professional reasons. The SEC is a way to jump past the first tough years of that associate situation, and is widely used in the law business like a vaulting pole. It is also an entry into the "old boy" network of SEC alumni in securities practice. It exists in the defense bar, that is, in representing Wall Street against the accusations of customers and the Federal Government. Common sense dictates that in presenting any case against the SEC, you hire one of their alumni. I never met a lawyer in the SEC who had been a broker, or who had a broker's license. I'm sure they must have a few, but I never heard of it. It isn't required.

Before you acclaim the SEC for its handling of Ivan Boesky and the insider trading scandals of the 1980's, let me remind you, gentle reader, that Boesky was undone by a letter sent to Merrill Lynch from Venezuela. A perceptive attorney working at Merrill had the good sense to send the letter on to the regulators with a sense of urgency, and from that the case fell in line. One target, when squeezed, turned in the others, who in turn, turned in others for insider trading. Mr. Boesky, accused of millions of dollars of harmful fraud, copped a plea, and is already out of jail, receiving leniency for cooperating against others. Securities criminals are wimps, afraid of real jail time. They linger under the constant threat, however, of tennis elbow or skin problems from too much tanning. Prison is no "picnic" for these fellows; it's more like scout camp. It's called "Club Fed."

Drexel, Burnham and Lambert, a power brokerage house and giant investment banker, pled guilty to several felonies, and settled with the SEC, paying a settlement of hundreds of millions of dollars to the US Government. They had plenty left over.

Drexel remained in business and ultimately fell in February 1990 because of the failure of the junk bond market and the credit squeeze forced on the commercial bankers by the FDIC chief, William Seidman. He generally insisted banks make responsible, sensible loans or their officers would face serious investigation, therefore Drexel's party was over. They couldn't raise temporary cash based on their "assets."

All considered, Drexel got an excellent deal from the SEC. The firm was in jeopardy of losing its license because it had pled guilty to felonies. Amazing! Remarkable - but not the SEC Deal Making Champ.

The absolute, all time champ has to be EF Hutton. This firm pled guilty to an astounding number - 2,000 - felony counts of check overdrafting in May 1985. I am unaware of any other plea to 2,000 counts of anything, ever, by a corporation!

What did the SEC do to EF Hutton? Essentially, nothing. Hutton continued in business, not missing a day. Their license was put on probation, but not revoked. Eventually, because of market losses in the October 1987 crash, Hutton merged into Shearson, Lehman Brothers, resulting in the present Shearson, Lehman, Hutton.

The facts show the SEC is willing to let gross, criminal activity slide when it comes to big firms. The big firms go on, without missing a beat on their license. The only forum that will ever uncover the reason for this policy of licensing felons is the US Congress, which, in modern times relies on the SEC to guide it through the maze of good and evil in the securities business.

The Congress has good reason to be suspect of the SEC, because the Commission has very few experienced securities lawyers who know how the financial community operates. It's a one way system - lawyers go from the SEC into the private sector, not the reverse. The principal reason has to be money. Chairman Breeden hit it right on the nose when he said success depends on attracting and keeping talented staff. Perhaps Breeden will be the real activist.

Remember my reference to liquidity earlier on?

It's the most important aspect of an investment. If it's not liquid, then an investment becomes useless. In my mind, former SEC Chairman David Ruder will always be remembered, not for the deal making with criminal corporations, but for his comment in the early afternoon of the October 1987 crash that the markets might have to be closed. I was in the office that day at my brokerage house, and saw the announcement of Ruder's quote on the video. I didn't believe it. I thought it had to be a misquote, an exaggeration fabricated in the rush of events. No, it turned out he said it, and the market went into a further dive as panicked investors rushed to get out while the market was still open.

In the Report of the Presidential Task Force on Market Mechanisms, (the Brady Report) issued in January, 1988, at page 111-20, special mention was made of this same event:

"At 1:09 PM, the Dow Jones news wire reported that the Chairman of the Securities and Exchange Commission (SEC) said that he had not discussed halting trading on the NYSE with the Exchange or President Reagan, although "anything is possible." He continued, "...there is some point, and I don't know what that point is, that I would be interested in talking to the NYSE about a temporary, very temporary halt in trading." Between 1:15 PM and 2:05 PM the contract plunged from 255 to 227; the Index fell from 258 to 246, and in the DJIA dropped from 2,081 to 1,969 breaking through the 2,000 level for the first time since January 7, 1987.

By 1:25 PM the Dow Jones news wire quoted the SEC as stating that it was not discussing closing the stock markets. However, the uncertainty created by the possible inability to sell may have exacerbated the dramatic selling pressure. In fact, between 1:30 PM and 2:30 PM, one portfolio insurer sold 1,762 Contracts, worth $200 million, which represented 20 percent of the total volume during that half hour. In addition, during this same time period, this portfolio insurer sold $500 million worth of stocks. Between 1:00 PM and 1:30 PM, index arbitrageurs sold $216 million worth of stocks, and straight program selling totalled $305 million of stocks. Together these two selling interests accounted for 39 percent of total volume during this period."

The Report is available for sale through the Superintendent of Documents, US Government Printing Office, Washington, DC, 20402 for $17.00. The "contract" mentioned above is the S&P Futures Contract. For a look at how this interaction of futures contracts and stocks works, skip ahead to the chapter on program trading.

What was happening after Ruder spoke was a stampede OUT of the market, with the big guys pushing their way past everyone.

In his December 27, 1989 comments about his new position, Enforcement Chief McLucas indicated the SEC will be making cases against more managers at brokerage houses for failure to supervise bad brokers.

In my opinion, branch and desk managers are hired to be sacrificed, if need be, in these cases to save the big shots who run the firm. It will be interesting to see if the Enforcement Department will make any cases against the very top leadership of the large firms. For all the hoopla, they haven't touched anyone at the bureaucratic top of Drexel or the old EF Hutton. My sad prediction: the SEC will continue to let the top leadership in major houses slide no matter what happens.

I propose a few solutions that will help make McLucas' job a lot easier. Make it a Federal Crime for an SEC attorney to represent anyone, in any capacity, in an SEC proceeding or SRO proceeding for 5 years after terminating employment with the Commission. Kill off the revolving door finishing school and the mega dollar recruiting of top officials.

It wouldn't be so bad. The SEC veteran could present cases in front of the Commodities Futures Trading Commission, the CFTC; well, that would be pretty bad. The SEC thinks the CFTC should be shut down and given to the SEC.

Under my version, the SEC veteran could present cases in front of the Federal Communications Commission, the FCC, or the Department of the Interior, and all the rest of the Federal Government. It will never happen, though, because the years at the SEC would be "wasted." Horror of horrors - the SEC veterans could even run cases against brokerage houses, that is, against Wall Street! A rare few do.

If my recommendation was passed, how many of the present staff at the SEC would stay on? THEY would stampede out!

In my opinion, based on the results so far, most of the SEC's efforts have been wasted on deal making with criminals for mysterious reasons, and plugging the occasional leak in the dam of insider trading to grab headlines. Rumors still circulate before almost every major deal, coming out of sources never discovered, and the deal stocks move. The best the SEC can do is pick off an occasional idiot who leaves a paper trail the blind could follow, and who, as confederates, hires contenders for a Three Stooges imposter contest. Everybody sings, once squeezed, because, while financial types talk tough, often in violent sports analogies, they are terrified of hard time in prison where they might have to mix with real criminals.

If the SEC wants to keep people under the present system of the revolving door, then pay them more. I favor paying US Congressmen a lot more than they make now, and if the SEC can't keep its people, then pay them more. What would it take? The present consequence is that the SEC legal staff will continue to be made of the inexperienced led by the courted, or worse, a professor!

The SEC cannot produce a well policed market for public securities trading. They cannot possibly catch all the bad guys, and can't catch even a significant minority of the rascals. When they do catch genuine, big-league criminals, the SEC makes deals, provided the "catch" is big enough, because the SEC is, in the end, bureaucratically self-concerned.

Consider: the only job you've ever had is in the Government with the SEC. You've never had any money so you have never had a securities account, and you don't know how an NYSE Member Firm's P&S department works. You don't know how a Bond Desk really works and you don't know how an OTC Desk operates or what an option straddle is supposed to do; you can't calculate margin. You decide to shut down EF Hutton because it is a criminal firm and should have its license revoked. It has 350,000 active accounts, many of them on margin and many with option positions. It also has another 300,000 accounts that have positions, but aren't terribly active.

Exactly how do you "shut down" EF Hutton?

My belief: no one in the SEC could run it for ten minutes. Could you imagine the customer panic if the SEC said it was going to take over a firm, and run it until it dissolved? You can see why William Douglas made the deal early on that the SEC would stand back and let the NYSE do the real work in its area, and the SEC would just check on the NYSE. Bureaucratic Nirvana!

The SEC wouldn't run it. They would run from it! They would get a court to do it. The SEC has very little responsibility. They don't approve corporate filings. They don't have to stick their necks out on anything. The US Attorney prosecutes the criminal actions, not the SEC.

I was at a conference in the Winter of 1989 concerning the changes to the 1934 Exchange Act which had just passed the Congress in November, 1988. The SEC speaker indicated that he opposed the inclusion of the bounty provision in the recent statutory amendments under which a reward could be given to a person who turns in an inside trader.

A bounty, or reward, sounds like a great idea, but the opposition from the SEC was due to the probability that litigation against its personnel would arise when a reward was not deemed sufficient by the informant! I was shocked!

The decision on how much to pay would be made at the senior levels of the SEC, and they didn't want the responsibility. My guess is that all the responsibility will fall to a poor non-lawyer, pay grade GS-12, in an obscure section of the archives of the SEC down by the literary boiler room. If he doesn't award enough, let the angered informant sue him!

Amazing? No, bureaucratic. Your SEC opposed the reward provision, but your Congress wisely put it in.

Congress was on the ball! The SEC also opposes any Congressional mandate that they examine and approve "blank check" or "blind pool" entities. They shirk responsibility with cunning regularity.

Think I'm way off the mark? In March, 1988, The National Association of Securities Dealers, the "NASD," put out the Final Report of the Regulatory Task Force, a self examination conducted throughout the organization, looking at ways to improve. The members of the NASD Regulatory Review Task Force, 8 securities industry leaders, had about 150 years of real life experience among them.

What a Report!

Get a copy from the NASD, 1735 K Street, NW, Washington, DC 20006. The NASD should republish the Report and REQUIRE its member firms to distribute it to all customers. It discusses problems and solutions for Wall Street issues.

When it came to Task Force Recommendations on Staff-Related Issues, the Report first called for salary and benefit reviews to get and keep the best possible employees. It makes solid sense. NASD veterans are not in the same demand as SEC alumni, but they suffer regular attrition.

The Report next discussed the need for additional training to cope with creative attempts at manipulation, but cautioned, "Although insider trading has generated substantial publicity, other abusive practices cause greater harm to investors as measured by pecuniary losses." Report, p.15.

Insider trading has taken the publicity spotlight, but is not the main event. It never was.

Take away the insider trading cases from the SEC repertoire of recent years, and what's left? Not much. While they were off on their Insider Trading Crusade, who was minding the store?

Let's review the numbers. The Ivan Boesky case was announced on November 14, 1986. In 1987 the SEC brought 36 insider trading cases and in 1988 they brought 27. In 1987, the SEC brought 303 Civil cases and in 1988 they brought 252. That's it. Civil cases cover the whole gamut of violations, not just insider trading. It covers cases against branch managers who fail to supervise brokers who are thieves, actions against firms that don't keep the proper books and records, and controversies over excessive commissions. It covers boiler room criminals and phoney stock promoters. A number of the most important cases concern firm capital violations. Insider trading counts for a small percentage of SEC activity, but it gets all the major press.

With that small number of cases, the SEC feels it has done its job!

The SEC's Enforcement Division - guess how many people serve on the staff, taking care of the nation's markets? Two maybe three thousand?

How about 245? That's it! They intend to add 100 more. Merrill Lynch alone has 12,000 brokers. About 30,000 financial industry workers were LAID OFF in 1987-89 in New York City alone. Based on those numbers, McLucas cannot succeed. He shouldn't feel abused, however, because the Investment Adviser watchdogs in the SEC have a staff of 225 and oversee over 16,000 Registered Investment Advisers.

That covers 100,000+ investment adviser employees! How much thinner can you be spread on a nation-wide jurisdictional mission?

NASAA and the US Congress end up minding the store.

Who? Congress we know; what's NASAA?

The North American Securities Administrators Association, Inc., is made up of state securities regulators. The men and women who work for you, the retail investor, in every state across the nation.

We'll look at that body of regulators, but first, a little sub-chapter on William O. Douglas, firebrand, raconteur, jurist and former head of the SEC. His career at the Commission highlights the problems in overseeing the securities laws.

William O. Douglas, Esq.

William O. Douglas is best remembered for his work on the US Supreme Court. He was born in 1898 in Minnesota. His family soon moved to Yakima Washington where his father, a Minister, died. Douglas had been a sickly child, having survived infantile paralysis. He pushed himself to physical prowess, to academic honor at Whitman College, then further academic heights at Columbia Law School in New York City. He was a brilliant self-starter.

Stories abound, perhaps true, that he hoboed his way across the US by train, or that he was a train-car cattle tender - however he managed it, he did show up in New York City, and worked his way through law school.

Because he didn't graduate number one is his class, he had to get a (ugh!) job at a major Wall Street law firm, the predecessor to today's Cravath, Swaine et al. He stayed two years as a starting associate grinding away in the back room. Number one graduates sometimes clerk for an important judge, thus jumping past a few associate years.

He bolted to teach at his alma mater, Columbia, then jumped again to Yale Law School, where he became the Sterling Professor of Law, writing a few books, lecturing, being an academic. Next, he rocketed to success.

He became an ardent New Dealer when the depression hit, and was hired/appointed to the Securities and Exchange Commission to serve as director of a special study examining how to protect the public from bond defaults and other abuses, which he had written about while a law professor. He also seems to have attracted the uncle-ship of Joseph Kennedy, Franklin Roosevelt's very strong supporter and confidant.

Douglas was named to serve as an SEC Commissioner, and when James M. Landis resigned as the Chairman of the SEC to become Dean of Harvard Law School, Douglas was named to succeed him, being unanimously elected by the other Commissioners to the Chair on September 21, 1937. Douglas was 38. He played poker with another gentleman who had suffered polio - Franklin Roosevelt.

When appointed to the US Supreme Court, Douglas had not tried a case. In his autobiographies he says he carried the bags for a litigator after law school. His appointment to the top court was the only safe place to send him, because a trial judge and an appellate judge have to be familiar not only with the substance of the law, but its application and trial procedure.

Trial judges are reviewed by appellate courts above them, and when the trail judges make a mistake, they see discussion of their error in print. Unlike professional baseball players who see the scoreboard light up for the rest of the game when they commit an error, but start each game with a fresh slate, a mistake by a trail judge is put into the case reporters where it lasts forever - worse, it gets cited by other judges and lawyers, even in matters before the same judge.

Being a trial judge is a very difficult job. Everyone watches what you do and say, and when the case is finished, one side will always say you made terrible mistakes, while the other will say you didn't, but that even if you did, it was only a little mistake with little effect on the case. Whole briefs are written to say that the trial judge didn't know what he or she was doing.

Trial judges aren't paid much, often work in older buildings, seldom get complimented, have to rotate around into areas that are fairly boring, and often get lousy parking spots. If a Federal District Court Judge didn't know what he was doing, he'd be a laughing stock. Before you are critical of the judiciary, go to the court house and see what they do for a living. They work hard.

If you don't have a great deal of experience, and have not tried any cases, the only safe court to be appointed to is the Supreme Court. You can't be wrong! You're "it," the court of last appeal, so whatever you say about an issue has to be right. No one can say you're wrong. You can dissent on opinions that go the opposite way from your position, and you are still right!

The real merit of the Supreme Court is not the raw brainpower of its sitting members. It was never intended to be a think tank, but rather a court of final resolution. A number of intellectuals reading this will howl, claiming that the US Supreme Court is supposed to be the top activist stew pot of swirling ideas and legislative usurpation on behalf of the people. The Supreme Court exists because a case ultimately has to end someplace.

Douglas was not the youngest man appointed to the Supreme Court, but he was the youngest in modern times. No matter what one thinks of his politics or intellect, Douglas was no pushover.

Let's go to 1937.

The New York Stock Exchange was under pressure in Congress to clean up it's act or face possible legislative actions in addition to the 1933 and 1934 acts. Senator Wheeler was the Chairman of the Senate Interstate Commerce Committee. In open hearings, he told Richard Whitney, the immediately past President of the NYSE, that he, Wheeler, felt Whitney hadn't done much to clean up the NYSE, and that things had better change. Whitney dutifully took this message back to the NYSE where he still served as a director. Poor Whitney went to jail shortly thereafter for embezzlement of funds from his own firm, sending shock waves through the investment community.

Douglas was a Commissioner, but not yet the Chairman of the SEC. He got along well with the press, was young and was always good for spontaneous quotes. He had become a close confidant of the President.

On March 24, he gave a speech at the New York Bond Club Luncheon that was nothing short of amazing! "Today, as you well know we have a practical usurpation of the rights of the great body of investors which can only be described as financial royalism."

He quoted Joseph Kennedy to castigate the investment bankers who had gathered too much power, were charging excessive fees and taking home unfair bonuses through their salesmanship, not from any benefits bestowed on shareholders.

Douglas explained that powerful brokers could force investment business from corporate clients by cunning or what amounted to extortion. He wanted to break up the underwriting process so that the underwriter had no control over the sales force that would move the shares to the public. The issuers could then make a decision to sell new securities because they really needed the money for a useful business purpose, not because brokers were looking for commissions on sales of the new securities to the public.

He felt that the real owners of a business were the stock owners, not the management. He wanted to make management respond to these real owners, and not allow management to ignore the needs of labor, investors and consumers. Douglas cautioned that any other course invited disaster. He called it "economic royalism."

It was, and is, economic royalism. It reads like today's press! This professor with no real experience was hitting the matter head on, accurately. Wall Street responded by claiming Douglas was a radical.

Earlier, in November 1936, Douglas had fired a broadside in a speech at the New York Stock Exchange Institute, claiming that the brokers had to be changed from a bunch of frenzied tipsters to a positive influence in the investment markets. No one was safe from the Douglas whip, not management, underwriters, brokers, investment bankers or even bond men!

On April 17, 1937, Douglas gave a speech at the Graduate School of Public Affairs at American University in Washington, DC. This time, in addition to again castigating management of public companies, he went after lawyers who supported corporate reorganizations meant to befuddle and strip away the rights of investors. He claimed that management bureaucracy was worse than government bureaucracy!

On July 11, 1937, Harold H. Neff, the SEC Director of the Division of Forms and Regulations in Washington, DC, gave a news conference to explain that the filings and prospectus materials the SEC was getting under the 1933 Act were too wordy. He felt that a prospectus of 250 words would suffice, not the extended legalese that went on and on. He claimed that the prospectus was designed to be read by people making business judgments. Meticulousness, which lawyers used in corporate documents was out of place in a prospectus.

On August 10, 1937 the news that Douglas was to be the Roosevelt choice for the next SEC Commissioner broke. The Wall Street choice of Commissioner George C. Matthews didn't make it. It followed, therefore, that after the official, procedural vote by the other SEC Commissioners, Douglas was sworn in as the Chairman and gave a short speech on September 22, claiming that he stood for the investor, but that he "wouldn't save a fool from his folly."

Within three weeks of Douglas' swearing-in, Kemper Simpson, an advisor to the SEC quit the Commission as they were abolishing his economics office. He issued a highly critical statement about the way the SEC was failing to do enough to help investors. He noted the Douglas statement about fools and their folly, asking where the buck was supposed to stop if not at the SEC. He felt the SEC had made too many concessions to issuers to compose and publish misleading filings in an effort to streamline the filing system. He charged that bondholders were the investors at most risk because their security may not have been what they thought. (Sounds like Junk Bonds.)

He claimed that the biggest weakness in the SEC was its lack of interest in putting together a professional staff of people interested in long term public service, and that the SEC was relying on staff who were there only to acquire prestige and experience before going into the business world.

On October 26, 1937, Douglas, as Chairman of the SEC, met with President Roosevelt in Hyde Park, NY, along with Joseph Kennedy.

On October 29, Douglas met with the heads of the various securities exchanges in Washington, DC, along with a special guest - the head of the Maritime Commission, Joseph Kennedy.

On November 23, 1937, Douglas issued a statement wherein he threatened to clean up the New York Stock Exchange if the NYSE didn't act. He attacked the membership system as being intended for the benefit of the members at the expense of the public, and implied that the historic relationship where the SEC was content to let the Exchanges police their own members was under scrutiny. SEC activism on behalf of investors was threatened.

This was very serious. Not just a statement, this sounded like an assault, a threat of future action from a powerful Douglas, Roosevelt's pal, who had expressed controversial opinions in the past.

And then? After all that talk, what happened? Nothing.

In 1938, John Hanes, formerly of Barney and Company, came to the SEC as the head of the Division of Research, lauded by the Wall Street community as the first of their kind to get inside the SEC. The Street pressured Roosevelt to get this appointment.

At the end of the year, in November, 1938, the NYSE announced changes in its capital requirements for Members and the way Members carried accounts. The special report also discussed creation of a central clearing house that would hold securities so that customers wouldn't have to worry about what their brokerage house was doing with their stock and bonds. While important, enforcement against bad brokers and manipulative houses was not on the agenda in any substantive sense.

The significant part of this announcement was the agreement between Douglas and the NYSE that the NYSE would do the enforcing and the SEC would only look to see that the NYSE was doing its job with its Members.

In January, 1939, in two political speeches in Texas, Douglas called for the creation of professional public company directors, individuals who were skilled and experienced in finance and management who would be available to serve on corporate boards in place of the management minions then serving. This idea had been debated in business circles since 1935. He also called for creation of more exchanges, even one in the South, in order to reduce the prominence of the NYSE.

And then, on February 9, 1939, Douglas, in a speech to the Fordham University Alumni in New York City, described big business as "evil." He claimed huge corporations degraded moral values, acted against the interests of workers and could ultimately lead to communism or fascism in the pursuit of profits at the expense of all else. He praised the New York Stock Exchange!

On March 20, 1939, Douglas was nominated by President Roosevelt to the US Supreme Court.

In brief, despite press rhetoric, the SEC had done nothing. World War Two was already in progress in Asia in 1937, and was expected shortly in Europe. It came in 1939. Wall Street was essential to any war effort. The Douglas verbal assault and rhetorical threats of 1937 drifted to silence in 1938.

Was Douglas fired from the SEC by Roosevelt and placed on the Supreme Court as an irresistible "promotion?" It makes sense. Douglas admitted he needed a pay raise. Roosevelt had a notoriously low opinion of the Supreme Court. Judges aren't supposed to speak out on policy issues because it creates the impression of pre-judging matters that might appear in later cases. Judges, like any citizen, have first amendment rights to speak their minds, but, as part of the burden of their jobs, they temper that right with judicial restraint to avoid having public positions on matters before them in court.

Douglas promised much, but the SEC didn't shake up the NYSE.

The Wall Street changes of November 1938 were old issues intended to address the stability of member's capital - not help the individual investor. The NYSE club was intact and ready to act to support business, which was tooling up for another massive war. Douglas' idealism couldn't produce one tank or ship. It wouldn't produce a single bullet, grain of wheat or bomber. Wall Street could raise the money to do all that. The fire of Douglas in 1937 was extinguished by the time he got to the Supreme Court. Today, we think of him as a free speech enthusiast, an environmentalist, and liberal. We forget that as a Supreme Court Associate Justice he had no problem with locking up native-born American citizens of Japanese ancestry in concentration camps in the Western US deserts.

Douglas was a sworn New Dealer, a favorite of the President, and hated by Wall Street. Douglas couldn't go to work on Wall Street, and didn't have any experience to avoid embarrassment on the trial judiciary level. There were no openings for deans at any of the Ivy League law schools, and Douglas couldn't get elected to anything. After insulting people all through the business world, there was only one place to put him. Imagine Joseph Kennedy and Franklin Roosevelt thinking about the solution to the growing complaints coming from Wall Street: suddenly, the answer looms: the US Supreme Court!

In March, 1939 Douglas was nominated by President Roosevelt and in April, 1939 he was sworn in as an Associate Justice of the US Supreme Court. His confirmation hearing took 20 minutes, in private. The only expressed disappointment was that he wasn't really from the Western US as had been quasi-promised by Roosevelt for his next Supreme Court choice. Douglas was identified as an Easterner because of his time at Columbia in New York City and Yale in New Haven, Ct.

Douglas served on the court until 1975 and died in 1980.

His reputation as an arch-liberal and conservationist live on, but his SEC period is the most interesting for our present purposes.

2 years on Wall Street, 2 years at Columbia, a few years at Yale, a few years at the SEC, then onto the lifetime tenure of the Supreme Court. He wasn't wealthy, didn't come from a powerful family, but he did make the right friends and swear allegiance to FDR.

In July, 1940, as the Democrats were settling into their convention and grappling with Roosevelt's third term nomination, Vice President John Garner was clearly "out." Douglas, then on the Supreme Court bench, was openly suggested as a candidate to replace Garner on the ticket, as the Vice President to Roosevelt!

Douglas didn't get the nomination and remained on the Supreme Court. If he had gotten the Vice Presidential bid, and remained faithful to Roosevelt through his third term, we might never have seen Harry Truman as the President after Roosevelt's death - it might have been "President Douglas."

Life is full of "might have beens."

The first lesson then: to be an SEC Commissioner, you must have clear political allegiance. Securities experience is interesting, but not terribly relevant. Minimum Wall Street experience is acceptable.

The second lesson: serve a minimal time, nail down the grand titles on the resume, and anything is possible.

Douglas wrote numerous books, two of which were about himself. He wrote to make money to supplement his bureaucratic and then judicial salary. His Go East Young Man covers his life through his Supreme Court appointment. It was published by Random House in 1974 and is probably in your public library. Get it. It's great reading. Douglas was an excellent writer and had a fascinating life as a young man. Commencing at page 312 Douglas spent four pages discussing the revolving door of government servants who sell themselves to the industries they are supposed to control. He called them knights in shining armor, who had sold their souls and corrupted their subordinates to do the same.

Douglas sadly felt, " By the late sixties and early seventies the industrial and financial powers were completely in control of the regulatory machines." How awful!

My belief: add on the eighties. Keep your fingers crossed for the nineties. Chairman Breeden has the opportunity to stand the institution on its ear to represent the people, or he can work on his resume.

Men seldom have such a singular opportunity to make their mark on history. There is no dollar yet minted that can buy honor. I urge him to identify the resume builders and get rid of them now, today! The SEC would be better off with a tiny, real staff, than ranks of pretenders.

Key Definitions: Brokerage Cash Flow

xxviii. Gross Production is the term applied to the total amount of revenue generated by a broker in all forms, from all products, whether it is from stock and bond transactions, sales of mutual funds or special, direct investments. In baseball, you would ask a player, "How many home runs did you hit last year?" In the brokerage business, you judge the success of a broker by, "What did you gross last year?"

xxix. The Commission Schedule is the list of potential charges for your transactions. It will be based on the number of shares and the dollar volume of the trade. Any reduction from the official commission schedule is called a discount. Your broker may or may not have the power to discount. His manager can. Always ask for a discount when you do business with a full service firm. Big customers never pay full commissions. No discount? Use a discount firm!

xl. The Grid is the way the firm figures what to pay the broker. It is made of a series of dollar amounts of gross production; for example, if a broker does $50,000 gross production for the year, he might get a payout of 25% as his W-2 income. If he does $250,000, he might get a payout of 38% as his W-2 income. The brokers watch their gross production to the penny because the impact on their pay is very direct and predictable.

xli. The Net is what the broker gets paid from the grid. This is the amount that hits his paycheck. While you are figuring profit and loss from a transaction, the broker is thinking "Net."

xlii. Direct Investments are things a broker can sell to you aside from stocks and bonds. These items usually have a higher payout to the broker, often approaching 50%. Examine a $1,000 transaction. You buy a piece of an equipment leasing deal for $1,000. The brokerage firm takes 8% as the gross sales charge, or $80. The broker gets 50% of that, or $40. That payout is too small to make the sale worthwhile, so the product is sold in larger blocks of $5,000 or more to make it attractive to the broker. When the broker can't get you to buy stock and bonds, there are always the direct investments or mutual funds. Some also sell insurance. They don't sell cars - yet!

xliii. Churning occurs when the transactions in your account are primarily intended to generate commissions to the broker. It's illegal, fraudulent conduct. If you find it, stop it!

xliv. Educational Seminars are put on by brokers to get you to use them as your investment broker. Sometimes the house will split the cost of these seminars with the brokers, but some very good brokers do this with their own money. Don't be afraid to go to one of these, but be prepared to say "No," to any solicitation of your account business based on one seminar. A lot of big firms have motivational speakers from the research department who are supposed to come in and impress you at these seminars so that you bring the account to that house. Ultimately, your commission dollars pay for the seminar even if there is no admission fee. You can learn something from these seminars, but don't be impressed with them. If you want to learn about finance, there is no substitute for the PUBLIC LIBRARY, where they aren't trying to sell you anything but unlimited ideas.

CHAPTER EIGHT

CROWDS, OBSESSIONS AND TULIPS

Heroic Leadership

Heroic leadership means you endure combat with your troops. You lead at the head of your followers, experiencing their pain and rightfully sharing in their triumph. You eat what they eat, take the same fundamental risks, and more. As leader, you affirmatively and publicly identify your presence to your troops to inspire them and therefore become a target of the opposition through that same mechanism of exposure. Heroic leadership incurs extra hazards, meriting exceptional rewards. It doesn't exist today in senior circles, military or industrial.

Heroic leaders were the norm in ancient times. They became the most celebrated and enduring of the world's great conquerors. Modern corporations use decision avoidance or decision by committees.

Alexander the Great, son of Philip the Macedonian, remains, to this day, as one of the great military leaders of any age. He was born in 356 BC, became king of Macedonia and Greece in 336 BC and went to war until his death in 323 BC from disease, at age 33, which was about the average life span for the time.

Alexander fought side by side with his troops, winning their praise and loyalty. He took numerous wounds in battle as a soldier's soldier.

He never lost a campaign, yet in 323 there was a mutiny among his old Macedonian Officers who felt Alexander had taken on too many of the Oriental trappings of the conquered regions of Persia and Northern India. He was dressing differently, socializing in the Oriental manner, had married a Persian Princess, Roxana, and was no longer, in the officers' view, one of them. At his death, Alexander had finished his conquests and was preparing to return home. The heroic leader was about to become a bureaucrat. Perhaps history was kind in bringing his early death, because he survived in fact and legend at the height of his power, the young emperor, the "Great."

Children study Alexander, if not as a historical military character, then as the spearhead of the Hellenistic Cultural movement of his time.

Misguided despots refer to Alexander as a model for the forceful spread of their social programs, claiming a legitimacy for the sword as an instrument of social change. There are no Alexanders today. Modern leadership avoids decision making. Groups make "decisions."

Sun Tsu

This brings us to a classic text of Military Science: The Art of War by Sun Tsu, an ancient Chinese writer who may or may not have existed, but is thought to have lived about 600 BC. Literary historians disagree as to whether Shakespeare's work was the result of one man or many, or if Shakespeare wrote even the majority of the attributed works. The Bard lived from 1564 to 1616 AD. Imagine the debate regarding this fellow, Sun Tsu, whose personality may have been a clever nom de plume used to present a set of "timeless" thoughts on the tactics of battle over 2,500 years ago! I cannot prove he existed. His book is out, however, and selling.

March off to your book store and buy a copy. It makes great reading. There are several editions, all in paperback. Take your time with it, because books filled with short proverbs must be reviewed differently than lessons drawn from historical narratives.

Proverbs can be misleading, especially military ones. Just because you see it in print, with an Oriental name from antiquity and see a retired general's forward to the particular edition, don't start believing that everything you read works exactly as it sounds.

I raise this caution because I have noticed an alarming trend among recent business school graduates, where they transpose the subjugation techniques of military science to business. Sun Tsu, in one liners worthy of Charlie Chan, recommended lying, cheating and stealing, using spies, bribes, and other methods of subterfuge. He cautioned against rash actions, but recommended that combat be as fierce as possible in order to be short. Under this ancient master, winning by any means was acceptable. Do you want to motivate your troops as a battle begins? Burn all your wagons and destroy your retreat routes. Faced with victory or death, says Sun Tsu, your army will fight like a tiger to survive! Unfortunately, I am seeing Sun Tsu a lot more on shelves in the business sections of upscale bookstores.

Like any military officer, I was trained in combat methods and weaponry, even combat ethics wherein the use of dum-dum bullets is illegal, but the use of nuclear ordinance is doctrine! While I agree that in war, winning is paramount, that is not so in business. They are radically different professions. I became an officer by taking an oath and pledging my life to the defense of the nation. Business does not operate anywhere near that level, and never has. Japanese Bushido in the American board room has a Gilbert and Sullivan comic opera flair. As increasingly favorable publicity and a conservative political climate bring business back into journalistic favor, business discussions are taking on a larger-than-life aspect.

Years ago, when I studied Sun Tsu, it was in a military application. A lot of it is sensible; a lot of it is weird! I can recall playfully inventing "Tsu-isms" that had an authentic ring, but were so shocking they were meant as ridicule of the old master. "Only take edible prisoners," comes to mind. Well then - if I, as a young pup, went about inventing Tsu-isms, how do we know that what we have got is not meant as an extended parody of the real thing? Ancient documents are not deserving of merit merely because they are old. I have been privileged to poke through a lot of old books, in world-famous libraries, yet I still don't believe in witchcraft, alchemy or astrology, despite passionate, literary arguments in old texts that they exist as real sciences. Healthy skepticism is a good companion on the road of ideas.

Professors - are you using Sun Tsu on your business students? Are you proffering that work as a legitimate guide to how business works? Are you implying that business works on this level?

Stop! Business is not war. Money does not justify EVERYTHING.

War is the most wasteful of state acts, compelling the destruction of some for the preservation of others, often for the profit of the war's promoters, but always at the expense of soldiers' and civilians' lives. No one opposes war more than soldiers, who pay most dearly for it.

Business is not war. There is no enemy. There may be competition, but it is not war. It hardly embraces killing and purposeful destruction. If the 1970's were a time of anti-militarism in the US, then the late 1980's has seen the reverse, the pendulum swinging to the other end. Business is creative, positive, and, best of all, enjoyable! Rather than leaving a swath of destruction, business leaves monuments of construction, displaying one of man's best traits: progress, resulting in a better world for all.

If your broker is quoting you Sun Tsu, watch out!

It's supposed to impress you, but it should DISTRESS you. He might as well quote from Mao's Little Red Book. Remember that best-seller, waved by Red Guards in China in the 1970's? They executed millions.

Brokers - if your managers are throwing Sun Tsu at you, find a new firm. Your old firm has gone Madison Avenue Macho. It's unbecoming.

If you need a lesson in what "tough" means, look at Mother Theresa, the missionary; then look at yourself. Open up the old Testament and read the book of Job; Job was "tough." The Romanian people, without regard for their own safety, recently attacked and overthrew a terrorist central government. That's "tough!"

Lessons can be drawn from military service which are useful in business and private life. The foremost is a sense of trusting comradeship with, and loyalty to, those involved in your unit. Another soldier's virtue is the ability to take abuse and still bounce back, and a third is to work with responsibility for others toward a specific goal. It teaches teamwork with lives and honor potentially in the balance.

Caesar's War Commentaries are filled with psychological observation, sociological reviews and military tactical theory, but war, for him, was a last resort even though Caesar was a heroic leader.

Military combat theory may apply in the National Football League or in organized crime, but don't use it as an excuse to brutalize people in business. If a firm wants to use Sun Tsu, it says a lot about attitudes toward innocent investors. Combat presumes an enemy. Whose "enemy" are you? Do you think you are an "enemy?" I don't.

Popular Delusions
Tulips

Charles Mackay is credited with having written a book in 1841 called Extraordinary Popular Delusions and the Madness of Crowds. Alas, we have no excuse now for crowd mentalities.

This is another standard business school text, but it's excellent. No book on the financial markets would be complete without homage to Dr. Mackay, who should go down in time as a classic bookshelf companion to Adam Smith's Wealth of Nations.

Mackay reviews several of the great manias of history, some of which had to do with investment schemes. He attempts to educate the reader to slow down and not go along with crowds unless careful thought has clarified where the activity is leading, why it's going there and what the danger along the way could be.

Get the book! Every large book store has it in paperback. The next time you see brokers pushing a stock as a unique opportunity - stop! Remember Mackay! Then listen carefully to the pitch to see what the broker is up to. The Mackay book is a great gift for friends who have been burned in any hot stock, or who specifically loaded up on oil during the oil craze, gold during the gold craze, or brokerage house stocks in 1986-87.

In tribute to Dr. Mackay, I note that the market surge in January 1990 led to headlines in reputable newspapers to the effect that the continuing eight year old business expansion might mean that traditional economic theory is dead. The suggestion was that governmental organs such as the Federal Reserve might be able to engineer around any recession, or dip in the business cycle. The writers were suggesting that economic expansion might go on forever, like a machine.

When you see that kind of thinking being seriously entertained in the business pages, take care! View it as a warning that danger is coming down the tracks, right at you. Periods of market largesse entertain the question of unending continuity, so don't take these musings seriously; the topic of unending good times seems to play out right before a bang.

Have respect for business cycles, for up and down markets. Don't be overly cynical, but don't be a part of a crowd that gets hurt by emotion and unfounded belief in an errant dogma. MacKay described the tulip craze in Holland with subtle humor. Her fleets had brought home great wealth from trading the world over. A fad developed: the search for a tulip bulb that would produce a completely black flower. Prices on certain bulbs took off! Fortunes were made. People were buying and selling bulbs as though they were jewels, looking forward to an ever escalating price scale. It crashed! When the fad abruptly ended, the bulbs had very little value. Fortunes vanished.

Historic Tragedy

I have the greatest respect for the fighting men of France, admittedly colored by their aid in the American Revolution, especially when they stood beside us in combat at the climactic Battle of Yorktown.

I cannot leave a chapter, having commented on Sun Tsu and Mackay without discussing one of the most tragic battles in Medieval European history.

From 1337 through 1453 the English and French fought a series of engagements that has come to be known as the Hundred Year's War. The cause was fairly straightforward: the English King claimed the French Throne and with it, most of France. Intermarriage of European monarchies is still commonplace. Various dukes and princes have claims to crowns in other countries through marriage.

Edward the Third used a series of armed raids as his method of warfare, trying to dislodge the hold of the French Monarch, Philip the Sixth, on the French Countryside. In 1346, Edward was busily out burning and pillaging when Philip finally caught him close to the Somme River, south of the modern Pas de Calais. Edward went into a defensive position with his 8,000+ troops. Philip's 40,000 knights attacked!

The result of the Battle of Crecy: the French learned that the English longbow could mow down armored cavalry at a distance with terrible efficiency. The French withdrew with massive casualties. Edward went back to work. The war went uselessly on.

New kings appeared as the English and French Thrones turned over through royal deaths. Another English raiding invasion was mounted by Henry the Fifth in 1415. The French gave him a very hard time, and again, the English were pinned down in a defensive action, this time at Agincourt, not far from the Somme River. The French King, Charles the Sixth has been characterized as insane, therefore his forces, 25,000 fighting men, were under the command of Constable D'albret. English Henry had just under 6,000 men at arms.

Each side was very familiar with the results of Crecy, fought less than one hundred years earlier about 10 miles away.

What did the French do?

They massed their attack into such a narrow field that as the English archers once again ripped French formations apart with their longbows, the congestion of charging and fallen troops made the attack fail. Over 8,000 French knights were killed! The English lost about 400.

In each case, the devastating losses occurred not to common soldiers, but to French nobility. The lesson of Crecy was wasted. Noble families in France lost sons in each battle.

Both engagements are studied as classics of defensive firepower supremacy over poorly led and improperly equipped offensive forces. The general lesson for all students - learn from history!

Can these harsh lessons be disregarded? Of course. It happened in the First World War.

Battle of the Somme

On June 23, 1916, the Allies opened a furious artillery barrage against the German positions at the Somme River, a scant 20 miles from the battlefields of Crecy and Agincourt. Over a million artillery shells rained from the sky on the heads of the German infantry. Both sides were stuck in trench warfare along a front that stretched the length of Europe. Barbed wire and seven foot deep trench streets replaced the flash and elan of 19th century cavalry battles, and destroyed the staff plans that had called for a fast war in the summer of 1914.

Day and night, thunderous shelling continued to soften up the Germans for the allied infantry attack. On July 1, the barrage ended.

Alert allied troops got ready to spring out of their trenches and advance on the shattered Germans.

Whistles and trumpets blew: English and French infantry went up and "over the top." Massed troops supported by the greatest barrage in history were thought to be invincible. Few Germans could have survived the artillery. It was all worked out in careful staff planning by some of the best military minds in Europe.

On the first day, the British alone lost 20,000 dead and 40,000 wounded. Whole regiments disappeared. Young men were stitched with machine gun fire and ripped by shrapnel as soon as they vaulted from the safety of their trenches. The Germans, dug in deep and tenacious as demons, had survived and were ready to fight after the historic barrage.

The Battle of the Somme lasted from that July 1 disaster through November, 1916, when the terrain became too muddy to walk, much less fight. Nature stopped the killing with rain, else the generals might have fought to the last trooper.

The allies suffered about 600,000 casualties; the Germans experienced the same. For all those killed, for all those whose lives were shattered, the "Front" moved approximately 5 miles in a small pocket.

How can these fields in Northwest France can be as peaceful as they appear today, with a history of such enormous suffering. In late summer evenings, one expects to feel the presence of ancient and modern warriors, restless through time, wandering. I pay homage to the memory of brave young men who went forward in honor and faith on behalf of their nations. I trust God damns the fools who, placed in command, sent them there to die.

Modern, Expensive Stupidity

The crowd is usually wrong! The crowd is made of followers who get caught in a collective momentum that stems from our instinctive need to do something when we are surrounded by activity. Mass approval implies the action must be right, the premise must be correct. Let's do it! What do we get in exchange: often, tragic results. Crowd approval is fickle, but it is also subject to manipulation by purposeful individuals who may have suspicious intent.

When you deal with a crowd, look to isolate the promoter. Who stands to gain? How will the promoter gain? How will the crowd gain, if at all? If you are investing, remember that prices are based on knowledge of what the investment is worth. If the crowd has formed and is buying in, the promoters have probably moved on, or are in the process of selling to the crowd just before moving on to the next idea.

Crowds do not invest based on fundamentals. A crowd assumes there is good reason to go forward, but individually, investors rely on the group momentum, not the group's knowledge. There is usually no widespread group knowledge in crowds - only momentum.

Then, bang! The momentum stops and no one is there to buy from the group at the price the group was willing to pay. That is MacKay's point about tulips. Does it sound extreme?

As taxpayers, you and I are paying for the death of the Savings and Loan Industry which rose and foundered on the Real Estate Mania of the 1980's in the US. Remember the phrases,"...buy before it's too late, before the prices get unreachable," or the classic,"...can't miss!"

The prices did become unreachable. When no one was willing to reach, they fell. "Can't miss," turned into "next time!" The underlying need in crowd investments is an unending crowd, always willing to put more and more money into the object. Once the crowd stops putting in the cash, that's the end. The price must drop, then the crowd starts to run away and the sellers become a panicked crowd.

Read Mackay's book!

Once in a while, as you read the financial pages, look to see if you can tell what the latest craze is. There is always a farce playing in the theater of finance that will bring Mackay to mind. If you try that exercise, cut out the articles that strike you as fads, put them away in your investment notes, and review the clippings once in a while. Watch how the balloon goes up, stalls and drops. At least keep Mackay's book on your active book shelf at home, where you see the title on a regular basis.

Tulips will never be the same.

Hopefully, Junk Bonds won't reappear in the future as they did in the 1980's. The largest Junk Bond owner in the land is the US Government, which got the bonds from the Savings and Loan mess. What would happen if the Government decided to sell the bonds for cash in a short time?

It would be "Goodnight, Wall Street!"

You and I, and all the taxpayers in the US are now subsidizing the fat cats that gave us junk bonds. We own, collectively, billions and billions of dollars of junk. Should we cower like fools, or should we be politically furious.

Perhaps it is "goodnight, Wall Street."

KEY DEFINITIONS: ANTI-LOGIC

xlv. Fear and Greed are the rhetorical underpinnings of a lot of market theory. Somewhat demeaning in concept, it is a loose term used to indicate that retail investors, you, are motivated by Fear and Greed, that you don't think logically, and that retail investors are like sheep. Fear and Greed do motivate a lot of things, not just in finance, but throughout life. Politics, philosophy, investments and more are influenced by these concepts, but there is, or should be, more. Fear and Greed do influence institutional investors, especially the ones who are "marked to the market" each month by calculation of their performance to the third decimal place. When the market drops a hundred points at a shot, you are seeing institutional Fear and Greed, not retail. Retail usually doesn't know what's happening until after it has occurred. Institutions and professional traders do panic. Some are the ones who try to convince you that they can calmly advise on your trades. Real fear is an autonomic reaction. It happens, and you can't control it because it is an instant, instinctive reaction of the body to danger, such as jumping back when you are startled. Investment fear is an abandonment of thought. It is not autonomic, but for some professionals, it is automatic.

xlvi. Manias are intense desires to get something or do something that goes beyond logical sense. People trying to quit smoking experience a mania for a cigarette. You have to stand back to understand a mania, looking to see if your thoughts are logical. Whole groups of people can get caught up in manias. It doesn't mean they are crazy. It means that something has become impulsively attractive beyond any logical level. Brokers can be involved in manias - sometimes they advise investing in electronics, or, alas, bank stocks to the exclusion of all else. Then the mania fades, the enthusiasm withers, and, in the cold light of logic, no one is excited about the industry. Prices drop. It happens time and time again. The Dutch tulip craze is the classic mania.

xlvii. An Obsession is a constant, relentless preoccupation with an idea, thing, activity, person, etc. Even in the face of failure or rejection, the obsession continues. Some retail investors can't stop. They shouldn't be in the market, they keep on losing but they can't say "no." The test: pull out for a few months. Don't do any trading. If you can't stop, you shouldn't be in the market. Some brokers get obsessed. When they lose, they can't accept they were beat. The tragedy is where they lose your money by their futile attempt to better the markets by their humble input. An obsessed broker doesn't care if he gets caught, or what the consequences are. He doesn't really care about his income. He wants to beat the system, to score and win. He can't stop. Manias fizzle and die. Obsessions keep going.

xlviii. Odds are used to bet sports and other occurrences. Odds in football or basketball use "The Point Spread" method. If New York is favored in a game over Los Angeles by 5 points, you can lose the bet on New York to win if they DO win, but only by 3 points. You win but you lose. When you hear investments discussed with "the odds" as a factor, watch out! You can win, but lose. Be careful about brokers that tell you "the odds."

xlix. Betting is not what the markets are about. Firms go crazy when they see brokers using this word because it is demeaning to the industry. The NYSE gets very upset when the markets are referred to as a casino, or the word "bet" is used because it hurts their image. Betting means you put down money on some event you have no control over, choosing one possible outcome as your "bet." Someone else puts down money on another outcome for his "bet." The key is you have no control. The event will happen. You are not supposed to have control, only a guess. If you have control, it's not a bet. The NYSE feels that if you believe the market is a bet, you will not invest. How much control do you have over the markets? Are all traders really bettors?

l. Investing means you think out your financial actions before you pay, looking at an opportunity as one where you might make some money because of a number of factors. In the markets, it means you will probably hold on for a while, that you are not a trader. Investors are long term. Traders are very short term.

CHAPTER NINE

TORTURED SENTINEL: THE BRANCH MANAGER

Under Section 15 (b)(4)(E) of the 1934 Exchange Act, the SEC can bring cases against brokerage houses and their personnel for failing to adequately supervise brokers who break the law or wrongfully harm customer's accounts. This is separate from cases that claim the house has failed to keep the proper records or capital levels, which, while serious, rarely has a direct effect on a customer.

This is important to the brokerage house because the case can result in big penalties to the firm, supervisors employed by the firm in its various departments, and to the branch manager.

The branch manager is Johnny on the spot for the firm. He has command of the local branch that services your account. He acts in a number of capacities, from logistical - light, heat and rent - to the professorial - teaching the brokers about new products. His most important job, however, is to watch what the brokers are doing - to you! He is supposed to watch, probe the broker's activity, and recognize problems before your account gets blown out by your broker.

Branch managers are hired by the firm with the clear understanding that they will be responsible for the office, from top to bottom. It's a lousy, dangerous job, but any manager can examine his situation and quit. If they stay, they take on the responsibility, not just a part of it, all of it. Before you feel any sympathy for these employees of the firm, remember they can hold out for more money, they can go into production and just do their own gross, or they can quit. No one has drafted them for the job; they're not missionaries. They are mercenaries, doing the job for money.

What is the job? Primarily, they are supposed to produce revenue for the firm by making sure the brokers have a good physical facility, that the machines work and that the flow of information from the home office gets through on a timely basis. Unfortunately for them, Federal Law requires that they do a little more by supervising the brokers under pain of losing their manager's license or getting kicked out of the business altogether.

The NYSE and NASD can also punish a branch manager who does not do his job with similar penalties. They can levy fines which must be paid or the individual cannot work for a Member Firm. The manager, today, gets a set of instructions from his firm, a manual, that tells him what he is supposed to do with a great amount of detail.

The manuals are composed because the SEC has threatened to bring actions against the senior officers of the firms unless the manuals are in existence and contain acceptable procedures to reasonably ensure control over the brokers. Get the picture? If the firm has composed a manual and given it to the branch manager, the firm and its senior officers can escape liability when a broker blows up IF the manual given to the branch manager was adequate, covered the subject area that the broker abused, and the manager missed the harm because he didn't follow the manual.

You can bet that the bigger brokerage houses put out extensive manuals covering everything imaginable so that when a broker does cause trouble the home office can point the finger at the branch manager and say he dropped the ball: blame him, not the home office. This goes on all the time.

It's not hard to hire a warm body as a branch manager, but it is very difficult to get a good one, that is, a man or woman who takes the job seriously, applies themselves to the task, protecting you, the customer, while, at the same time, making money for the firm by squeezing the best performance from the brokers.

While some managers keep their clients, their "book," others walk the razor's edge by not having their own clients. No "book" means the manager is salaried, and probably needs the job to pay his bills. Larger firms occasionally insist the manager give away his book in order to manage.

This kind of professional manager is the most prone to succumb to the pressures of the every day conflict of interest: control or production, because the firm never has enough production. As soon as the firm makes money, the firm spends it; therefore, any manager that meets his quota is immediately met with a higher quota, then a higher quota, and higher and higher. He can't win. If he falls behind, the home office will threaten to fire him unless he gets the gross production up.

Imagine getting "the call" from the regional supervisor who tells you that you are an easily replaced jerk and that you WILL be replaced unless there is a 20% increase in revenues within the next three months, and that you'd better not lose one more broker to another firm. You put down the telephone as your stomach rumbles from too much acid. Your palm feels sweaty against the telephone's cool plastic. You stare at the ceiling, look out the window, tap the desk top, and rock in your swivel chair in an effort to calm down. 20% more gross; three months. As you look around the room you see the typical, meaningless trappings of brokerage house "impressabilia." "How did you get this lousy job," you wonder. Family pictures, bronze bull and bear - and the damn Compliance Manual. You know very well how to get more gross out of the brokers, and as you look at the manual, you know what it could cost if you get "caught" because one of the brokers blows up.

Your office has large glass windows so you can see a lot of the work area. Low producing brokers are in the open space, the bullpen, and the big producers are in private offices with windows. Occasional secretaries' stations block the clear view of the private offices, but, as times are tight, half the secretaries are long gone.

The brokers are on the phones, reading the papers, playing with the video tubes - God only knows what they are telling people. "What promises are they making, what half-truths are they tossing, what flat out lies are they inflicting? Which one of them is going to get me?"

It's not paranoia. The brokers aren't out to get you by abusing customers, but they don't care what happens to you, either. They want you to stay out of their way. They want you to fight with the back room for them, to get breaks for them from the product desks and keep the Compliance Department off their back. They want you to block for them. They don't care if you die for them.

You're the manager.

What they absolutely don't want is for you to say "no." Say "no," and they'll go! No, not the little ones, but the big ones will let you know they carry you, that their gross is the only reason you have a job.

The regional manager tells you he carries you. The brokers tell you they carry you. The Compliance Department tells you they are watching you. The rest of the firm won't talk to you because you're nobody unless you do gross production.

The pressure's on. What do you do? Your kids have school bills, dentist bills, and one's off to college next year. You have bartender bills. Your new, $200 shoes, and lots more, are on your American Express Card, and you need a job to pay the bills, bills, bills.

You look at your desk.

There is a copy of the blotter, a document showing trades from yesterday. Rasputin the Animal bought 1,000 shares of Big Doggie for the retired school teacher, another 1,000 for the retired cop, 1,000 for the Temple, 1,000 for the Church, 1,000 for the guy who runs the newsstand, 1,000 for the elderly widow, 1,000 for the kid's trust account, 1,000 for the guy in the Peace Corps in Senegal, 1,000 for the college kid, 1,000 for the house painter and 1,000 for the secretary on disability since her fall down the stairs. Oh, and he sold 11,000 of Big Doggie out of his brother's account - essentially to them!

Rasputin the Animal does about $ 800,000 gross per year. He pays the rent, and more! They love him in the home office. He was recruited by the Regional Manager with a bonus of $ 200,000 two years ago, so there's about $125,000 left on the books for his five year deal.

You know you should fire him. You know you should bust the trades from yesterday.

You know Rasputin will explode if you do either! He'll be on the telephone to the regional manager and the president of the firm telling them he's had it and he's going to quit unless they fire you right now. You have to wonder - will the home office consider firing you if you try to fire him, or will they make the pressure so unbearable you'll be gone in six months? Will they stand behind you?

If you do nothing, maybe Rasputin will get caught, maybe not. Even if he does get caught, maybe the regulators won't get to you. Even if they do, maybe you can make a deal.

What do you do?

Bounce it around for few moments as you sit comfortably reading this book - what would you do?

If you had a "book" that grossed $500,000 you could act and let them fire you. Without the problems of the manager's job, you could do a lot more gross. They'd do you a favor if they fired you as manager, provided you had a book.

But, you don't have a book. What do you do?

A manager can fold; others, to their lasting credit, do the right thing, come what may, restoring faith in integrity.

The Manager's Routine

The manager is supposed to make sure that all correspondence is examined when it comes into the branch, BEFORE it gets to the brokers, because this is one of the ways the firm finds out about complaints.

Customers don't know the manager is there to examine all complaints, and they send them to the brokers, who can bury them. The manager is supposed to personally examine the mail or get his assistant to do it. This includes any apparently personal mail to the brokers such as their club dues, school alumni letters, letters from creditors and relatives. If it comes to the office, the manager is supposed to open it. Managers find securities, checks, lawsuits, subpoenas, complaints, inquiries and requests for adjustments in the mail.

The manager is also responsible for reviewing the outgoing mail to see what the brokers are sending out. If you get a letter from your broker, the manager has seen and approved it - well, he is supposed to have seen and approved it. He is looking for outright lies, and other excesses, but he is also looking for technically inappropriate comments that you wouldn't know are prohibited. The most important items to catch and stop are home-made research pieces and other essays that make excessive promises or guarantees. The haunting hazard they try to catch is the broker who gives specific tax advice.

As the day goes by, the manager is supposed to sign off on any new accounts opened by the brokers. The manager doesn't just stamp them and pass the account on - he signs to indicate that he has inquired about the suitability of the client for the kind of account being opened, that he has deemed the broker as competent for the type of account, and that he, the manager, will thereafter be aware of the account and will supervise the broker's handling of that particular client. This is part of the paper trail of your account.

The manager must pay special attention to discretionary accounts, the ones where the broker will be making the trades as he sees fit per the written permission of the client. A lot of firms require clients to renew that discretionary permission on a periodic basis. In Commodity trading, it has to be renewed each year.

It sounds simple. The manager reviews the way the account forms are filled out to make sure the required information is properly filled in, and that the tax forms, cash account, margin account, options and other account forms are sent on their way to the main office for recording in the master archives of the firm's official records.

In the headquarters, the firms use micro film or electronic data imaging to make and keep copies of all account forms. SEC rules are strict - records have to be made and kept. Certain forms have to be kept in the branch and in the home office, but be assured, they are kept and they must be retrievable! If you want copies of these forms, you can get them. If the broker puts you off, go right to the home office. They will send them, unless they want to fight with you.

Forms are lost. It happens for a number of reasons, more often than you think. If the broker needs new ones, don't give him a hard time: give him new ones - but, always keep a copy of what you are signing! Don't sign the form unless you read and understand it, because many forms are filled with technical, legal language. If you sign, it looks like you understand the agreement and have approved it. You could be signing margin, option or discretionary trading forms!

The average margin agreement is two sides of standard sized typing paper, with small print, that you cannot possibly read and understand in less than ten minutes, unless you are a lawyer who does brokerage house work. Don't sign these things on the run!

You sign lots of forms to open an account. It's part of the business. Don't sign unless you understand it! Don't sign in a hurry and NEVER SIGN A BLANK FORM! Forms can come back to embarrass and haunt you. If you don't understand them - don't sign.

The manager is supposed to review your financial data to see if you should have an account. If you don't have any money, you shouldn't be buying stock or other risky investments. You can go and buy a sports car, a pair of platinum ice skates, but you are not supposed to be in the stock market unless you are suitable for it.

When the manager approves the account he is making a decision that you are suitable to be in the market based on what you are telling the firm. If you lie to the firm about your income, savings and experience, that's your problem. The manager is not supposed to check out everything you tell them; but if you do tell them the truth about your finances, he has to make the decision.

The broker is supposed to go out and get business. Sure, he is supposed to look to suitability, but the one with the first level of control is the manager, and he looks. If he doesn't, he isn't doing his job.

Once he looks, he has to keep looking. He doesn't just sign off and thereafter ignore your account. He watches what the brokers are doing to make sure that very active accounts are suitable for the activity. He can pull your forms out whenever he wants, to see if you are suitable to buy 100 IBM or 10,000. It becomes important when your account trades every day, when it buys high risk securities, or if margin is used.

Don't lie on your forms. Don't stretch the truth. Brokers may ask you to sign blank forms which they will fill in - don't! Don't leave anything blank. If you don't understand it, don't sign it! The form is there to protect you. Signed, blank forms are extremely dangerous.

Managers pay close attention to option accounts. They are told they have to be very careful by the firm, by the regulators and by their common sense. The manager is a Registered Options Principal and has been approved to specially watch this trading. This is probably the most dangerous activity a customer can commence. Many managers will require any trade over 10 or 20 options contracts to be personally signed by himself or his designee BEFORE it can be sent by the cage. This is a practical, recommended rule for the cage.

Managers may require the same "sign off" on the order ticket for an equity trade over a certain size, for a very large bond trade or for commodity or mutual fund trades.

The manager's office can get like a train station in busy times with brokers coming and going, asking for help in getting forms filled out, arguing about why an account should be allowed to make a large trade despite what the forms say about income and net worth, asking for help with an obstinate desk manager in the home office - now you see why the manager doesn't have time to do gross production!

On top of that, he is supposed to recruit from other firms!

The manager is supposed to review daily trading. He looks at all the order tickets to see what the brokers have done. He's a broker himself, and he knows the products. When you look at tickets, you can tell what's up by the size of the trade and the nature of the underlying security, and, even though you are seeing the activity after it has occurred, if a trade is peculiar, the manager can discuss it with the broker, get the facts and "bust" the trade if it was wrong.

It sounds easy, but in an office with forty brokers, there may be hundreds of order tickets per day. The manager has to make fast determinations based on the size of the order and the nature of the security, or he will be overwhelmed! The best thing for the manager to do is not wait until he looks at masses of tickets, but rather, to go into the cage during the day and review tickets several times. He can also look at the broker's book periodically to see all the trades for any particular customer.

The manager doesn't have to be suspicious; it's a good practice to review the broker's book on a regular basis with an open mind, just looking. Patterns are apparent in the book, whereas a single order ticket will stand out only when it is exceptional on its face. An experienced, bad broker will try to beat this kind of ticket review by doing a steady stream of small tickets, which, when you add them up, day after day, show a pattern of conduct. That's why the manager can't just look at the tickets.

He also gets the copies of the monthly statements that go to the brokers before they get them, so he can review the last month's activity easily, in hard copy. The manager has a video tube that can go back for several months activity in all the accounts in the office. The broker can only get his own accounts on his video, but the manager can get all the accounts being serviced by the office without the brokers knowing. If the manager wants to see the activity for the past several years, he can get it from the home office just by asking. The broker won't know.

The manager gets a commission breakout by product for the brokers, intended to help squeeze more gross production from them. It is a great control tool, however, because it tells about activity by another method that everyone in the firm can understand - income; cash; money! On top of that, in large firms, the manager gets a copy of a special customer report which highlights accounts that have done a combination of commissions and trades, perhaps five trades and/or $500 gross commissions for that month. The number of trades and the amount of commissions can vary from firm to firm, but the manager gets a report that highlights the active accounts. These reports show the activity for the month and the cumulative for the year.

They get reports showing a comparison of the gross commissions generated by the account in comparison to the equity value in the account. If an account is worth $50,000 and generates $15,000 in gross, the activity is very suspicious.

The manager can't miss! Activity is reported on paper in black and white, on the video, in the tickets, and posted in the book.

They "miss" it all the time. How? The manager doesn't bother to read the material because he's too lazy. He reads it but doesn't act because he is too afraid. He would take action, but he's too busy doing his own production with his own clients. He wants to act but he has been told by the sales chain of command to let the brokers do business and let the Compliance Department catch the activity, making them wear the "black hat," and leaving sales to wear the "white hat."

The first question in an account blow up is, "how could the broker have done that to the client?" The next is, " where was the manager?"

It's a fair question. The broker does it for the money. For the manager, in the end, it's the same: the money.

Make no mistake, they know their job is no picnic, but managers are supposed to look for trouble using all the skill and intuition they can bring to the task. If they don't measure up, then the SRO's and the SEC have declared open season on them and are gunning for manager scalps.

If the choice at a firm is to sacrifice a manager or a president, who do you think will go? The manager is always in the middle. Good managers work very hard to help all the branch's clients. As I said before, they are typically underpaid and often unsupported by the celebrities in their senior management.

Either his fingerprints are all over the documents because he was watching the situation with all the data at his disposal or there are no prints because the manager didn't bother to look.

Look at the letter in Appendix F - use it! Make the manager get involved in your account. That's his job. Get his fingerprints all over your account, even if you are presently happy. He is supposed to look at it: <u>make</u> him look at it. Make him "sign off!"

You are paying for this protection with your commissions. Good managers like to hear from customers. If you believe you are getting good service, call the manager and say "thanks." Good ones earn it.

I watched a lineman work on a powerline after a storm one day: one mistake and he would have died. While dangerous, the branch manager's job isn't THAT dangerous!

CHAPTER TEN

CHINESE WALLS: KEEPING SECRETS

A Little History

"Chinese Walls" comprise an intellectual concept that brings out the best and worst of the scholastic gang. Serious thought went into the creation of this device, and even more serious examination has condoned the concept which is all built around the idea that it is possible for the left hand to know nothing about what the right hand is up to. This is pure think tank wizardry.

The Great Wall of China is vastly misunderstood in the present age. It is not one wall, but a series of fortifications built over the course of hundreds of years. What we all think of today is the series of fortifications that date from approximately 1645 AD, most prominently the part outside Bejing where regular tours go. That part is a restoration.

The actual Wall is about 1500 miles long, stretching from Manchuria down around the Mongolian plains, ending in the middle of nowhere, about 500 miles north of Tibet. It never worked in military terms. It was never manned as a precise barricade or disciplined fortification with any success. It never stopped an invasion of coastal China by the barbarians from the Northwest - the Mongols and their allies. It was a quaint relic when China opened its doors to the West in 1834 at Canton. It had absolutely no effect in the Japanese-Communist-Kuomintang struggle. China suffered constant, mobile war from 1917 through 1949, right through the "Wall."

The Great Wall is a quaint idea, but an ineffective reality.

Ignorance Remains Bliss

Naturally, therefore, the securities industry and the SEC have ignorantly latched onto the myth and use it for desperately real purposes to create the illusion that a firm can deal with public retail customers and at the same time conduct its own independent trading and further, conduct extensive activity in the corporate finance and syndicate areas. Why? Because "Chinese Walls" stop information from crossing among the different areas as though there were different firms under the same umbrella that didn't talk to each other.

Consider: if a firm has a corporate finance area, it solicits fund raising business from corporate clients. What if, after getting the potential corporate client interested, the corporate finance people sit down, open the books - and walk out because the potential client is in terrible shape? The brokerage house now knows that Big Doggie is in bad shape. Who do they tell?

No one. Certainly not you.

Even if you are buying Big Doggie stock through the same brokerage house at the recommendation of their broker, they won't tell you that it's a bad stock. You keep buying away, and one day Big Doggie rolls over and dies, so you get wiped out.

If you find out they knew and decide to complain, "Chinese Walls," says the brokerage house. "We couldn't tell you without passing on inside information."

Pilgrims, once the firm took a close look at Big Doggie do you think they bought any more? They aren't stupid. Do you think they kept it to themselves in toto, or do you suppose that this information, valuable to the "Shorts" wouldn't wind its way about the markets.

How about the case where Big Doggie turns out to be great, super, the best thing since sliced bread? Do you think they keep it to themselves? Do you really think they do? The senior officers of the brokerage firm and Big Doggie aren't dumb. They are not going to go out and buy Big Doggie stock in their own accounts because computer surveillance will find them out. What about the brokers?

Theoretically, they don't know that their own brokerage house is out talking to Big Doggie because of the Chinese Wall, but in reality, the introduction to Big Doggie probably came from one of the big producers who has an "in" with the company. You can trust all the big producers, right? Corporate finance people depend on the brokers to get introductions to companies on a regular basis. The brokers know the senior officers of the companies as clients, friends or relatives. The company can't exactly advertise its desire to get financial advice on raising money for secret projects, so they rely on introductions - enter the brokers. The brokers love it because they get a piece of the corporate finance fees, if any result.

Once the broker makes the introduction, he is supposed to be muzzled by being brought "inside the Chinese Wall." If he tells anyone he could get into serious trouble. If caught.

What's so interesting about the corporate finance people crawling over Big Doggie's books? The only genuine reason to go to the capital markets for more money through an issue of stock or bonds is to get a major effort going in a new direction, usually to finance a new product or research effort, or a Big Doggie effort to buy out and take over the Little Doggie company.

If you know that Big Doggie is going to do something major, you can make money. It doesn't matter if down the road the "something major" turns out to be a dud; the information is valuable NOW.

If you know that Big Doggie is going to buy Little Doggie, you can start buying Little Doggie stock and make money when it gets bought out by Big Doggie. If you know that Big Doggie has secretly discovered a new laser beam that carries telephone traffic at a 90% price reduction from the best, present technology, and that they want to raise money to build a mass production laser plant, you can start buying Big Doggie to make money when the stock rises when the discovery news is announced. You could also buy land around the plant area or buy a McDonald's franchise down the road from the probable main gate.

Remember the research department - what if they are secretly working on a piece that will be very favorable about Big Doggie? If you find out about it, you can start buying Big Doggie. When the research piece comes out, the stock should rise and you can make money.

The Gray List

The brokerage firms claim they can keep it all in bounds by use of a spider web of control that stretches over the firm. Somewhere in the bowels of the house, usually in the compliance department, there is a "gray list."

This list tells everything the research department is working on, everything on the corporate finance agenda, and everything that is being traded in the firm's own accounts. This master list is probably the greatest secret in the firm, next to the president's expense account. With this list, the compliance department can tell if any of the brokers or employees are trading in the gray list stocks. All firm employees have to have copies of their account statements sent to the compliance department if they have accounts at another house. Brokerage houses are getting to the point where they are forbidding their employees from having accounts at any other houses. In theory, the compliance department can see all trades done in gray list stocks by the brokers and all the employees, all the firm's customers and the firm's own accounts.

If the employees obey the rules and send their outside statements as they are supposed to, all employee trades should be available to the internal "cops," because all the internal trading records are readily available. But, since it is a federal crime to trade on this inside information in the first place, what further threat can the firm make to force the employees to obey the internal prohibition?

None. The gray list is a paper tiger. Only a dolt would buy Big Doggie in his own name while using hot, "inside" information. Derivative investments such as the land and franchise described above can be more profitable than a stock transaction. Suppose I confidentially learn that a truck depot will be built on River Street. If I buy the River Street Garage, next to the proposed depot, have I broken any securities laws?

Recent amendments to the 1934 Exchange Act force securities firms to have these Chinese Wall procedures in place, but you can see that it is all theory and little substance. The real problem with market manipulation is not going to be controlled by rhetorical fences that sound secure, but mean nothing. Brokerage house ABC has no idea if their broker, Nuclear Rasputin, has an account at brokerage house DEF unless Rasputin tells ABC. There is no central clearing house of names and address of accounts because the houses compete against each other and they won't give up the information.

Bluesheets

When a takeover deal occurs, when a new product is announced, or when earnings are announced, the information is controlled. Precise times can be associated with the public news announcement. The NASD and the NYSE can look back on the times of the announcements and compare the prices before and after the announcement, looking to see if any prices took off before the announcement.

If prices did move in a way that indicates insider trading may have occurred, the NASD, the NYSE or the SEC can make an inquiry of individual firms to obtain their records of who traded the stock on suspicious days. If it looks even more interesting, the regulators can get copies of the order tickets from the brokers to show exactly when a suspicious trade order was taken, sent and executed.

The only entity that can chase a civilian bad guy is the SEC. The SRO's have no power over a civilian. When they get information they consider suspicious, the SRO's hand it over to the SEC fast, and step back. The SEC gets the right to make the serious inquiry first, then the SRO's grill the broker and the branch manager or other employees that work for the brokerage house. If the house employees refuse to cooperate, they are immediately suspended from work.

Many stocks are "thinly traded," which means they don't have much volume on an average day. It may be a great company - some stocks just don't trade a lot of shares. If volume picks up right before an announcement, one can infer that information "leaked," but it's hard to figure out the source. Serious detective work is required to reverse-engineer the process and catch a wrongdoer.

Let's consider a different situation. Suppose a big company with a lot of average volume makes a public announcement that does affect the stock price. A sharp operator can be an inside trader and never stand out because so many people trade the stock every day in big and small pieces for pure speculation. He can use a number of accounts to make small trades that blend in with all the other legitimate ones.

The SEC and SRO practice of asking for specific trade data is called "bluesheeting," after the color of the pages used in the old days. Without bluesheeting, the law is blind. Bluesheeting is done by letter to the firms. The firms respond with electronics because the data is so extensive. Smaller firms can still respond by handwritten entries.

The Coattails of Anarchy

The SRO's do not have a copy of the gray list put out by the firms. The SRO's do not have a list of all the customers at any house. Neither does the SEC. No one does. Ah, you say, this is America, and no one should have any such lists. Perhaps so, but then, at least the charade about full and fair disclosure should end, and caveat emptor should prevail. Then you would know you can't compete and you could invest on the coattails of daily anarchy if you so chose.

Are You Impressed?
Rumors Still Run

You are supposed to be impressed by all this "Chinese Wall" insulation of one area from the other. Such clumsy dissection of raw trade data, while delightfully Victorian in appearance, is the present state of the investigative art.

Turn on your evening financial news. Not the 30 second round-ups on the networks, but the half-hour programs on cable and PBS each night. Rumors abound, with price movements all over the charts.

Chinese Walls are effective against you, the customer. You won't get wind of the research department's next reports, the corporate finance department's opinions and you will never get to see the firm's accounts. Chinese Walls make sure you, the retail customer, are completely in the dark. It won't stop a bad broker.

Go back to late 1939. William Douglas had already insulted the brokers, the bankers, the bond men and the legal community, calling them greedy, bent on havoc. He called for the break-up of firms so that one firm could not be selling stock to the public at the same time it was acting as an underwriter. Douglas would be horrified today!

Nothing I have pointed out in this chapter is new. It's very old. The only thing that's new is my accusation that the Chinese Wall system enforces the status quo, acting against the investing public by keeping things proprietary, but not exactly secret.

By now you should be extremely curious about the firm's accounts, its own trading with its own money. Now, THIS is secret.

Why is it secret? The firm may have several accounts where it trades in pursuit of any profits it can get. It may trade throughout the day, right alongside you, or in front of or behind you. Serious bonus money comes out of these accounts. Careers are made and destroyed by them. Houses die when they have trading losses in these accounts.

Open Their Books

Many firms do trade like maniacs, hoping to make a profit. They can trade on the moment, as they feel, with direct word from the exchange floors about activity and the latest data supporting their choices. How can they resist a little mischief to make a few dollars - to feed the beast. If commissions aren't coming in, how do they expect to pay the rent? From trading.

They see your accounts. Wouldn't you like to see theirs? They are licensed to be in their business and their trading affects their ability to stay in business. You should be able to see their accounts; let's be a little bit revolutionary at this point and call for an open book policy from the SEC.

The best way to stop insider trading by the financial community is not the ludicrous fiction of the Chinese Wall - let us see the firms' accounts, the chief officer's accounts, what the research department is doing work on, and who the corporate finance people are talking to as soon as they start. There are two ways to do it.

One is to have the firms make a monthly disclosure filing with the SEC, but that is too slow. Make it weekly. Every Friday night. It can be done easily, just as the firms can produce reams of data about cash flow and commission income. They do it daily, with detail, when it comes to their own money. Send the Gray list to the SEC on Friday, at the close of business, then let the public see it if they want. If everyone does it, what's the big deal? What assurance is there that all trades in the firm will be covered by the Gray List?

Another way is to have the firm send a copy of its own "monthly" statement with yours, to you, each month. See what they are really putting their money into, no matter what they're telling you to do.

The brokers would love to see that list of firm trades, just to see if they are getting double crossed. They really don't know.

The first howl from the securities industry would be that this would cause foreign capital to stay away from the US because they would not understand or appreciate this invasion of their privacy. Lately, every time the industry is upset, they wave the phantom image of "foreign capital" around as the reason to stop any regulation. It's a hollow, rhetorical cry. Foreign capital loves the US because we don't nationalize assets on political changes. We have law, unlike most of the world.

So, firms give you Chinese Walls, the SEC applauds, and rumors still move the markets. The only thing Chinese Walls do is keep information tight enough that bad guys can use inside information to attain trading profits. If everyone knew, there would be no advantage. Chinese Walls cause an advantage to occur, and a false sense of safety to prevail. It's not safe and it's not fair. Prices move.

The firms would be mortified to show their activity to the public. They want to show you the same syrupy nonsense in their commercials, over and over, hoping you will come back for more.

Your choice is easy - don't go back.

How do you know if your brokerage house is trading against you, that is, not only selling what they are recommending you buy, but selling in advance of when they tell you to sell, or buying before they tell you to buy. This practice is called "frontrunning." It's illegal.

Remember, major public announcements can cause a stock's price to move, so you logically look to see what happened close in time to the announcement. Why does it have to be close in time? A corporate finance department may have months of lead time before any announcement of major corporate activity is made public and may be advising on when and how to make the major announcement! Suppose the department knows not what will happen next week, but four or five months from now? Lead time can be the best camouflage. A patient criminal can sit back and move in small increments, never standing out beyond the background, but covering great distance over time. If you know how bluesheets work, you know how to beat them.

Common Sense

We've been discussing secrets. Big secrets. What happens when two people know a secret? How about three, ten, twenty or fifty people? Suppose all the people that know the secret could, if they chose, make money from the secret? How long would the secret remain intact?

Have you ever seen twenty people keep a secret that was worth money?

On this planet?

The SEC encourages the use of Chinese Walls in gigantic securities firms. If firms have one set up, they're OK, because the only alternative is to make the firms break up into segments based on their activity and the firms wouldn't like that. Firms hold grudges FOREVER!

What do you think the answer should be? Should houses be chopped up into pieces? Would it hurt if they were chopped up?

Think about it! Pick up a pen and paper; send your thoughts to Congress; they'd like to know!

It is time to chop up the industry according to specific activity!

Just as the SEC threatened 50 years ago!

There are thousands of broker-dealers, all of whom are used to taking investment risk and conducting hard competition to keep customers who might otherwise go off to the big wire houses. "Big" does not mean better. When new issues of bonds or stock come out, firms get together in "syndicates" in order to spread the risk of failure around, and to get as broad and BIG a distribution network assembled as is realistically feasible. These syndicates form over the telephone in little time. The resulting syndicate may have far more selling power than any one firm in the world!

If the industry giants are chopped up into smaller firms that specialize in their activity, the flow of capital will not be harmed. The flow of secrecy will be more naturally limited by the walls of the organization's size than by the fiction of Chinese Walls within an organization.

Secrecy will also be promoted if law breakers are more readily and more severely punished. Why make deals with them?

First we saw Sun Tsu misapplied to business, and now we see another Oriental concept, Chinese Walls, used in error. What will the bureaucrats and industry wizards think of next?

Why do they keep making excuses and complex "solutions" when chopping the firms up and disclosing activity would take care of the problem better than any rhetorical controls? If a firm wants to trade its own accounts, then make it stop handling accounts for retail customers. It's not a big deal. If they don't want to give up retail accounts, then make them disclose their accounts.

William Douglas discussed the same concepts over 50 years ago. The problems he saw have become worse. The time for active, public discussion is now! The time for action was 1938! It's still not too late.

CHAPTER ELEVEN

MOVIES, HORSES AND OIL: DIRECT PARTICIPATION

Beware Random Evil
Danger and Trouble

Every once in a while, we encounter ideas or objects that have little or no redeeming value. Cocaine is used in eye surgery to stop bleeding in the small veins that clamps can't hold. It is a killer when used in the street.

Automatic small arms in the hands of civilian mental defectives can be used to tragically massacre innocent civilians in California or, in the hands of our soldiers, to defend our nation.

These are emotional topics. We have opinions based on fact and our hearts' direction. Yet, no matter the tide of your interest, no matter what attracts you for whatever the reason, finance and investments call for logical actions. Try to keep emotion out. Avoid pressure. Think!

Direct participations are special products with large commission possibilities for the selling brokers. They are inherently dangerous, frail yet powerfully destructive. They are put together to finance particular deals that require your money because the deal can't get it anywhere else at the same, cheap price, and same lack of investor control. Please read that last sentence one more time. Promoters go to the public after considering the big guys.

How Big Guys Do Deals

If a promoter wants to execute a shopping center deal, he puts a road show together and tries to get backing from major investors such as insurance companies or pension funds. The insurance companies and pension managers are no fools. Slides and charts are not conclusive.

They have experts in house that know the shopping center game down to the smallest detail, so they can tell a good deal from a bad one. They know what land costs are in the subject areas if it's a land deal, what horses cost if it's a horse deal, and what wire costs if it is a cable TV or radio station deal. If they don't have the information right at hand in house, they have regular, trusted consultants who can get the information or review the deal in confidence. The professionals can check out the promoters by word of mouth in ways you cannot.

When they find a deal they like from among the THOUSANDS presented to them, they try to take it over as much as possible to keep control. A lot of business experience is required to keep the appearance of a loan, because the lender wants to be in control, but not liable if the deal blows up. Lenders don't want to become partners if they can help it because partners open up to the full liability of all the bills - they want to be lenders and that's it.

After their experts scrutinize the possibilities of the proposal, the lenders require regular reports of progress when the deal begins to build. The contracts allow the lender to fire builders, demand letters of credit if the promoters fall behind, foreclose on the property if need be, and do a lot more to make sure their money is not at risk. These professionals get beat sometimes - witness the real estate debacle facing the Savings and Loan Industry and many New England Commercial Banks. Still, a private deal involving insurance or pension money means that someone is always looking over the promoter's shoulder.

The professionals use every tool they can to examine a deal before they leap in. For promoters, this is the best kind of money to get, because it is directly placed and may avoid full SEC registration with all the subsequent, public reporting. It also saves time, because the money comes in big chunks and doesn't have to be assembled from little pieces.

There are plenty of deals that the professionals throw out, or that the promoters never show to the professionals because they know the deals will be tossed. Guess where they end up?

You Get the Call

You are at home, minding your own business, when Rasputin, your broker calls and tells you he would like to send some information about a new shopping center deal. It might be a cable TV deal, or a business condominium, residential condo conversion, horses, gold mines and a lot more. One day, it will be space stations.

The literature arrives a few days later. You open a large mailer to find slick advertising covers, endless descriptions with artists renderings of lovely stores in a not-as-yet-built shopping center in Chernobyl, Ukraine, former site of the infamous atomic reactor, the most intensely polluted land in the Soviet Union (that we know of), which is why the land was so cheap. Read on.

The deal can't miss. The projected numbers prove beyond the shadow of a doubt that once the stores are up, they will prosper, pay their rents and the shopping center will return a proportional amount of that profit to you. No problems - the Russians are now our "pals."

As a limited partner, you are told, you will have all the income advantages of a partner, but none of the risk. You cannot be assessed for more than you put in. It sounds like stock, except you get a direct income flow from the deal when profit rolls in. The major advantage: the partnership will avoid the income tax corporations pay on profits before they can pay you a dividend from those SAME profits that you have to pay a SECOND income tax on. And Chernobyl? It's going to be a winner, shown by the pages of narrative and statistics. It's in print; it's typeset, with color photos, positive momentum and lots of legalese. Yes, just imagine - downtown Chernobyl, the Rose of the Ukraine.

Stop!

You are getting a look at this deal because no professional lender took it. The typical direct participation investment will be set up as a limited partnership and will indeed offer to give you a direct, partnership stream of future income - IF - there is any!

Putting the deal together is expensive.

Once the promoters decide to go the brokerage house route to raise cash, they have to give up 8% on sales of partnership interests as a commission to the selling house, travel and prize costs to promote the deal to the brokers, registration costs, etc.

For every dollar you put in, about 25 cents goes out the window on day one.

To make a profit in the first year, the deal has to do better than that 25%. In a shopping center deal, the promoters may also have an interest in the mortgage company, the builders, suppliers, building management company and more. You may be paying them fees, fees and more fees every year through all of these suppliers and servicing entities.

To make this project a success, it will have to earn a fortune, not just a regular profit. In baseball terms, if the project doesn't hit a home run, you will lose. A triple won't count.

The broker will make his commission, the promoters will make their fees, and you will get nothing but papers, papers and more in the mail. Your initial objective was to make some cash in a deal that could not fail. The great ones don't get to you. The ones that might fail are rejected by the professional lenders, who get burned nonetheless by their own visions of fantasy. The difficulty in investing is the uncertainty of future conditions. Large institutions encounter it, despite their best efforts. Bonuses, commissions, promotions - each is a subtle promoter of investment activity in addition to logic.

Get In Now!
The Ground Floor!

These deals are sold with a sense of false, promotional urgency, claiming that the deal will "close" in the near future and you have to get in now, or miss the opportunity. Here is how a deal closes: the promoters need to line up money to start real development of the site. They figure out how much that is. A large part will come from people like you, and some will come from a bank, but the bank is no fool - it wants to make sure that the partnership has money in it before it lends to the project. The bank will give a mortgage. It will be secured IN FRONT OF YOU, so that it is secured and you are not. Once the public puts in a certain amount of money, the bank promises to make the mortgage loan. The target amount to be raised depends on the deal.

Once the target amount is raised, the deal "closes," the bank lends the money, and the tractors roll. If the target amount is not raised, the deal does not go forward. It doesn't "close." The bank won't lend.

The promoters take their materials, change the name, advertising materials and sales scripts, and try to sell it again, any way they can. The brokers don't get paid unless the deal closes, so they keep the enthusiasm going, selling, selling and selling. No one wants the deal to close more than the brokers.

Some brokers don't waste time selling stock any more because that market never recovered from the 1987 crash, but the direct participation investment can be sold as an alternative to stock. One line from a slick direct investment specialist is to tell you this is far safer than a stock because it exists, has intrinsic value, doesn't depend on traders, specialists and the fickle nature of the SEC.

This kind of broker wants to get your confidence by telling you everything that distinguishes this product from the stock market, as though that was a positive factor. It's irrelevant, because the investment has to be judged on it's own.

What do you know about horses, gold mines, biotechnology laboratories, shopping centers in another state or part of the country, or cable T.V.? Movie deals are done this way, too. Yes, you can be a limited partner in the next film starring Macho Starissimo, and this film will surely make as much money as his last. Right?

How about this pitch: "real estate is the backbone of the nation. Aren't you sick and tried of all those foreigners buying up the best opportunities, kicking Americans out of the way. This deal will provide jobs for Americans right here in the good old USA, just like the old days. Forget those swine on Wall Street! In this deal, you are part of the ownership; you are in charge. The people behind this are committed to its success on a personal level."

"What are you, un-American?" That's one pitch for this kind of deal.

There are others even more vile. In the times before Reagan tax reform, tax shelters were put together as limited partnerships. To the extent that there are still exceptions to tax reform, shelters are still made this way. Limited partnerships have a tax exemption at the partnership level that is the envy of corporations. Profits and losses flow through without tax at the partnership level. Losses can be used to offset other limited partner income. I never understood why outwardly rational people put money into tax deals to get losses. Losses are easy to acquire. It's not hard. Partnerships that had tax losses either ended up as big, overall losers, or had tax re-capture gains at some time in the future, requiring purchase of two, new tax deals to offset this income. Depreciation was the usual tax advantage. If you buy a property for commercial use, it depreciates. If you later sell it for 100% of what you paid, you may recapture all the depreciation you wrote off as regular income. Highly taxable regular income. Real Estate shelters are tricky.

While some of these deals are huge, requiring thousands of investors signing up for thousands of dollars each, others are small, requiring only a few million which can be raised from just one brokerage house.

The deal may call for you to put up $5,000 this year in cash, $5,000 next year, and on and on. When you sign up, the investment may not be a one-shot cash outlay. If you don't pay in year two, when the partnership calls for the next $5,000, you may lose it all. The commitment may be long term. The broker gets paid up front. Once you've bought, he gets paid. Make sure you understand payments due.

Information on how the project is doing will come from the general partner of the deal, not the broker. If the general partner is tardy, it's your problem. The broker will tell you there is nothing he can do if you badger him for information. He's right. There IS nothing he can do.

If the deal goes sour, your broker will tell you that there is nothing he can do, and that he sold it to you on the basis of all the papers he sent you - AND - that you signed.

And you signed a lot of papers to indicate you understood the risk, the possibility of failure and the method of project management. When it fails, there is nothing left except "assets" that are pledged to others in front of you.

Here is another problem. Suppose you buy one of these deals: what happens when you want to sell it to pay for an unexpected expense, or because you are tired of the investment and could put the money to work elsewhere?

Good luck! You can't take it and sell it on an exchange, because it isn't listed. You probably can't sell it. It may have ZERO liquidity. Some deals tell you the investment cannot be transferred without the consent of the general partner. Some are illiquid because no one will buy it.

There are times when a brokerage house will buy a deal from you. The deal has to be viable, that is, not dead. You look for a buyer to take your piece because you want to pay tuition, hospital bills, etc. The expense came on suddenly, and you have to get out. Eventually, you hear of a firm that will buy the piece, but at a huge loss to you! It's tough, but you have to sell.

Once they buy it from you, they have one of their brokers sell it to someone else. They aim to buy low and sell high as fast as possible.

Don't misinterpret what I have said - these things are basically ILLIQUID. You might be able to get a buyer, if you are lucky, but you probably are stuck once you have bought it.

The promoters are not stuck. When they structure the deal, they have plenty of outs for themselves through all the servicing entities created to make the project go. They can always walk away from a project and leave it to the mortgage bankers and you, the limited partner, after taking down fees for all the service and contracting. In short, they make money if the deal fails in year 2 - you don't. They are ready to walk away in year 2 - you can't.

Even if the deal is marginal, but has some cash flow, the promoters in their various servicing capacities can sell their service contracts to other promoters who might be interested in taking over the deal. You can't. The obligations you committed to are themselves negotiable, not by you, but by the partnership. You are still in.

As you read this, do you have a desire to be a gold mine operator? Do you want to be in the equipment leasing or condo business? Do you understand how commercial real estate operates, how to price it, dump it, exchange it? Don't be fooled by a broker telling you that this is a great "investment" for you. Think of it as going into business.

Are you ready to go into the movie business with a bunch of guys you have never met from New York and Los Angeles, for a film project that doesn't have a script yet, with a cast that has not been finally set (Macho Starissimo departs in favor of new, rising star, Minimo Talento), in a business with special accounting rules regarding copyrights, royalties and distribution rights? The promoters may own the movie company, the trucking company that hauls the sets, the support company that makes and rents the sets, the caterer that prepares lunch on the set, the distribution company, the security force, the prop supplier, the talent agency handling the star - have I left anything out?

If the film makes any money, it may be eaten by hidden expenses that turn up in the books of one of these servicing agencies.

What to do? Hang up! Question your broker for trying to sell you this illiquid "stuff."

If you have been stung by one of these deals, the broker will not help you. The brokerage house will not help you either. Before the brokerage house committed to the deal, it made a conscious decision to sell based on the merits of the deal, but remember, the firm is made up of financial pros who know what they are doing.

Which is why they don't commit the firm's money to the deal, but are eager to get you into this great opportunity. The firm makes money on the sale and is ready to disavow any responsibility as soon as you complain. They were your "agent." The house doesn't buy any.

Are there any good direct investment deals that will be offered to you by a brokerage house? Sure. It will be good for the brokerage house, good for the promoters because they get your money to close the deal, good for the mortgage bankers who need some real money in the deal before they will commit to their loan from which they generate their own fee, and good for your stockbroker who gets a very nice commission check, and, if he sells enough of this "stuff", may get a free trip to learn more about the deal he just sold. By some amazing, unnatural occurrence, you can make money in these deals, but, think of all the people in line for their cut BEFORE you have a chance. Think of the incredible earnings the deal has to generate before it trickles all the way down to you. Don't do it unless you understand the investment and the underlying activity.

If you want to buy a piece of a shopping center, go find a deal in your area with people you know and trust. Go into business with them, if you dare. That's the real test: would you go into business with the other actors in the deal? Do you know them enough to say you "trust" them? Do you know the specific business like a professional?

Don't touch these things unless you absolutely understand the deal, can afford to lose all your money, and don't need future cash flow. Then, one more thing.

Take it to your lawyer or accountant and try to get them to give you a letter saying they have read it and recommend you consider the investment. No way. It will never happen, unless, (oh no!) they are the ones that are showing you the deal. While this book is about brokers, your accountant or lawyer may also be a broker, trying to sell a deal. Don't buy a deal from a lawyer or accountant, unless you clear up their capacity and cash flow from your possible purchase.

OK, let's try something more direct. If you have gotten the materials from your broker, get the broker and the firm's president to sign a letter saying they have read the deal and recommend it to you, understanding your suitability limits and the non-liquidity of the deal. They probably won't do it! I wonder why? It's a fair proposal. They want you to sign, not them. If they won't sign, don't buy it!

Oil wells, cattle, cable T.V., radio, gold mines, horses, railcars, and much more. Leave it to the pros.

If you really want to get into this action, buy stock in a company that specializes in cable T.V., oil, gold, etc. - whatever you are interested in. Look at mutual funds that specialize in these sectors of the economy. Listed shares are more liquid than a direct deal. A mutual fund may be more liquid, too.

CHAPTER TWELVE

THE BAND WAGON: MUTUAL FUNDS

Safety in Numbers
Trend Investing

Mutual Funds are a method of investing that has been historically popular for big and little risk takers. Notice I said risk takers - all investments involve some risk, because prices can change as various economic factors change. Don't think that mutual funds are any safer than picking a particular bond or stock, or that a mutual fund that buys only US Government Securities is somehow immune from price declines. Review our discussion about bonds and US Government Paper to be familiar with that sense of value and risk.

In our discussion of the Roman shipping merchants, we saw a group of investors getting together to finance a commodity shipment - grain. They shared the risk in the face of grave consequences for business failure, such as slavery. It was safer to risk a little in many efforts then put all one's capital in one project and risk destruction. Our discussion showed how this led to the "invention" of companies and then the democratic institution of the modern corporation.

A mutual fund is similar in shape, but a little different in purpose. Whereas most companies have a direct productive business function such as manufacturing or providing services, a modern mutual fund is a pooling of money for the purpose of subsequent investment in securities of other companies. Think of it this way: instead of raising funds to buy the ship and the grain for import, a mutual fund raises cash to look around for opportunities to make a profit, which might include buying a share in the grain operation. The mutual fund doesn't own the grain. It owns shares in the companies that own and use the grain.

Investing in a mutual fund makes you a financier. You put in capital to get a return without direct labor. A Marxist (if any remain) would be disgusted.

There are investment partnerships that operate with enormous amounts of capital to invest in sky scrapers, build baseball stadiums, marinas and airports. These investment partnerships are different from mutual funds because they have a specific partnership form, restricted participation and their stated purpose is usually quite limited: the airport, marina etc.

A modern mutual fund is an Investment Company, defined by the Investment Company Act of 1940 and regulated by the Securities and Exchange Commission.

The law is concerned with entities that have 100 or more participants, where investors pool their funds together to get professional management in the business of investing, reinvesting or trading in securities. The investors are passive owners.

There are mutual funds that take the pooled funds of their investors and direct the fund's investments in specific sectors of the economy, such as high technology, hi-yield or "junk" bonds, US Government Securities, European growth companies, US Growth companies, Japanese Giants and Japanese lesser-fry companies. There are all kinds of funds that offer selective investment targets that the ordinary investor or even an institution might find desirable, but difficult to maintain on its own.

Add professional management to "mind the store" and watch the target investment area, and you have the best theoretical combination: diversity of risk, target by sector, professional management and bulk buying discounts on trades that the small investor could never get.

Market Risk
It's Always There

Sounds great. But, you can get hammered by putting funds in a mutual fund because nothing, absolutely nothing can remove the underlying market risk that you will buy something that will drop in value. What a fund attempts to do is cut down the odds through the use of professional techniques that keep the fund in closer contact with the Street. It takes the broker out of the picture, because the fund shops all around for the best price and execution on its trades. Fund trades can be very large, therefore very profitable to the brokers, so they want to get the fund's commission business by low-bidding for it.

Modern mutual funds are bundled in "families," that is, fund promoters don't have just one fund to offer, they have many funds in the same family. You can typically switch from one fund to the other at no or a low service charge. The advantage to you: when you feel the equity market is in for a drop, you can sell out your equity fund and switch to, say, the bond fund or the money market fund in the same "family" of funds. There are independent researchers who, for a subscription price, will tell you when to do this kind of change.

House Funds
Revenge of the Spurned House

Many funds are "above board" and offer great advantages to the retail investor - you. Some are run by Street-wise salesmen who are out to get you all over again. How can you tell what's up, and protect yourself from the same old gang? Just because an investment is a mutual fund, don't forget RISK. Financial institutions have been dropping with alarming frequency because their investment portfolios collapse. And they are the professionals!

Don't buy a mutual fund that is an in-house fund for a broker-dealer, unless you think it out carefully. The brokerage houses start their own funds to keep your money under their control, because they see retail customers showing more and more dissatisfaction in the ranks by the way you vote with your feet. You keep leaving.

So they say, quickly switching hats, "why, we're not stockbrokers, we're, uh, mutual fund managers!" Thus the fox becomes the alleged guardian of the hen house.

The house sets up the funds, registers them with the SEC as Open End Investment Companies under the 1940 Act, with a mix of Junk Bond, Equity, Growth Equity, Bond, Foreign, and others. They get a fee for managing the funds. They get a fee as the investment adviser to the funds. They try to squeeze maximum profits by running these funds while wearing several hats, just as last Chapter's movie promoters.

I want you to understand this quite clearly. The fund gathers assets: hopefully yours. Now that they have it, they have to figure out what to do with it. If it's a high yield fund that buys junk bonds, someone has to make the selection of the actual bonds. The fund hires an investment adviser to make the selections. The fund gets paid a management fee. The investment adviser gets paid a fee.

The investment adviser is also licensed, but under a separate Federal Law, the Investment Adviser Act of 1940.

Brokerage houses create these investment advisers in a flash. By the way, if you wanted to become an investment adviser, all you do is fill in a Form ADV and send it in to the SEC. No qualifications, no tests, unless your state insists on it. The Feds don't.

So, who is this investment adviser running your money in the brokerage house's funds - he's probably one of their employees! You didn't want to buy stock because they kept feeding you doggies, so they changed their costume, put on a moustache and glasses, and came at you again. If they can't get a commission from you for buying/selling IBM directly, they will get it from you in fund fees and investment adviser fees. This can add up to several percent of your investment per year, so you are behind the curve before you start out. Each year you will have to make a larger profit to break even to feed the same old beast of many colors, essentially the brokerage house.

You get the benefit of their same old research and their same old execution - they do the executions, too, with the excess trading capacity left over because they are seeing less and less of your regular trading. They need trades to pay for the computer beast. When "they" decide the fund is going to trade while wearing their investment adviser hat, they send the order to themselves at their own trading desk. They get the best possible price for the execution, right? What do you think?

Because the funds in this example are in-house, the brokers get the sales routine in their internal mail, on the squawk box and through personal visits of the fund wholesalers, their fellow employees.

Personal visits of the "wholesalers" means that the brokers get wined and dined in order to "educate" them about the fund. The wining and dining is charged as an expense to the fund; you pay for it. It's not a fee, it's an "expense." You pay for it.

Managers get pressure to sell the funds and regional managers get it, too. If you buy a house mutual fund because the broker told you that they have a hot adviser and that no fee will be paid which allows 100% of your money to go "to work", watch out! You bought it through the broker, and he got paid a commission on the sale - otherwise he never would have sold it to you. The house is not about to pay the broker a commission unless they have a way to be covered. If you want to get out of the fund, you may find that the "No Load" fund he sold you actually has a hidden sales charge that pops up when you exit, a "Rear End" load. That charge may be 4% in the first year, 3% in the next, and so on.

The time you want to get out is usually when the market is in some decline or you need the money - and then you have a hidden sales charge to get your money back. Don't buy the house fund unless you have a valid reason, like the investment adviser is a relative and really needs the job. You keep paying the house fees instead of commissions. It is all in the prospectus that you're supposed to get before you buy the fund.

A prospectus is a small booklet that tells you how the fund will operate, not just the sector it will invest in. It also explains what fees will be charged against the assets (you) of the fund, how much the management fee will be and how much will be paid to the investment adviser, if any will be used. It's all there, in small print. Most people don't read it. Every time the fund makes a dollar, several hands reach in for their cut.

If more investors read the prospectus, the surprise of these rear-end sales loads wouldn't exist because investors would know it was there - they saw it in the prospectus.

A prospectus is free. Get them from the real mutual fund companies that advertise in your Sunday paper's business section. Clip the coupon and send it in. When it comes in the mail, read it. If it is hard to read, keep trying. Get on the telephone with the real mutual funds and ask them about the parts you don't understand. They will explain it to you.

Go to the Public Library and get the annual issues of Money Magazine and Forbes Magazine that rate the mutual funds for the year by their performance. See who was hot last year. The accompanying articles will describe the latest trends in funds, the latest charges being worked out, and the reason that some were hot - and some not.

If you can't or won't read the prospectus, you are a sucker for a bad broker's pitch to buy a house fund. If you simply cannot read the prospectus and make any sense out of it, please, don't buy ANY fund. Don't be ashamed to say you can't understand a prospectus after you have really tried - a lot of it is written in legalese, and the fund managers might not understand it all. For example, the fund might be a corporation or it might be a Massachusetts Trust. How many people in the US understand that distinction?

If you feel you don't understand the prospectus, don't buy the fund. If you want more information about the fund's investment adviser, ask for it. DEMAND IT! If no one will give it to you, don't buy that fund. Funds don't like to tell you who the specific person is at the investment adviser who is calling the investment shots. They fear making that individual a superstar who will demand more compensation. Hollywood worked on that same system in its early days - there were no stars' names in the credits, only the studio's name.

There are plenty of above board, excellent mutual fund companies that offer value and convenience to you and charge a fair fee. They are entitled to a fee and there is nothing wrong with their making a profit by offering their service to you. They exist for that profit; they aren't charities.

Many real funds have a front end load, or sales charge. It can be pretty steep, up to approximately 8%. Brokers love to sell these funds because they get paid a piece of that sales charge or load. They won't show you a fund that has a very low sales charge, or a true no load fund, because they won't make any commission from the sale.

The load is important. If you pay an 8% load, that means only 92 cents of your investment dollar goes to work. The fund ate the other 8 cents as soon as you handed it over, with a large chunk of that going to the broker. The broker won't put it to you that bluntly, but you must understand how much the load hurts you. Next, add on the same fees for management of the fund and the fee to the adviser to the fund - why buy a fund that starts out the first year by taking 10% of your money? To make 7% on your original money the first year, you actually have to make over 17% on funds that "went to work." How can you win with that kind of situation?

You can understand why the broker wants to sell you his house fund. The commission on the independent, loaded fund is not the only reason the broker offers these funds to you. The outside funds also have wholesalers.

A wholesaler is a salesman. He sells the concept of the fund to the brokers, who, in turn sell it to you, hence the term "wholesaler." He figuratively goes around with bags of money from office to office in his territory, from house to house, without allegiance to a given house, because he works for the fund, not the brokerage house.

When he gets to an office, he takes the crew out for dinner and good times and pitches the fund to them. No pitch: no sales by the brokers. That's why he needs "bags of cash" or unlimited credit cards as he travels. A fund can have a seminar about how it works, its investment philosophy, its history - all very educational. They can have it at Pebble Beach, California, near Carmel, site of some of the most beautiful ocean beaches along the Pacific, south of San Francisco, where the senior house managers sometimes meet. The brokers who get invited to this are usually the ones who are selling the daylights out of the fund, in order to get the "education." You pay for it as a fund expense.

The brokerage houses are no fools. They get commission business from the outside funds for all the trades the funds do. It's an interesting circle.

You are paying all the time. Understand how and why before you decide to buy a fund that has a big load.

One of the broker's big games is to get you to first buy Fund B which does bonds. The load is 6%. Then he calls you and says that it's time to get out of bonds and into equities, so he gets you to buy Fund S, which does stocks. It has a 6% Load. Then he calls again: he says, it's time to get ready for 1992 in Europe when the European Economic Community becomes one nation for trade purposes, so you buy some 92 Fund. To pay for the Stock fund, you sold the Bond fund. Then, to buy the 92 Fund, you sold some of the Stock fund. Instead of churning you with stock transactions, the broker is doing it with mutual funds. It's called "switching."

Switching

Switching is a form of fraud. The best loaded funds can be misused by a bad broker when he has you in his sights. Mutual funds are not meant for trading when they have a load, unless you buy into a family that, once in, allows you to go back and forth from one fund in the family to another with little or no charge. You can find that in the prospectus.

If you find a good "family" of funds, even if there is an initial load, this free transfer of funds within the "family" means you may not have to leave the "family", even when markets change a LOT. You get in, and then you can go from one fund to the next. You don't have to pay a new load each time you move.

Gurus

There are guru funds; watch out for them. Suppose some famous T.V. talking head starts a fund and gets your attention with commercials. It sounds catchy. You identify the fund with the individual. Image, personality, marketing - it all works against you. Don't invest based on the name; look at the prospectus and see what the fund is about. If it depends on the supposed unique qualities of the guru, stand back!

What if the guru dies? What if he has only been lucky for a while? What if all he ever amounted to was a T.V. commentator. How much time can he devote to the matter and still be a public guru? Will he be the marketing device, while the fund will be run by others? Logical questions. Get answers!

The key, no matter how you think about it, is to get the prospectus, read it, not just casually - seriously! Don't sit down and try to digest it at one time. The biggest mistake you can make is to try reading a prospectus in a rush, with the phone ringing, kids running about, or worse, with a broker sitting at your elbow, either in person or on the telephone. Set aside a few spare minutes on several evenings. Take your time. Read it through, make notes, write down questions. If you use this method with several prospecti, you'll notice they follow the same format, and you'll be comfortable and informed. If you do some homework, you will know more about funds than your broker. You'll be able to pick your own, and more importantly, REJECT them, too!

No-load funds are available for your consideration. Forget that old saying about "You get what you pay for." Most of what you pay for in the investment business is grief. Some experts are not experts at all: except at marketing. A no-load fund doesn't charge you to get into the fund. Brokers won't sell them because they can't make any money doing it; they react with alarm if you bring up the idea, as though you had mentioned vampires or the IRS!

No-loads can give the same good performance as the loaded funds, and they can give the same services - check-writing, free or minimal charge movement between funds in the same "family," and telephone contact for any questions or to effect activities. The no-loads make their living by charging a management fee, just as the others. Read their prospectus. While they charge a management fee, they aren't out there wining and dining the brokers, because the brokers won't touch it. Some spend big money on newspaper and television ads.

When you are in the library, reading the ratings on the funds in Money and Forbes Magazines, you'll see some no-loads at the top of the chart along with some of the loads.

The moral - make up your mind. If you think paying the load is worth it, then do it - after you have read and analyzed the prospectus in the peace and quiet of your own house or in the library.

Got a newspaper handy? Turn to the financial section, and look for the mutual fund prices. It used to be a pretty small column, but now there are plenty of funds; it takes up most of a page. The Federal Law that covers these companies was passed in 1940. That's over fifty years ago. How many of those funds are 50 years old?

Funds come and go. Uh oh! That's right.You can buy into a fund and it can crash. Be careful. The law stops funds from going on margin, but it cannot stop them from losing money. When a fund becomes a loser, its managers may decide to liquidate. When you look at the ads for funds, they will give performance statistics for one, five and ten years, but how many do it for fifty? Suppose I manage 10 funds, and two are real losers. I don't want to be associated with them because the hard numbers show I can win AND lose, and I want to be known only as a winner. I shut down those two, losing funds. In their place in the "family" I start two new funds in the same sector of concentration. Killing off a fund because of its performance is nothing new; replacing it with a similar fund with no adverse track record is an old technique.

Don't buy a fund unless it has a track record. If it is new, let someone else test it out.

If the investment adviser was really hot, he'd spend all his time managing money for the big guys who do the airports, skyscrapers and hotels. He wouldn't be looking for your business. Reality is a harsh teacher. When it comes to loans or investments, humbling events in the press should make us all pause and wonder at the mistakes that are made after the most careful thought and research.

Remember Campeau Corporation's billion dollar bankruptcy? You know that banks and investment bankers don't want their clients to go bankrupt. They are not that devious - or purposefully dumb. Before they commit to these multi-billion dollar deals, the big institutions plod carefully through numbers, data, references and comparable experiences with other clients. Technical and fundamental analysis are used.

Who is involved in the Campeau/Allied/Federated loan situation: First Boston, Manufacturer's Hanover, Irving Trust Co., Security Pacific National Bank, Chase Manhattan, and on and on and on. What? you weren't involved?

Do you own Chase Manhattan stock? Do you own a mutual fund that owns Chase Manhattan stock? Does your pension fund own Chase stock or does it own a mutual fund that owns Chase stock? You might not know. You may be indirectly involved for a lot.

How about Citicorp? It's the largest bank in the US, although not in the top 10 in the world. In January, 1990, it set aside a billion dollars as a reserve for bad loans to the third world. Let me be fair to Citicorp: they are one of many American banks that are setting aside reserves for developing nation defaulters.

These are the top pros. How can they be wrong? They don't get too bent out of shape - they are right a lot, too. Act like them. Learn to recognize a loss, accept it and move on. Enjoy it when you are right, accept it when you are wrong.

When you are constantly told about safety in diversity, remember that very few funds go back 10 years, let alone 50. If you buy a fund, constantly analyze it. If the situation calls for it, be ready TO DROP IT. Add up those fees and loads. You paid them.

The Newspaper

Back to the newspaper. The mutual fund page is put together by the Associated Press and is standard throughout the US. Look at the listings under Vanguard - see all the "NL" listings? That means no load. Now look at Dreyfus - some are "NL" and some have two prices. Finally, take a look at the brokerage house funds under the Merrill Lynch, Smith Barney, Paine Webber, and Shearson headings. These are loads.

The prices you see are from last night. Mutual funds get priced, or marked to the market, each day. If you buy today, you pay the price set at the end of today's market, so you don't know the exact price you are going to buy at.

Because mutual funds own securities, when they are priced, you can add up the value of all the securities easily, right off the tape. If the fund owns IBM, the price is ready any time. If it owns any NYSE listed security or a NASDAQ security, it's also available. Pricing the value of every share in a fund is not a problem. That gives you ALMOST the regular Net Asset Value, the NAV listed in one column of the price reports. NAV includes not only the value of the shares the fund owns, but also any cash sitting around from dividends and capital gains. We'll touch on that more, below.

The next column shows you the "buy" price. This means that if you bought a share of the particular fund, you paid the buy price per share. Get out a ruler to help you look across the page.

With Vanguard, the net asset value is what you pay if you buy, which is why they said "NL" for the buy price.

Go over to the Merrill Lynch listings, and you will see an NAV to show what the fund was worth per share the night before, and you'll see the buy price. The buy price is higher. If you subtract the NAV from the buy price, you get the load. Divide the load by the NAV and you can see the percentage you are giving to the house. This does not include the management fees down the road.

Why pay a load of 75 cents on a share of NAV at $12.10? Would you pay that much commission per share if you bought a share of regular stock for $12.10 per share? Do you know what an institution pays when it buys a block of stock? 75 cents a share? No.

6 to 10 cents. What do you pay?

There are approximately 2,000 mutual funds. Get a sector direction YOU are comfortable with. Get a prospectus and do some homework. The worst you can do is act like Citicorp! Don't buy a junk bond or High Yield fund unless you absolutely, positively are ready to walk the razor's edge. High Yield should really be called, "High Risk." There are very risky mutual funds, very conservative ones: there is a fund for every profile. This does not mean there is a fund for everyone. If you can't understand how they work, don't buy them.

Let's Get Technical

An open end mutual fund has no limit on its size. It can grow for as long as the managers want. You can put money in and take it out, depending on the rules in the prospectus. Think of it as a balloon that can change dramatically in size. When you take money out, you actually redeem shares with the fund. You don't sell them into the market.

A closed end fund is different. It is closed from birth. You can't get out by redemption. It has a fixed number of shares, just like any other corporation, and it trades on an exchange or in the Over the Counter Market - just like a regular corporation. If you want to buy it, you pay a broker a commission on the way in, then on the way out, just like buying IBM common stock.

A closed end fund is priced by the market every night. An open end fund is priced by its asset value. The price per share of the closed end fund will be related to demand on its selling exchange for its own shares, not just the shares held by the fund. Suppose people get very bearish on the market in general. It is possible for the closed end fund shares to trade below the fund's NAV as marked to the market on a given day.

An open end fund cannot sell any shares for less than the NAV. A closed end fund cannot issue shares for less than their NAV, but after that, market forces take over. The market price for a closed end fund can be less than the NAV. It can be more.

You sell shares in an open end fund by tendering them to the fund. If you are holding the investment in certificate form, DON'T LOSE THEM. If you are holding them electronically you're OK. To tender, it depends on how the fund is set up. If the shares are held at a custodian bank or transfer agent, you will probably have to send a letter to the bank. In some funds, they will ask you to call, and will redeem on the basis of your telephone call.

The prospectus will explain redemptions. The open end fund cannot refuse to honor the tender. They have to send the proceeds within seven days of your tender, unless the SEC says they can take longer or if there are emergency situations.

If the markets crashed as in October, 1987, and you wanted to liquidate, it might take a little longer than seven days. If you call on Tuesday morning to tender, and even ship off a letter by fax the same day, you will get that day's price as of the Tuesday close. Therefore, if the market crashes in the morning, you will get the crashed price.

When you are in a fund, you cannot just get out intra-day. You have to stay for the whole day.

Cash

Funds own securities. The securities are usually being traded, resulting in capital gains or losses, and the shares may be paying dividends or the bonds may be paying interest. This complicates things because you have to pay attention to when the fund passes on these cash flow items to you. Professionals watch to see when funds receive dividends from their holdings and compare it to when the fund will pay them out. The fund can sit on capital gains during the year. It becomes a little tricky to figure your taxes.

Keep track of open end fund shares as you buy them. You can buy a lot at one shot, or you can buy some on a regular basis using "Dollar Cost Averaging." When you average, you don't care what the markets are doing; every month you buy $100 of the fund as a discipline. I think averaging is a sales tool for the funds and makes little sense for the investor, but you will read about averaging and you must consider its relative merits on your own. For taxes, when you make periodic purchases of an open end fund, you will have different purchase prices for groups of shares. If you go to sell 50% of your holdings, you may have to figure your taxes on the basis of many different purchase prices.

Keep those confirms! Get a free copy of the Internal Revenue's Publications 17 (a big book) and 544 (Sales and Other Dispositions of Assets) from your IRS Service Center. The IRS will tell you what is required for records and they will insist you have specific data for any audit. Basically they want to see every purchase price compared directly to the sale of those specific shares.

KEEP THE CONFIRMS! Next: think about what cash in an open end fund means. Suppose a fund maintains a tax year that ends on December 31 of each year. Also suppose it has a bunch of capital gains. It doesn't matter what they are right now, long or short, but it might matter in the future if tax rates change. The NAV in the newspaper will include the value of the shares the fund owns, AND the cash. NAV is the result of Fund Assets minus Fund Liabilities.

If you buy a fund that has cash, understand that the fund is going to have to make a tax decision: if they don't pass it on to you, they have to pay taxes. If they pass it on to you, the fund doesn't pay any tax on the interest, dividends and capital gains. Obviously, funds like to pass on the cash flow and advertise this benefit to get new investors. If you buy the fund when it is cash heavy, you may get a distribution.

Suppose you buy November 1. The fund declares a distribution on December 21. You will get a big check on January 21 of the next calendar year. Are you happy? Maybe not.

Suppose the cash you got was in the fund all along and was part of the NAV on November 1. When you bought the shares, you effectively bought the cash as well as the value of the securities they owned. When you got the distribution in January, you really got a part of your own money back, but the fund will say it is taxable to you as dividends, interest or capital gains. It is not really income to you because you just bought it, penny for penny, but you may have income tax liability. Cash tax liability on what is really a distribution back of your own cash.

That's right, income tax liability! You don't get the check until January, in the next tax year, but the tax liability will be for the year the dividend is declared. Get IRS Publication 544! Make sure, if you buy a fund, that you understand how they pass on income, and WHEN they usually pass it on. Find out how much of the NAV is drawn from securities prices when you buy and how much is drawn from cash on hand.

Special note: a few funds do not distribute their capital gains. They keep it, pay the income tax on it, and reinvest it. You get a form that tells you what your proportionate share is, and you have to include it in your taxable income. They tell you how much tax they paid. Your share can be used as a credit on your taxes. Your tax preparation becomes more and more complex.

Ask about this before you buy. Look in the prospectus.

One more tax item: if you buy a municipal fund to keep on the tax exempt side of life, you may have to pay a capital gains tax if you are lucky enough to sell the fund at a profit. The interest passed on to you may be tax exempt, but any capital gain is not. The same holds true for municipal bonds bought directly in the bond markets. The interest may be exempt from federal taxes, but any capital gain is not. Don't get too upset - you can also claim capital loss in the proper situation.

What happens to the NAV when the open end fund pays a distribution? It drops. Imagine you bought at 12 per share on November 1. On December 22, you may have income tax liability for a 50 cent per share distribution of cash, and a resulting NAV of 11.5 per share. It happens. Be careful.

If you want to calculate the selling or "offering price" of a loaded, open end fund, find the NAV. Look in the prospectus and see what the sales charge is. If it is 6%, then divide the NAV by the sales charge subtracted from 100%. Example: the NAV is 12.5; the sales charge is 6%.; 12.5 divided by .94 equals 13.30, the selling price of the share. The Load is an amazing 80 cents per share. No wonder the funds make money! The prospectus will explain exactly how the selling or offering price will be calculated.

If you want to get into mutual funds on a cost averaging basis, read the prospectus and see if the fund has Rights of Accumulation or if you can buy under a Letter of Intent.

ROA's
Letters of Intent
Discounts - Break Points

Suppose your broker says he has a good fund; yes, it's loaded but it has great performance and a famous guru at the helm. You know you should hang up, but you ask for the prospectus. The broker sends it. You study the material and decide that it really is worth the investment. The broker says you should buy some every three months, a kind of extended averaging. It sounds sensible.

You have $60,000 from an inheritance, so you agree. Every three months you buy $20,000 of the fund. When you get the confirmation, it shows you have paid the correct 6.5% load that the fund carries.

Stop! Get out the prospectus. When you buy a lot of one fund, you'll find discounts for bulk purchase, just like buying macaroni at the grocery. Your prospectus might say that if you buy $ 25,000 or more, the load goes down to 4%, and, if you buy $ 50,000 or more, it goes down to 3%. You paid 6.5% each time because the broker wanted to get more commissions. You bought $60,000 overall, but got no discount.

Even if you are not going to buy the $60,000 worth at one time, you can file a letter with the fund that tells them how you will purchase, and how much you will invest. That way, they will credit you with the lower load and more of your money goes to work from day one. They can't force you to go through with all the purchases. If you don't buy all you said within the time allowed for this Rights of Accumulation period, the fund will just recharge your account for the full load appropriate to your actual purchases.

A similar situation occurs when a broker shows you a lot of mutual funds and advises that you should spread your investments around because the greater diversity makes it safer.

Using the same $60,000, you buy not one, but five funds. All target similar sectors, but have different Investment Advisers. No one investment gets you past the $25,000 and lower levels needed for a "Break Point" discount on the various fund loads. You pay the full load rate for each of the funds, and the broker is happy.

If he sold you $60,000 worth of one fund, he'd miss the full load and therefore his full commission. If he broke it up, $30,000 in one and $30,000 in another, you would pass the $25,000 Break Point on both. If he put you in a family that allows free or low cost switching, he would get the commission this time, but he wouldn't be able to make a commission in the future when he told you to sell the fund to buy another.

Branch managers are supposed to review order tickets to look for possible violations. This is a classic. He should catch it.

If the manager sees any mutual fund purchase of approximately $24,500, he should inquire about the Break Point, which is the dollar level when a reduced load comes into play for that fund. He'll get the prospectus and look it up in 30 seconds. A lot of break points on loaded funds come in much lower at 5, 10, 15, or $20,000. Look for it.

If the manager is reviewing the broker's customer posting book and sees that Customer Finegan has bought a fund on several occasions well under the usual Break Point (but adding up to an aggregate above the Break Point when all the transactions for the year are added together), then an inquiry should be made to see if the Rights of Accumulation for the fund have been overlooked in an attempt to perpetrate a fraud on the customer.

The benefits of these rights can extend to purchases made by a whole family, not just an individual! It can make a loaded fund much more attractive. You must understand Break Points, Rights of Accumulation, and Letters of Intent when you deal in funds sold by a broker. It is all in black and white - in the prospectus.

If you have been a regular buyer of mutual funds and your broker has never discussed this with you, call the branch manager and demand an audit of the buys and sells to see IF your rights have been abused. The mere fact that your broker has not mentioned Rights of Accumulation, Break Points and Letters of Intent to you is a very serious matter. If you have been buying funds, you should have known about this all along. It is not a simple mistake. These rights are a fundamental part of how a fund should be sold.

As a customer, you are entitled to reject their use, and decide to buy ten funds investing in the same sector, if that's what YOU want. A bad broker is forbidden to "switch" you because of what HE wants. He wants gross commissions.

Some brokers make a living selling just mutual funds. Watch out! Bad ones look for big commissions from big dollar purchases now and in the future without regard for your interests or the rules. If you buy a fund through a broker, be very cautious if he calls and says it's time to sell. Don't trade loaded, open end mutuals. It's too expensive. One of the reasons you buy a fund is that you want the professionals to do all the work, to worry about all the trading. You pay fees for this. Why not hold onto the fund for a while? If you feel the time is right to trade, even that the circumstances demand a trade out of a fund, just be sure it's your idea and not the broker's.

The NASD is considering a new rule that would limit the "charges" that can be levied against your money in the so-called 12b-1 funds. These are the funds that don't charge you to get in, but charge you a large fee to get out in the first four years. The industry knows the "charges" game very well. If they don't tackle it, they may lose you. Find out how much you have paid in loads, investment adviser fees and other charges for your funds - you will be amazed! You are supporting a lot of people with your mutual funds. Demand performance!

CHAPTER THIRTEEN

DAS NET CAPITAL
S.I.P.C.

It's Not Insurance

When you get mail from your broker or if you go into his office, you will see a logo "Member SIPC," which you might have heard about, but probably haven't inquired about.

It's not insurance.

If your broker tells you it is, he's wrong. He doesn't deal with SIPC to make commissions, so don't presume he is lying on this one. He may sincerely think it works just like insurance.

The brokerage industry has suffered extensively from cycles in the market and the increasing cost of the back room. As I have indicated, houses come and go without any need for a crash. Houses manage to destroy themselves in the best of times, because they can lose in their own accounts or on major deal-sized investments.

In 1970, Congress created the Securities Investor Protection Corporation, referred to as "SIPC." Congress acted because the late 1960's saw a number of securities firms go under. Who should be responsible for business failure? Historically, if a house went under, no one was responsible. If it was a corporation, a liquidation occurred. If it was a partnership, partners could be wiped out, but the magnitude of losses could far outstrip personal assets of the partners.

There have been times where the NYSE stood ready to inject millions of dollars into a failed firm in order to keep public confidence in place. This unspoken, yet real form of "insurance" was funded by voluntary contributions from the members through a combination of dues and special assessments - passing the hat. If the Exchange wanted to ignore a failure, it could; investors would stay away, hurting all the Members business and the future of the Exchange itself, therefore the "hat" is really mandatory. Part of the Congressional effort has been to create a level playing field for investors - the Congress has tried to make the industry as safe as possible; not investments, the houses.

Commercial Banks are covered by the FDIC, the Federal Deposit Insurance Corporation. That has "insurance" right in the title. It's also an independent agency of the US Government that was set up in 1933 to backup the banking system. It has 15 billion dollars in reserve.

Brokerage houses are different, though, because they have always dealt with risk. Investors almost expect to lose money when they put money into an account, not from the failure of the house, but from the market. SIPC is not insurance. The word is "Protection," and there is a marked difference. SIPC is not a US Government Agency and it is not a securities regulator. It is a mere nonprofit corporation.

SIPC was not created to seek to limit market risk. You can buy Big Doggie stock and lose your shirt. That's your problem.

SIPC assesses securities firms for dues and creates a reserve, which is the only asset of the SIPC corporation. If a SIPC Member Firm fails and is not immediately merged into a solvent house, or otherwise taken over by an Exchange, then SIPC is prepared to go in and take over the firm, liquidating its assets and distributing securities to the rightful owners. It can be a laborious process, depending on the financial shape of the house before it went under. The FDIC has a Congressional promise of potentially unlimited financial backing. Not SIPC.

SIPC has a war chest of about 500 million and can borrow 1 billion from the US Government in an emergency. For your information, that's peanuts if a real market emergency occurred with the death of a few major houses.

Get the SIPC brochure from your brokerage house - it doesn't say how much the SIPC Corporation is worth, only that they can borrow the 1 billion.

SIPC has no governmental authority to examine the books of any securities firms. It has no field examiners poking around, asking to see a firm's stock record or trial balances on net capital calculations. It's purposefully blind as a bat because the SEC, the exchanges and the NASD are supposed to do all that probing.

Why Houses Die

What makes a house go under?

It's easy to use a colorful example of a failed house where cash went into wild bonuses, condominiums, yachts and more, but they also go under because they lose money in their own trading accounts or because they have an enormous back room and cannot get the revenues to pay for it. Embezzlement can kill a house.

Customers can kill a house by being on margin for a lot of money, suffering losses that wipe out the equity in the accounts and run the accounts into the red. Then the customers can't or won't pay. The house has to cover its positions and must absorb all the red ink while it is trying to collect. If there is enough red ink, the house can die for want of net capital. It's like dying of thirst for lack of fresh water while adrift on the ocean.

They go under, therefore, like any other business. Expenses exceed revenues. They fall on their faces because of business failure for all the traditional reasons. It is usually abrupt. The employees are suddenly dumped. The customers are quite surprised.

Houses compute their capital each day. Under Section 15(c)3-1 of the 1934 Exchange Act, the SEC sets standards for minimum capital of all broker dealers who are federally registered. The whole point of this section was to make sure that reserves were set up on the firm's balance sheet to account for the custody and use of customer securities and credit balances. SEC Rule 15c3 covers the area in great detail.

Suppose you and I set up a broker dealer, but we clear through another NYSE member firm. We don't hold any securities on the premises. We don't hold any money, credit balances or anything else of value. Whatever comes in, we ship out to the clearing firm. If we fail in business, all the customer securities should be safe at the clearing firm.

Net Capital
$ 5,000

The SEC isn't concerned with whether the telephone company gets paid, or even if we can pay our taxes or payroll - all they are concerned about is the safety of the securities. If we don't become market makers in a security, don't trade for our own account, don't jump into underwriting, and clear all our business through another firm, we need only $5,000 of capital. Don't jump up and start a broker dealer on that basis alone. You need to have securities-licensed individuals and a set of books, a location and business licenses. Don't equate the minimum net capital with the full cost of the operation. Overall, however, you don't need much.

If a firm has possession of customer securities and credit balances, the whole picture changes. Another test on top of net capital is used: the aggregate indebtedness test, which concentrates on how much money the firm owes to its customers for credit balances and securities and how much it owes to other broker dealers.

I don't want to make you all auditors, but I want you to understand that the law requires brokers to add up their balance sheet in a special way, and if they fall below certain minimums, they get into trouble.

The calculation reviews the location and extent of assets sufficient to provide the customers with safe return of their cash and securities. The broker dealer could own all of Manhattan - real estate is irrelevant. Net Capital and aggregate indebtedness look to cash assets and the location and kind of securities in the control of the broker dealer. Most broker dealers compute their capital this way, which requires the greater of $100,000 or 2% of the amount of its aggregate indebtedness to customers.

I warn you that a lot of houses that use a clearing firm to carry their accounts have next to no capital, either under the net capital rules or under regular accounting. They don't have to. Firms that carry customer accounts have to have some capital, but note the 2% mentioned above. It's not much. A firm can go under in a flash. The real danger is not that your securities will disappear, but that once the house goes and you see what really happened to your account, there is no one left to sue. It's a corporation. When the house goes into bankruptcy with its pittance of capital, if you realize that your account was churned or that the transactions were not suitable for your needs which caused losses because of increased risk - there is no one to recover from even if you have a serious case. They are shells compared to the value rolling in and out the door.

Every firm, giant and tiny, must do this capital computation and every firm must have a Licensed Financial and Operations Principal for this purpose.

The SEC was given the tools to identify firms that looked like they might fail and therefore jeopardize customer property. If a firm gets into this technical net capital trouble, it has to report itself to the SEC. If the firm tries to cover it up, people can go to jail.

The SEC Regional Administrators run the audit of the broker's books on a periodic basis to see if the calculations are being correctly done. This is probably the primary benefit of the regional system. The audits are not done by the attorney staff - the auditors are usually accountants, so they know what they're doing because they are long-term, professional employees.

The single greatest compliment that could be given to the SEC and the regulators is that since 1975, no major brokerage house has blown apart from losses which then fell completely on the shoulders of the retail investing public. The SEC does deal with criminals in cases involving prohibited activity, and the markets may be as driven by rumor as ever, but the underpinning of the financial marketplace has been shored up by forcing broker dealers to keep a timely set of books that go the heart of the system's frailty. Note: I said major houses, and further, I emphasized firms that went out of business where the firm's death caused the losses. I did not say that the SEC has prevented houses from abusing customers over time by using wrongful discretion in their accounts, by dumping unsuitable, dangerous investments in customer accounts - and then going bankrupt. The harm was already done before the bankruptcy. When big firms like EF Hutton, Thompson McKinnon, and others disappear, with no harm to their many thousands of customers, credit is due to the SEC and the capital requirements system.

SIPC has worked. So far. It hasn't faced hard adversity, but that may be coming.

Any lender can ask a broker dealer for its net capital computations before making extensions of credit. Firms send formal capital reports to their regulators to keep the numbers flowing. If insider trading grabs headlines and is otherwise the sensational activity of the SEC, this capital surveillance mechanism is far more serious, and so far, it has worked well.

In times past, when a house went under, it took banks and other houses down with it to continue the ripple effect. It hasn't happened lately because the capital inspection system tries to identify the weaklings, follow them closely and take action before they fall. It happens quietly. Mergers are prodded by the regulators under threat of a closure. Weak firms had better find a partner fast - or else! If a bank goes under the FDIC can step in to cover the bank.

What If?

Suppose a major brokerage house was in touch with a takeover promoter who needed to raise money to buy out a series of liquor distilleries. The promoter wants to be the biggest liquor king in the country. He needs money to make it work. The brokerage house says it will raise the cash by selling bonds.

The bonds get a non-investment grade rating, making them Junk Bonds. They are placed with pension funds and other institutions because the promoter has a good track record and the brokerage house has a good reputation of success. So far.

In order to make the deals, the promoter needs bridge funds, which are short term loans of less than one year, sometimes less than two years. Where can he get these funds?

From a consortium of banks and the brokerage house. Bridge loans command higher interest than permanent loans because of the urgent need for the cash. "Need" translates into a market force where lenders charge more. The brokerage house lends cash, looking to close the deals and make a series of fat fees from placing the bonds, advising the promoter, making the bridge loans directly, and getting fees from the consortium of other bridge lenders.

Then, one day, the deal goes busto after all the little distilleries are bought up and the empire is in formation. People don't stop drinking; the interest cost of the bonds and the loans just can't be met from the revenues of the empire. The empire files bankruptcy.

What happens if a big house goes under, not gradually under the net capital wind down, but suddenly? Suppose, without any real warning, when the liquor empire filed for bankruptcy, the next day the brokerage house did, too, due to losses as a bridge lender.

This brokerage house not only does these big deals, it has customer accounts, little ones and giant ones. Who takes over?

Probably no one at first because the matter would be in bankruptcy and the court would take it on. The New York Stock Exchange would be rushed to the consultation table to get some action going, calling around the Street to get a match for merger with the bankrupt house. Promises will be made of financial support, to certain limits, to make sure that the accounts will transfer smoothly. If it's a big house, the call has to go to another big house. Not many others could handle a big merger on a fast basis. The NYSE can't force them to take on the bankrupt firm, but the Street has a way of getting these things done. Technically, a broker-dealer has to surrender its license to the SEC before it can file in bankruptcy. Suppose the SEC said, "No, we won't accept your surrender of the license. You can't file." The house would send a messenger to the SEC and drop off the keys to the front door, telling the bureaucrats to have a nice time running a real, live business, because no one else is going to show up tomorrow at the firm. The NYSE took care of its own in the past. If no firm would absorb the bankrupt firm, then it could fall onto SIPC.

SIPC Steps In

SIPC would take control of the firm by kicking everyone out and starting to count securities. If you have option positions, tough. SIPC will probably close them out. If you have equity positions held at the firm for your beneficial ownership and the position is correctly entered on the books, you'll be fine. The same for bonds and other debt instruments. Under the net capital and books and records rules, your positions have been accounted for on record. SIPC protection is limited to $500,000 of which only $100,000 can be cash.

But suppose some really bad guys ran the firm into the ground, and played with the numbers and papers so that what was supposed to be there was now in Switzerland or the Bahamas in secret bank accounts? It may have been spent in Las Vegas.

SIPC takes out the checkbook and goes to work. They have to figure out what you owned. If your 500 shares of IBM is gone, stolen, SIPC will give you 500 IBM. If the cash is gone - all $ 60,000 - they'll give you that, too. Again, they only protect you up to a maximum of $500,000, of which $100,000 may be cash. They further protect you under a number of accounts, so your personal account may be treated differently from the trust account you have for your child or grandchild. SIPC is not a bottomless reservoir of cash. Some houses buy "excess SIPC" insurance and get coverage from a private insurance underwriter like the Aetna in Hartford, Connecticut for $10,000,000 beyond SIPC protection. There are other insurance underwriters out there that have excellent ratings and can write this excess SIPC coverage that kicks in after the SIPC level has been exhausted.

Every broker dealer has a brochure from SIPC that they can give you, which explains how SIPC works. It is not put out by the house; it is put out by SIPC for you. Ask for it. It's free and available. Ask if your house has a private underwriter for excess SIPC coverage. This is valuable for another reason - it means that the brokerage house's books are under the scrutiny of another financial professional with an interest in how solvent the entity is: the insurance underwriter! Insurance people hate to pay. They issue insurance only for the best risks.

Big Dollars

The Savings and Loan debacle is estimated to be heading to the 400 or 500 BILLION dollar level over the next several years. Congress is honoring its moral commitment to the S&L investors by authorizing this expenditure, a piece at a time, and by creating the bureaucratic machinery to administer the situation. SIPC has a 1 billion cushion.

No such promise of insurance was ever given to the securities industry. "Insurance" is not a part of SIPC. SIPC has never worked on a really big failure, raising the question, " What if..."

What if Merrill Lynch went under? Don't ask. SIPC would be completely overwhelmed; Shearson - the same answer. SIPC has never been in action in a depression, and has existed only since 1970. It has never faced a major financial test.

Richard Nixon was the president in 1970, just twenty years ago. The SIPC fund is not backed by anything more than the ability to assess members for contributions. If there is an economic collapse like that in 1929 through 1932, many brokerage houses will go under and the assessment process will be meaningless. While larger firms tend to have excess SIPC coverage, smaller ones do not.

Allen Greenspan, Chairman of the Federal Reserve, said in early 1990 that no brokerage house was so big that the government could not allow it to fail.

The Paper Tiger

In the face of a major economic shock, SIPC has neither the manpower or monetary commitment to cover the industry. It is a paper tiger, as they say in the Far East. SIPC will give you back your IBM if the records show you owned it, but the IBM may be worth 70 per share if a crash dragged it down and caused the house to go under. The key to the present web of financial regulation is regular financial reporting; the danger is the debt market, especially the junk bond market and its ability to end abruptly in bankruptcy with little forewarning. SIPC does not save the house, and when a big house goes under, it will drag down banks. SIPC does not protect the industry against risk. It is nothing like the FDIC.

If the next economic decline sets off a further junk bond disaster, many brokerage houses and their clients that have bought these low-rated bonds will fail. A lot of these bonds may have no trading value. Yet, brokerage houses have junk bonds in their inventories and count them as assets, even though the Street knows there is no liquid market for junk bonds even today. If you own them, you are advised to hold them by the firms that issued them. If you sold them, your actual market price would be plugged into the Net Capital computations required by some of these advising brokerage houses. It would be plugged into valuations used by lenders who have given funds to the same houses and cause the lenders to call for more collateral. A lot of selling would collapse the junk prices, killing the houses.

How many billions, from whose pocket, are available to bail out the securities industry? One. Maybe one and a half.

Is Congress willing to write a blank check for Wall Street, when Wall Street has acted with moral abandon in the 1980's creating and heavily marketing the potential instruments of its own demise - low rated debt? Let's talk about it now, when the time for discussion is liberally at hand, and not when we, as a nation, are reacting to economic pain with intellectual spasms.

It Can't Happen

Sorry, sooner or later, "it" has to happen. Bear market time.

When you see newspaper articles heralding the end of economic cycles, be on guard. The history of economics and commerce is one of dynamic change where the rise of one power is marked by the decline of another. History displays achievements of brilliance, bravery and rank stupidity, some of which have been discussed in this book. Dishonor and thievery have ruled at times.

Why can't we have another episode of economic disaster? Because the media say, "No?" Because the politicians say, "No?" When it comes, we will express surprise at its ferocity because the last great downturn was distant, the stuff of stories from the past.

The NYSE Dow dropped 500+ points in one day in October, 1987. Why not 1,000 points; why not 2,000? Is the safety feature of the "circuit breakers" so reliable? What are we doing about the financial integrity of the markets and the houses now? Not much. The center stage has been stolen by a mis-emphasis on insider trading. "Circuit breakers" will not stop anything. If the NYSE stops trading after a 250 point drop, it might as well shut down entirely. The professionals will dump their assets overseas. A circuit breaker is like the Roman Emperor Caligula fighting with the ocean, declaring victory over the tide by edict. If the NYSE shuts down, YOU can't get out; the big boys can, overseas. In the face of a collapse, there is no time for retail hedging.

A spider's web is strong because of the interrelated strength of all its threads; it can capture and hold a large insect, but it can't catch you or me. We would fall right through the web.

October 19, 1987 was interesting, because of the big decline. It was October 20 that was dangerous because that was the time to see who was left on the Street, and if the Street would still work.

What about the next time?

I know, "it can't happen."

Humor me, get in touch with your US Congressional representatives in the House and Senate and let them know you are concerned about what happens when the big debt promoters disappear. The Congress is interested, and they'll consider the matter if you show it's worthy of their time and attention. It is.

Call. Write. Send telegrams. Get in touch with Congress and tell them that you don't want to see the Savings and Loan debacle show up in the securities industry. No one thought the Savings and Loan mess could occur. It happened because of wild appraisals of "assets."

Some ready solutions: make firms that carry customer accounts disclose their balance sheets on a monthly basis to all their customers. One more thing: make the firms send a copy of their house trading accounts activity statements to each customer, each month.

The financial statement would explain how they stand. The trading account statement would explain how they got there and, besides, wouldn't you like to see if they were selling Big Doggie stock when your broker was telling you to buy? Your monthly statement comes with marketing pieces every month, usually a several page flyer that resembles a high school newspaper. What are their "assets?"

The industry would howl at the idea of customers seeing how they spend their money! They only want to tell you how to spend yours!

CHAPTER FOURTEEN

PRECISION ANARCHY
PROGRAM TRADING

No Penalty for Piling On

In football, if the defensive team tackles the player with the ball, but some of the defensive players jump on the downed player for hard "sport," it's called "piling on." Such conduct is illegal and draws a big penalty. It is a dangerous practice, likely to cause harm to the players on the bottom of the heap.

Like you.

We have reviewed the workings of the NYSE, with specialists, brokers, members, floor governors, traders and staff wandering around. It remains a physical place, subject to the limitations of any physical market. Physical crowding out can occur when a lot of brokers run to a given post to make trades because of sudden news. The big guys push the little guys out of the way.

Because the action is happening on the floor itself, your broker can hear about it only AFTER it occurs. He can't see it from a branch office. He can't see who, ON THE FLOOR, is up for fast action, who's yawning and reading the newspaper, or who is taking feverish notes from his trading desk upstairs, getting the "play."

Back to football.

Even if you don't follow the game, you know that the offensive team has the ball. They get into a huddle, call a play they have been practicing before the game, break out of the huddle and line up, ready for action.

The intrigue is trying to guess what they are going to do. The offensive team tries not to give it away; the defense tries to guess and stop offensive gains.

When the ball is snapped, the play begins. The eleven members of the offensive team perform their predetermined roles and the defense adjusts as best they can. Sometimes the defense decides to ignore what some of the offense is doing and smash through to the quarterback to tackle him before the offensive play can develop. The planning and execution of football plays is an art.

Program trading is similar.

Planning for trading models goes on in the home office to anticipate what to do when the market goes through the one thing it reliably does: it changes.

The plan hopes to use "what if" logic to make profits for the firm or for large institutional clients. You need big bucks to play this game. As a retail investor, you can't get on the field.

The Arbs

IBM is traded on the NYSE and on the Pacific Exchange. Both exchanges are open for some of the same hours each day. You might think that the price for IBM on the NYSE will be exactly the same as on the Pacific. It usually is, but not because of any exchange price control system. It works because of arbitragers.

Arbitragers, "Arbs," are traders who notice slight discrepancies in price. If you can buy IBM for 99 on the NYSE and sell it on the Pacific for 99 and 1/8, they will do it. As they do it, their purchases of IBM pull it up from 99 on the NYSE to the same 99 and 1/8 as on the Pacific. The arbs have an almost molecular role in keeping an equilibrium going in the smallest increments. The markets are actually never in balance, but are in a constant state of being balanced by tiny movements back and forth. The arbs are essential to the process of price, working on direct supply and demand on the floor, generated from the floor itself.

You cannot know what an arb is up to until after he does it. Your broker has no idea. He hears about it after it occurs.

Arbs are at work all the time on all the exchanges. They're like ants, always in motion.

The Programmers

Forget what you read in the papers.

There is nothing bizarre about program trading. The gates of hell did not open and let program trading loose upon the world. The only reason it exists is the inefficiency of the New York Stock Exchange.

While the trading on the NYSE may be fast and furious at times, it is not fast enough. Information is not disseminated as fast as it should be, there is no level playing field, and being on the floor, seeing the action flow, is worth something.

Remember Charles Dow? He used an average made of thirty large NYSE industrials as an indicator of market performance.

The stocks of the NYSE are used to figure various indexes aside from the strict Dow Industrial Average. On other exchanges, those indexes are used as trading vehicles themselves. Think about it. Traders away from the NYSE floor are using the NYSE prices as the foundation of their trading.

Suppose you could take a shopping cart onto the floor of the NYSE and pick up 1 share of stock at each specialist post for the Dow Industrial 30. When you finish, you've got 30 stocks. It takes a while to make the rounds and get one of each, but it can be done.

Let's assume there is an exchange in Chicago which has a commodity futures contract, which promises to deliver to the owner of the contract a basket with one share of each of the Dow Industrial 30, exactly three months from today. I own the contract. I don't own the stock yet, but in three months I will, unless I sell the contract to someone else in the meantime.

If you own the 30 shares, you can see their exact value as they trade throughout the day. You can't keep track of this with a pad and pencil, but you can with a computer. My office PC can do it every few seconds. I need the data on prices and a small program. Put the data and program together and I get the average for the 30 stocks.

If the arbs are doing their job, price discrepancies quickly disappear between equity exchanges in ordinary markets. But I am over in a commodities exchange. I see the situation in different data, because I don't own the stock, I own a contract that gives me a right to own the stock in three months.

My contract is worth something. If the general consensus is that the market is going to drop and be lower in three months than it is now, my contract may not be worth much. If the feeling is that the market will go up, then my contract has value. You might object, saying that the present value has a great deal of speculation involved because three months is a long time and the markets can change every day.

True.

That's why, as the value of your 30 shares changes, the value of my contract to get those shares in three months changes, too. If your stocks drop a lot, my contract value drops a lot.

Suppose one of your thirty stocks drops a lot, but the others are stable? Your average value dropped a little. My contract value dropped a little.

Or, it should have dropped a little.

What if the value of my contract didn't drop at all? Is there an arb to take care of this? We are dealing with a basket of stock and a commodity futures contract, different markets, different market sales mechanisms, pricing and timing. This is not a time for a simple arbitrage.

As the day goes by, to keep track of both your basket and my contract, you have to have a computer. You have to have a program that tells you when the relation between the 30 shares and the futures contract is in or out of balance.

If it is out of balance, which side is up? Is the stock average priced below the balancing price of the contract, or is the futures contract priced too low? How long has the imbalance existed?

If you know that a lot of other firms are doing the same thing, you can draw up a few battle plans, figuring that any imbalance will draw computer arbs to close it. If you see an imbalance develop, you can make money if you get there first and close the imbalance. Speed is essential. Sun Tsu is back!

If the futures contract is apparently correctly priced, but the stocks are a little low, you rush to buy the stock so that you own them when they rise to the balance level. Then you sell the stocks. The profit may be quite small per share but quite large if you take positions with a lot of shares.

Likewise, if you see that the futures contract is priced too high, you sell it short. When it falls into price balance, you cover your short position by buying it back at a lower price.

Want some fun?

Suppose the prices are in balance, but you know that if you sell a lot of XYZ common on the floor of the NYSE, you will drag down the stock average. That should cause the price of the futures contract to drop. The reverse is true: if you buy a lot of XYZ you might be able to make the average go up, and the futures contract should rise in price.

Break out of the huddle, line up and get ready to execute the play.

In close cadence, the ball is snapped. Some of your players quietly buy futures contracts, and if they are successful in not causing that price to rise above your target, you proceed to the next phase: your other players loudly buy a lot of XYZ causing that stock price to rise, attracting other buyers, causing further increase.

The price of the futures contract starts to move up because XYZ is going up causing the "index" to go up. When it hits your target, you sell the futures contracts you bought earlier and dump your XYZ stock. You end up owning nothing, and making a profit. Total elapsed time might be three minutes or less. You made it work.

That's theory.

How does it really work?

Trading on the floor of the NYSE is not as efficient as you might think. It went wild in October, 1987. It can race, stumble and fall on any given day.

99.9% of all futures contracts are liquidated, that is, sold. No delivery of the stock in the contract takes place. It's pure speculation.

Commodity speculation and NYSE inefficiency cause the turbulence we call "program trading." One house makes a stab at evening out the balance. If ten houses have similar secret programs, the same numbers may trigger all ten to make a run at a program, resulting in wild, simultaneous selling or buying. It happens fast, with efficiency.

Thousands of "rocket scientists," the title given to computer compulsives on Wall Street, are at work with secret programs that kick in when there is an imbalance, or when other programs kick in, or when it looks like other programs are about to kick in.

You don't stand a chance.

You are not on the floor; your broker isn't on the floor. He can't see the floor people rush out to execute the program for their house. If you own one of the program stocks in the basket, you could be in for a ride.

How big are the baskets - try the S&P 500; that's 500 securities and a corresponding futures contract! That calls for a computer!

The Chicago Mercantile Exchange has traded the S&P 500 futures contract since 1982. It doesn't require actual physical delivery of the 500 underlying shares. It is based on a cash settlement. The CFTC approved the CME's application to trade the S&P 500 because it met the objective criteria underlying creation of a futures contract - real pricing based on widely available, reliable data.

The S&P 500 stock index futures contract has a dollar value of $500 times its presently quoted price. The $500 is an arbitrary number called the "index multiplier."

Another vehicle used for program trading is the S&P 100 option traded on the Chicago Board Options Exchange, known as the infamous OEX option. This tracks 100 stocks.

If your computer is big enough you can track the value of the related stocks to the S&P 500 and the OEX and then the related value of the OEX to the S&P 500. You can program trade among the three.

There are others! There are other index options, other stock index futures and the same old stock. The lagging item is usually the stock price. Moving around blocks of stock takes a little time, and the tape can run late.

You are powerless in this. The general concept is not difficult. It's just arbitrage. It's legal and goes on all the time.

Some brokerage houses do it, some say they don't. All the big houses trade their own accounts using computer models of some kind. They may not be doing index arbitrage, but they are probably using various models from technical analysis, looking for trends or trying to guess when someone else's program will go off so that an advantage can be gained by being there "first."

All the computer does is take the pricing data, sort it, apply it to a program that says "If the price is xxx, then buy the S&P Futures Contract up to a price of zzz." That's it. The computer isn't doing anything evil. It delivers speed. It sorts bulk data.

Does your brokerage house send you research? Do they tell you how to program trade? Even if the house has agreed not to program trade, how can you tell if they are or not? It's not illegal.

Why is everyone concerned about program trading? Because it makes for volatility which embarrasses exchanges. Retail customers can't compete, and when they see their stocks gyrate points per day, even the lowliest of retail customers knows a game is afoot among the houses and institutions. Large institutions can program trade, too, provided they have a few million dollars to play with at a time, have their own programmers, and command good, confidential execution from their servicing brokerage houses.

You will see advertisements and planted news articles about how one brokerage house or another is stopping program trading. This has been a quiet campaign carried on by the NYSE to restore public confidence.

Forget it; programmers are everywhere. Electronic arbs have to work to keep the prices in line. The wild gyrations occur when a number of programmers play the same futures contract or index option, or chase the same stocks. It's an intellectual, mathematical exercise.

According to the Brady Commission Report to the President in 1988, which investigated the market crash in October, 1987, "Although the value of the open interest in the futures contracts is only a small fraction of the value of NYSE Stocks, the value of the stocks represented by the volume of futures contracts traded on the CME (Chicago Mercantile Exchange) daily is typically about twice the value of stocks traded on the NYSE daily."

That SHOULD knock you over. Who is the chicken and who is the egg? The securities exchanges hate the pressure from the Chicago commodity pits. New York and Chicago fight every day.

Why do you think your broker has any influence over what happens to your positions or that he can foresee what is going to occur? When you hear from firms that complain about program trading, listen closely! All they are saying is that they can't do it, so don't let the big guys do it. The houses that complain about program trading being underhanded are really saying they can't compete.

YOU can't possibly compete. If you buy IBM, put on your seat belt. It's not IBM's fault - they keep plugging away. Their stock price is out of their control.

Marketeers used to be direct. They would grab one stock and shake it. These days, if you want to shake a stock, you can do it from afar. You can manipulate the Dow 30 from a different market, with a commodity futures contract.

The SEC wants to wrest control of the commodity futures contracts based on stock indexes. The Commodity Futures Trading Commission, the CFTC, presently has control, but has suffered a major embarrassment over recent, major scandals on the commodity trading floors in Chicago.

The FBI broke the case for the Chicago US Attorney, not the CFTC. Massive price shaving and gouging is alleged against many traders.

A bureaucratic turf battle is in progress, SEC vs. CFTC, while the markets bounce along. The SEC was caught short by the 1987 crash. It took a Presidential Commission to figure out what happened.

Giving the SEC jurisdiction over stock index futures contracts is like putting a plow horse on ice skates. If the metaphor is unwieldy, the prospect is frightening.

Program trading could be defeated if the floor of the NYSE wasn't so entrenched in history. The specialist system is the problem.

The solution: kill it.

In the future, a programmer with steel nerves, a hot computer, and a lot of money will play off the Tokyo Nikkei Index against the soon to be born Budapest Index on the floor of the London Exchange.

The world is changing.

The time for a physical trading floor dominated by specialists is long gone. It interferes with effective, electronic arbitrage and creates the environment for disruptive program trading. If you accept the prohibition on program and computer usage, we will next remove engines from ships and revert to the glory of sail. Let's give up the telephone. Ban ball point pens!

Fight the ocean tide with swords!

The answer is apparent: get rid of the specialist. Get rid of the physical floor and "go electronic." Accept change. If the archaic system is removed, perhaps the imbalances that allow program trading will disappear. The difficulty for the NYSE is that program trading spells the end for the Membership system.

CHAPTER FIFTEEN

Statistics, Please!

The National Association of Securities Dealers and the New York Stock Exchange have to report a variety of statistics to the Securities and Exchange Commission each year. So do the rest of the Exchanges and SRO's, but they are so much smaller. Let's put some numbers together and make sense out of all the reporting.

Make it a practice to get a copy of the SEC's Annual Report and the Statistical Abstract of the United States, the latter being put out by the US Department of Commerce. Both are available from the Superintendent of Documents, US Government Printing Office, Washington, DC 20402, telephone (202) 783-3238. Both books are crammed with data.

How Many of Them Are There?

At the end of 1987, there were over 9,000 broker dealers in the United States and they had over 21,000 branch offices! Only a tiny fraction were NYSE Member Firms. Brokers are all over the country. I haven't been able to find a statistic that would explain how many states each of the brokers was registered in. Let's assume there are 300,000 registered representatives left in the business at this time. If each of them is registered in 4 states, that's 1.2 million state registrations. The total is probably much higher.

That number rose dramatically during the recent bull market. In 1981, there were just over 5,700 Broker Dealers and a mere 7,693 branch offices. The number of branch offices almost tripled by 1987, while the number of broker dealers didn't quite double. The increase in size reflected the profitability of the industry. Another indicator - right before the crash in October, 1987, if you wanted to buy a seat on the NYSE, it would have cost you about $1,100,000. In January, 1990, you could have gotten one for $390,000, IF you wanted one. The Dow Jones Industrial Average in August 1987 and January 1990 was about the same, approximately 2700+. The price may go lower as firms in liquidation have to sell seats, affecting the law of supply and demand.

You can bet that all those branch offices were filled with selling brokers. There were over 350,000 registered representatives, licensed stockbrokers, in 1988, after the big crash. Many back room employees who do not sell are registered because they have control or possession of securities, or they supervise a trading desk, wire, or other sensitive facility involved in the receipt or transmission of orders. A lot of boiler room operators, the real bad guys, don't bother to get registered. How many of them are there - they aren't saying!

Brokerage Revenue

According to the SEC, every dollar of revenue in 1987 for a brokerage house that carried customer accounts was broken down as follows:

> 23.3 % came from commissions on trades;
> 21.1 % came from trading their own house accounts;
> 9.7 % came from underwriting, doing deals, or corporate finance;
> 6.2% came from charging you margin interest;
> 29.1 % came from other securities related activities such as lending securities to other brokers, investing in subsidiary securities, charging fees to introducing brokers, management fees for Investment Advisory activities, etc.;
> the rest came from miscellaneous activities.

Want to know where their revenue went?

> 29 % went to pay interest on money they had borrowed;
> 19.9 % went to pay compensation to the brokers as their net of gross commissions;
> 17.6 % went to pay for clerical and administrative employees;
> 6.5 % went to Communications and Data Processing;
> 5.4 % paid for rent and equipment;
> 4.1 % paid for commissions they were charged on their own transactions by other firms and two dollar brokers on the floor of the various exchanges;
> 2.9 % went to pay for general partner compensation in the few firms with partners, and
> 12.4% covered all other miscellaneous expenses which includes paying on lawsuits.

Those are average statistics that may have no relation to the house you favor with your business. You can see that trading their own accounts was a major part of revenue, in fact, if a firm was smart and daring, there would be no need to have any brokers at all - just trade the firm's account, cut the expenses to the bare minimum, and keep the profits.

Retail Has No Value

Why do houses continue to keep the brokers around? Some don't. Drexel got rid of its brokers in 1989. They dropped their whole retail network of about 1200 brokers in a surprise move. When Drexel tried to sell their retail system, no one wanted to pay for it, so they had to effectively give it away to anyone willing to pick up a piece. True, Drexel died later, in February, 1990 when its parent filed for Chapter 11 bankruptcy, but when the firm was healthy, they dumped their retail.

Now you can see why program trading is so important to the house. In 1987 21.1 % of their revenue came from trading their own accounts. They were hurt by the October 1987 Crash because the stocks they owned fell in value. Some firms disappeared, some suffered slow, lingering deaths, and some skated by. A lot of the firms' expenses came from the retail, selling end. It costs a lot to keep a broker going in the field. Innocent errors cause problems even when the bad guys are not conspiring on more evil matters. It's hard to make a buck, bring it back to the home office and keep a large part of it in the retail business.

Big
Very Big

How big is the brokerage business?

In fiscal 1987, Broker Dealers had total revenues reported on their SEC filings of 66 Billion plus. In dramatic numbers, that looks like $66,343,000,000.00. Of that figure, registered representatives (stockbrokers), were paid compensation of 11 billion plus, but the firms paid over 16 billion in interest to carry on business! They paid a total of 431 million as regulatory fees to carry on business, including SEC, State and other licenses. The brokers are always told they are the big expense.

In 1983, a pretty good year for the business, firms had total revenue of about 40 billion and total expenses of 31.7 billion. The pretax profit margin in 1983 was 14.1 %. The return on equity was 30.7%! In 1987 the return on equity was down to 9.2 %. Not too good.

My prediction for 1990: total revenues will be exceeded by total expenses, and ownership equity will drop to somewhere around 23 billion by December 31, 1990, but, if truth be known, very few firms that carry customer accounts will have real value!

Maybe Not So Big

Who would buy them if they were for sale?

Are there still insurance companies so dumb they would consider buying cyclical, uncontrollable firms with such weak management and such heavy regulation? They didn't bite at Drexel.

Here is a scary number: In 1987 the total receivables due from other brokers were 61.8 billion dollars. The industry's total assets, per regulatory reports, were worth 479 billion but the ownership equity was a mere 47 billion. Receivables includes stocks, bonds and other securities that firms owed each other, including cash due from transactions. Don't be impressed by balance sheet numbers attributable to assets until you compare them to the liabilities. A lot of the equity ownership of securities firms is tied up in non-existent value. Drexel, above, couldn't sell it's retail broker network to any other house for a big profit, but you can bet the network had a "book" value on the balance sheet.

What's so scary? The equity ownership may really be worth zero, yes zero, on a real market basis. No one wants to pay real money for a brokerage business. The Drexel bankruptcy shows that what they have in the inventory, even in the home office, may be worth a lot less than the paper value. What is a vault of junk bonds worth? To whom?

If I buy IBM through Merrill Lynch, they go to the market and may get it for me from Smith Barney. Merrill owes money to Smith and Smith owes IBM to Merrill. The total receivables due around the industry in 1987 exceeded total ownership equity by approximately 16 billion real dollars. What if there was a sudden, big crash? Not just 509 points, but say 1,000? Even SIPC, the much publicized Securities Investor Protection Corporation has a value of only about 500 million in its war chest and a line of credit for 1 billion with the Federal Government.

The single greatest problem with the industry is not insider trading, but who's minding the piggy bank?

Trivia

Trivia Question: as of September 30, 1988, which state had the largest number of brokers and dealers registered with the SEC? The answer is Illinois with 3,326! New York was second with 2,712.

Wyoming had but 4 entities registered as BD's.

Here is the ironic twist: Illinois had 2252 sole proprietorships and 727 corporations, while New York had 771 sole proprietors and 1544 corporations. There are about 550 Member Firms of the NYSE, nationwide.

If you live in Tennessee, Arkansas, South Dakota or the Virgin Islands, a broker in Illinois, New York or Wyoming can reach out on the telephone and try to get some use out of your funds.

The NYSE Domination

The domination of the markets by the New York Stock Exchange is to the NYSE's credit. While there are laws against other monopolies, the NYSE has a federal license and works right out in the open. The SEC is their sponsor, protector and muscle. One of the best ways to appreciate how effective the NYSE has been is to look at the dollar volume done by all the licensed exchanges expressed as a percentage attributable to each exchange.

In 1987, the total dollar volume of transactions of the registered exchanges was $ 2,286,902,788,000.00 The New York Stock Exchange handled 86.79% of all that. The Midwest Stock Exchange was next with 5.32%, then the Pacific Exchange with 2.53%.

In 1986, a bull year, the total dollar volume was an amazing $1,707,117,112,000.00, of which the NYSE did 85.02% and the Midwest did 6%.

Since 1973, the NYSE has done better than 80% of the total dollar volume of all exchanges combined.

At the end of 1987, the total dollar market value of all securities listed on US Exchanges was 3.8 trillion dollars. This includes stocks and bonds. The value of just the stocks was 2.2 trillion.

Of that 2.2 trillion dollars in stock value, 2.1 trillion dollars worth was made up of stocks listed on the New York Stock Exchange. The

NYSE had 97% of the dollar market value of all preferred and common listed on all US Exchanges!

The other 3% - mostly the American Stock Exchange with a mere 67 billion worth.

If one goes back to 1938, the NYSE had 47.5 billion worth and the Amex had 10.8 billion. In 1955, the NYSE had 207.7 billion worth and the Amex had 27.1 billion.

The NYSE has blown away the competition to a point where there isn't any.

By September 30, 1988, there were 7,890 securities admitted to trading on US Exchanges. This includes bonds, stocks, warrants, etc. These securities were issued by 2,558 companies. In 1987, there were 3,145 companies issuing securities. A few disappeared between 1987 and 1988.

Of the total 7,890 securities issued in September 30, 1988, 5600 were listed on the NYSE.

Since the early 1980's the number of securities and the total market value of securities issued has skyrocketed. New securities have come onto the market with amazing frequency since 1985.

SEC Numbers

Have you ever wondered how many people work for the SEC? In fiscal 1983, there were a total of 2,021 employees. With the rapid rise in the markets of dollar value and number of securities issued the SEC ballooned - to 2,267! That's nationwide, in every office plus all 9 Regional Offices from New York and Washington to Los Angeles. New York city has approximately 25,000 police. There are about 650,000 police nation wide.

The SEC has been in existence since July 2, 1934. Charles Breeden is the 24th Chairman. That's an average of 2 years and 4 months per Chairman. Why do they turn over so fast? It's certainly not a dead end job; rather, it's a stepping stone to other positions. Pity the poor staff that has to deal with commissioners playing musical chairs.

The Smithsonian, that wonderful institution devoted to the arts and science in Washington, DC, has more employees than the SEC. The Boy Scouts of America outnumber the SEC by over 2.5 to 1.

The Architect of the Capitol has about the same number of employees as the SEC. The US Supreme Court has a little under 350 employees.

The Target

That's you! The census people are knocking on doors to find out how many of us there are in the US, what we are like, how much we make, and all the trivia that is useful in commercial and political databases.

To the securities industry, the part of the population with spendable income is the part that matters, and the senior crowd is especially attractive.

According to the US Department of Commerce, in 1988, the total population of the US was about 245 million souls of all ages. This is not just citizens; it includes everyone in the US and even the military stationed overseas. The median age of the population was over 32 years!

In just 1970, that median was only 28. People are living longer. The longer we live, the longer we serve as potential customers of the securities industry. As we age, raising children, selling off the big house, and settling to the 45+ age group, we become the most prime of all targets.

Have you noticed the desperate commercials from the full service houses that ask you to trust your retirement funds to them? Having killed off a lot of customers with speculation in the Bull Market, they want you to "trust" them with the last dollars you have left.

Why? The marketing people know that in 1990 there are roughly 46 million people in the US between 45 and 64 years old, and another 30 million over 65. That's a target group of about 75 million people.

The brokerage marketing people also know that a lot of these folks have serious pension dollars to their credit in 401K plans, profit sharing, retirement plans, etc., and that as people move about in the present economic flux, these dollars are paid out in lump sums for placement in IRA Rollover accounts or other forms of retirement re-investment.

The brokers want that money.

In 1970, 640 billion dollars were spent on overall personal consumption. In 1988, that number was over 3 trillion dollars. In 1970 the personal income for the nation was 832 billion, but by 1988 it was close to 4 trillion dollars!

In 1988 the median family income was $30,853, and the disposable personal income per capita was $13,157.

Forget the median and the per capita. Averages include children and the unemployed. Brokers are out there buying up every mailing list they can get to select their target audience. They advertise on the evening news shows, in the big glossy magazines and the national newspapers.

They want you - actually, they don't want you; your money will do fine, thanks.

You, the investing population, are rejecting retail full service brokers. They smell it. It scares the daylights out of the brokerage industry, so they are coming at you as the same wolf but in a different disguise. Now they want to be your investment adviser.

Like Drexel, they can advise themselves into the ground. Investment advisers are everywhere. The entity, the adviser, can have a lot of agents. Sound like a broker? A number of brokers are also investment advisers.

The US trade deficit has been enormous during the 1980's, fueling a world boom. What happens if the US slows down its spending? Do economies limp along? While the boom has been going on, the number of manufacturing jobs in the US has been declining and the nation has moved over to the service sector. In 1955, 30% of all Gross National Product goods and services came from manufacturing. By some estimates, by 2000, that will be down to 17%. It is headed that way now.

Service industries tend to have wider swings in income between the high and low paid, and require fewer employees than manufacturing. The Japanese industrial base has been the marvel of the 1980's. They are a tough competitor. Yet, a lot of manufacturing in the US will be lost to productivity, not foreign competition.

Fewer young people are entering the work force. By the year 2000, the number of workers in the 16-24 age group will not just level off, it will drop by about 2 million. Older people will have more opportunity to work as they live longer and are not displaced by younger workers.

Important forces are shaping up that will have a profound impact over the next 15 years in the makeup of the labor force, the occupations people follow and the quality and cost of our lifestyles. Workers under age 45 tend to have a present savings rate of 3%. Workers over 45 leap up to 11%. It may not sound like much, but it is a gigantic leap. That savings rate is what the brokers want, any way they can get it. It is the pot at the end of the demographic rainbow, without which the brokerage industry will starve to death. It shouldn't be trading money. It should be invested to secure retirements. The marketing is directed to retirement-type accounts and managed accounts, which should render fees, not commissions, to the brokerage houses. The brokers are seen as dinosaurs at "progressive" houses.

The Chameleon

If you won't go back to them as stockbrokers, how about investment advisers; how about as mutual funds? There has to be some formula to get you, think the wizards of Wall Street, and they will go on trying.

If they can't get you directly, they will work on your pension fund, and get revenues from "them," which is, indirectly, YOU!

I have another homework assignment for you. Do you have a pension that depends on the investing acumen of professional managers? A lot of Americans do. Are you a teacher, fireman, airline pilot, professional athlete, etc.? Who is managing your benefits? The assignment: find out how much of your pension is invested in junk bonds. Who do you think has been buying most of the junk?

Drexel laid off a whole stable full of Street professionals when it finally rolled over and died. Where do you think they will end up? You had better pay very close attention to your pension funds. What are they buying, who is managing them, and what is their track record?

If you don't pay attention, you may have to keep on working, not for the pleasure of activity, but to pay the rent. The only institutions routinely greedy enough to buy huge blocks of junk bonds were insurance companies, pension funds, and Savings and Loans. The rest of us were chased to buy little pieces either directly or through the humorously titled "High Yield" funds that spread like dysentery through the investment world.

New York State's government employee retirement fund has close to 50 billion in assets. California's has close to 60 billion and New Jersey's has almost 40 billion. By some estimates there are close to 700 billion dollars in state pension funds, when you add them all up. That represents a lot of commissions and a mountain of investment advisor fees. It's brokerage heaven. The only problem is how to get inside the pearly gate, considering the industry's past sins.

The brokers are changing their song, but you are still the target. Invest with great care as you and I get (demographically) older.

Debt Collecting

We have heard a lot of chest thumping from the SEC about how they have taken down huge fines from Ivan Boesky, Drexel and then in the Michael Milken Guilty Plea Deal.

They don't get all cash. They get securities <u>and</u> cash, which they have to liquidate. How efficient are they? When Drexel made it's deal with the SEC for several hundred million dollars, the papers were filled with balance sheet reports of how Drexel could afford to pay and have plenty left over. The SEC was going to distribute the bulk of the "funds" to the harmed public. Now that Drexel is liquidating, the SEC is claiming that over 100 million dollars is still owed on the original deal! In late 1989, Drexel reportedly paid out over 100 million in bonuses to key employees. Nothing has been paid to investors. Drexel "went" in February, 1990. In the theater, comedy is "all timing." The same is true on Wall Street. Even in court.

Michael Milken hasn't been sentenced as of this edition, but he will probably be socked with tennis elbow at a federal club/farm/minimum security prison. He might get a consecutive sentence to unlimited golf, following upon the tennis. During his guilty plea, he broke down and cried. Ah, the crocodile tears! A defendant in Federal Court must convince the judge that he, the defendant, is guilty of the offence, that he really did it, and that he understands a guilty plea BEFORE the Federal Judge can accept the plea. If the defendant says he didn't do it, but it's a deal to avoid heavier prosecution, the judge will not accept the plea. Milken pled to several felonies. Insider trading was not one of them. Many reports say Milken's net worth is over 1 billion. So, he pays 500 million in cash <u>and</u> securities, and he keeps the rest. Not a bad deal. Guilty pleas are great theater. Such tears. Why? Sentencing will follow shortly. If the play works, champagne corks will pop as a light sentence is announced to the "remorseful" defendant. What rubbish! Deals, deals, deals, deals, deals, deals, deals, deals, deals.

CHAPTER SIXTEEN

THEY GO BANKRUPT

Watch Out!
They CAN Disappear!

This should follow within the chapter on net capital, but bankruptcy has to be examined on its own. Brokerage houses can and do go bankrupt. They make wild mistakes that would cause your head to spin, ironic because of their constant reviews and recommendations of many other businesses.

Drexel.

The next time you see an ad for a brokerage house claiming they know what they are doing or that you should trust their ability, think of Drexel. There is good old EF Hutton and Thompson McKinnon, too!.

Babe Ruth hit a lot of home runs. He regularly struck out even as he was hitting home runs at a historic pace. Drexel did great until they struck out in February, 1990, but they didn't keep on hitting home runs. The Babe's strikeouts were offset by his reliable, productive hits. He was the "Sultan of Swat" beloved by fans to this day because he gave them great memories. Drexel doesn't have that legacy.

The Wall Street Journal wailed that former United States District Attorney Rudolph Giuliani had killed Drexel by heavy handed use of the Federal RICO criminal statutes, which caused Drexel to plead guilty to its felonies and pay its enormous fines or face the prospect of being shut down. The Justice Department didn't kill Drexel. The SEC helped keep them IN business! Drexel killed Drexel.

The Journal ignores the 1990 bankruptcy filing of Campeau Corporation which cracked the junk bond market. When a billion dollar giant like Campeau went under, that was it for Drexel, whose inventory was filled with junk that had lost its allure and could no longer be used to raise cash or forestall commercial bankers who had the FDIC looking very closely over THEIR shoulders as major S&L's and commercial banks were on the rocks. The falling dominoes cause a de facto debt control.

Once the bubble burst, the Drexel empire went.

The last ones to know were the employees. It was fitting that the same firm that had abruptly dumped its retail brokerage operation should dump the rest of the operation with no notice to the rest of the staff.

Sympathy?

Save your attention for a worthy cause.

If you have considerable investments in a brokerage house, you should be concerned that in a serious economic downturn, your house will go bankrupt. Think it out, and see where you would stand. If you are a business credit manager, how much credit are you willing to extend these days to cyclical business?

How to File

In order to go bankrupt, you get a lawyer, fill out a form listing your assets and debts, file it in the US Bankruptcy Court and wait. Corporations are just like individuals, except that they come under different "chapters" of the US Bankruptcy Code. As I mentioned earlier, a broker-dealer has to surrender its license before filing, but that is not difficult. They aren't supposed to file under Chapter 11.

Most corporations file under Chapter 11; here, they are looking for protection, a time delay, while they re-organize. As soon as the filing is made, the corporation is "in" bankruptcy. It doesn't have to pay its bills, and you can't sue the corporation like before. All claims must be put into the bankruptcy proceeding, including claims for regular funds or for harm you suffered due to fraud.

Chapter 7 is death. All the assets of the firm are gathered up, then paid out to the claiming creditors, pro rata. If the assets equal $100, and the claims are $1,000, each dollar of valid claim gets 10 cents. That's it. This is where you expect a broker dealer to file.

The people who ran the corporate entity are not personally liable for the debts of the company. If they paid themselves enormous salaries while the going was good, and procured lavish perks, you will find the debts high and the assets low. In fact, one of the curiosities about bankruptcy is that it is like an autopsy. The entity is dissected and analyzed by specialists. The cause of death is the object of the search. Sometimes the real cause is surprising. When a brokerage firm goes under, the cause of death may well be "starvation," because the house died from lack of capital. Where did all the money go - "expenses" along the way. Brokerage houses run lean on little capital, not to be competitive, but because every dollar that comes in is grabbed by a hundred hands that want it NOW for salary, bonus, perks and fantasy projects.

With some companies, when they make a dollar, they use some to pay expenses, some for salaries, some for future research and development, etc. Hopefully, some is kept as a retained earning. If, after all the expenses are paid the company has an after-tax profit of 15 cents, it may decide to pay 5 cents to the shareholders as their dividend. That leaves 10 cents as a retained earning to be devoted to expansion of the company's real assets. Not the brokerage business.

Retained earnings are used up. Shareholders don't get a lot of dividends from brokerage companies, and they should question where the retained earnings are going. Lately, they have been going to pay for losses in firm trading accounts.

Drexel wasn't a public company, so it's death came as something of a surprise, yes? No. Once Campeau Corporation went into bankruptcy, Wall Street was waiting to see how long Drexel would last. It wasn't a question of "maybe" but "when." Drexel's demise caused hardly a ripple in the financial markets, where the professionals had seen Campeau go into bankruptcy, but it must have been a shocker at the SEC where they bent over backwards to save Drexel. The SEC now claims to be a creditor!

Chapter 11 is aimed at reorganization. Suppose a company has a regular payroll, telephone bills, and inventory costs. If it's a gas station, the gas in its tanks is essential to keep going. That's the inventory. Suppose also that the gas station has a large bank loan to pay next week, but it doesn't have the funds and the bank is demanding timely payment. No extensions. If the gas station files under Chapter 11, it does not have to close its doors. It can ask the Bankruptcy Court for permission to stay open, to pay the wages of the employees, and keep gas deliveries coming for cash payment. BUT, the gas station may ask to delay paying the bank loan. The Court will probably agree. The bank has to wait.

Some law firms specialize in bankruptcy, especially on Wall Street. You may smile or smirk at this, but good legal talent makes money when the market goes up and when it goes down, either building corporate structures or tearing them down. It's just business.

As soon as a bankruptcy filing is made, the creditors are frozen out. When you have traded securities with a house and it files for bankruptcy, you have trouble. The firm may or may not want to come out of bankruptcy. It can file under Chapter 11 and then go into chapter 7. Creditors can force the filer from Chapter 11 into Chapter 7. If the house isn't around to support the price of your penny stocks, who will?

What Are the Assets Worth?

What are a brokerage house's assets worth?

Very little. True, they spend a lot of time recruiting brokers from each other, but they have little in the bank and less in assets. The retained earnings have gone up in smoke on peculiar projects, and there are no hard, salable assets lying around. There is no vault loaded with gold, only paper.

Because real estate cannot be used as an asset when computing net capital, they rent space. They don't own it. If they own the buildings, they can't use them in net capital, so land owning firms are the first to go when times are tough.

They own leases.

In theory, a lease has some value because it contains the right to occupy a premises for a set time at a set price. That's great if prices for rents are going up, but a disaster if rents are going down. In the entire Eastern US, they are going down. In Manhattan, they are plummeting.

The leases, therefore, don't represent an asset that could be sublet for a profit - they represent a liability. The desks, lights, wall coverings and file cabinets are worth very little. I go to used office furniture auctions to bargain shop, and the prices are great - for me! The books and records are worth something IN THEORY because they contain the trading histories of all the firm's clients, client lists and other items of commercial worth.

But, the client records have no value because the accounts usually go with the broker. The house doesn't own your account - you do. The house can't sell your account to someone with an assurance that you will decide to do business with the buying firm. Customer lists are available from a number of sources. The corporate books and records have no value. The computers are usually set up to run with special software and are not readily transferrable to another firm's records without some tinkering. "Book Value" is very, very subjective.

The brokers can't be sold. Slavery is illegal. They can go where they want. Purchases of a brokerage firm concentrate on keeping the brokers by promising bonuses, higher payouts, and special perks. You buy the brokers one at a time from the brokers themselves, not the firm. The traders who manned the central desks and traded the firm's own accounts are usually the ones who delivered the disaster on a lead platter. Wall Street "Boat People."

What's left? The securities left in the firm's own trading accounts. Be very careful about this.

Suppose a house has been hyping the daylights out of a bunch of cheap stocks or junk bonds. You may own some of these hot items. Usually, it's a stock that costs under five dollars and has had a sudden rise from under a dollar. The house was probably a market maker in the stock - AND MAY HAVE BEEN THE ONLY MARKET MAKER OR ONE OF THE MAIN MARKET MAKERS.

When that firm folds, the value of the stock folds. The house is no longer supporting it. Like a tire running over a nail, the price blows out, and goes flat. The house inventory, full of former $3 stock is now full of the same stock with no value. The "inventory" has no distribution value.

Who gets paid what?

It depends.

Ultimately, a decision on value has to be made. Your defined, segregated positions are yours. They don't belong to the firm. The value of your penny stocks has probably been killed. If you were on margin, watch out; you will be sold out as the firm goes to complete cash positions. You may see enormous losses because all the penny stock is being sold out at the same time to reduce the margin exposure. Why the sell out? When you borrow from the firm to go on margin, the house, in turn, borrows money for your margin loan from a bank. The securities you buy on margin are actually pledged to the bank to secure the loan which went from the bank, to the broker, to you. If the broker can't pay the loan, the bank will foreclose. If the broker goes into Chapter 11, the stock will sooner or later be sold out to pay the bank back on its loan.

With penny stocks, you will get "murdered" in a big, forced sell out if your now-bankrupt firm was the principal market maker. The same will happen with junk bonds.

If your brokers were a bunch of crooks who literally stole some of your securities, SIPC may come along to settle accounts, but remember, SIPC has nothing to do with losses that come from decreased value. No one insures against a loss in market value.

SIPC is not insurance. I apologize for the repetition, but it's a concern of great magnitude. I am not aware of any firm that carries bankruptcy insurance to cover resultant market losses of firm-supported stocks or of any insurance carrier crazy enough to issue it.

What do you do if your brokerage firm goes bankrupt? Get a lawyer right away. You may have to get into the bankruptcy proceeding, but think this out carefully. Counsel is not going to act on your behalf for free. It can cost you a lot. There may be no assets in the failed firm and even if it filed Chapter 11, it may go into Chapter 7.

Don't worry about the brokerage firm's principals. They will probably do fine, because they have seen it coming for a while. You won't be able to get at them for all the salary and bonus they took out of the brokerage firm in the past.

The brokerage house reports its finances to you every six months by enclosing a financial report with your monthly statement. They report to the SEC. Can you read the brokerage reports about its financial condition? Have you ever tried to read it? Even if you did read it, could you tell a bankruptcy was coming? Probably not. Sudden reverses in trading the firm's accounts may not be predictable.

If you understand that the typical brokerage house doesn't have a lot of hard, liquid assets, then you must sense they can go at any time, especially if they have to borrow on a regular basis to meet cash flow needs. If the bankers, who DO know how to read those financial reports, say "NO," that's it. No more short term loans. Chapter 11.

A banker in 1990 is not like a banker from 1988. The FDIC is all over the bankers because of numerous bank failures.

Brokerage houses run on such thin capital that they can disappear in a flash. Some have. More will. Big ones and little ones.

Suppose you kept the penny stock at home? It wouldn't help. Taking delivery would mean you couldn't go on margin. Margin stock must be kept at the house because it is pledged against the loan from the bank. If you pay 100% of the purchase price you can take delivery and keep the certificates in a vault. If the firm files Chapter 11, and if the certificates are for penny stock or junk bonds principally supported by that firm, it doesn't matter whether you have the certificates at home or in the brokerage house: they have little value.

Once you are wiped out, if you want to pursue a claim for fraud, you may be cashing a phantom, a firm with no assets, already in bankruptcy.

The best lawyers cannot squeeze blood from the proverbial stone. No assets - no recovery. If you want to pursue the individual officers and directors of the firm, it will take a massive effort. You will have to prove a virtual criminal, fraudulent conspiracy on the officer's part to chase them as individuals. Even if you can pursue them, do they have any assets you can get at?

Forget the SEC. They won't help. They can't: no staff. They may bring some administrative actions against the failed brokerage firm and a few officers of the firm, but that won't get you a cent.

Do you own penny stock? Do you own junk bonds? Why?

Who is supporting the price? How many market makers are there? Who are they? How solid are they?

Why do you trust them?

As long as you own penny stock with tiny market makers, YOU DO give implicit trust. Some brokers are small and honest. Some are small and bad.

Do you see that owning junk bonds supported by a giant can leave you in the same position - with assets that drop in value no matter where you have them: at home, in a vault, or at the house.

Think about this very carefully. If you own penny stock or junk bonds at the recommendation of your broker, why do you trust that broker?

In bankruptcy, the United States protects the filing party, the SEC may pop in to protect the quantitative "public interest," but no knight in shining armor is there to protect you.

Just you. You may be a creditor in a crowd of equally distraught and confused creditors.

Some Data

October 19, 1987. The Dow drops 508 points.
October 13, 1989. The Dow drops 190 points.
October 26, 1987. The Dow drops 156 points.
January 8, 1988. The Dow drops 140 points.

Read the financial press about who's filing for bankruptcy. You should be concerned when billion dollar giants file because the ripples go far beyond the wreckage in the Federal Bankruptcy Court. What happens to their creditors, to the suppliers whose bills can't be paid on time, to the telephone company that may never get paid?

Look for quality in your investments; don't be impressed by the "quality" of the house. It can be a giant and go into bankruptcy. Mistakes kill these firms because they have no room for error. Their capital is too thin. When they get into trouble by trading their accounts, they can't go to the bankers anymore and say, "How about a loan with the big 'inventory' as your security?" Brokerage houses haven't any hard assets. They go to the bankers and say, "how about a loan for old times' sake?" The bankers decline. There are no real assets, only paper investments and leases.

Do you remember how large corporations in the late 1980's filed in Chapter 11 Bankruptcy as union-busting tactics or as a way to settle major lawsuits? Those were real companies, with real assets. They can go into a reorganization and come out. A brokerage house will have a hard time. It has to give up its license. As soon as it goes into bankruptcy, its accounts will probably be distributed to other houses. If it is a member of the NYSE, the Exchange gets on the telephone with its members and divides the accounts, even creating a pool to provide cash to the accepting house to make sure it will not have a loss if it stands up for the Exchange community.

The car, by analogy, is stripped as soon as it stops.

The Double Pump
Borrowing on Borrowed Money

We are now ascending to very thin air, the altitude where you can have delusions about the physical reality around you. You can even get knocked out by the lack of oxygen. This is high finance.

Margin is a very dangerous form of investing. You borrow value from the brokerage house in order to buy more stock than your cash allows. If Finegan Motors is selling at 100 per share, you can buy only 100 shares with $10,000. If you go on margin, however, you can buy 200 shares. The account has a total value at the moment you buy the shares of $20,000, but you have only $10,000 of equity in the account. You have borrowed $10,000 from the brokerage house, and you will pay interest on that money you borrowed. If Finegan Motors goes down 10 points, you have lost $2,000 or $10 for each of the 200 shares. You still owe the brokerage house the same money - the $10,000 you borrowed to buy your shares.

With margin, when you win, because you have used leverage, you can increase your profits. When you lose, however, you lose a lot, because leverage works on the way down, too. Under NYSE Rules at this time, you cannot go below 25% equity on stocks.

Remember how the account was set up - you put down 50% of the purchase price, or $10,000 on the total price of $20,000 for the 200 shares of Finegan Motors at 100 per share. If the value of Finegan Motors drops, it is your equity that drops. If all your account has in it is Finegan Motors, it is concentrated. Concentrated accounts are not allowed to get down to the 25% floor because it might drop right through to 0% in a flash.

In our example, suppose the price of Finegan Motors dropped to 50 per share. The account would have a total market value of $10,000 and the margin debit would be $10,000 which means all your equity has been wiped out and you are now risking the firm's own capital. You will probably get a margin call from the firm when the price of Finegan Motors got to somewhere around 15 per share. This would mean that your equity in the account was down to $5,000, and the total value of the account was $15,000. The house is free to require MORE than the NYSE floor of 25%, and in my little example they required 35%. They will call you for the money. If you don't pay it, they will consider selling out some or all of your position to raise the amount of equity in the account to a level they are comfortable with. You will be selling, paying a commission on your involuntary way out of positions.

If the account got down to 25% maintenance of equity, they would again have to sell you out. That would happen when the market value got down to 13,333.33 in this example.

How do you calculate the 25% call level?

First, find the total debit balance in the account. Here it was $10,000. Divide that by 1 minus the percent maintenance requirement, which was 25% here. Thus, the divisor will be 1 minus .25 which equals .75. $10,000 divided by .75 equals $13,333.33.

You can use that formula to calculate margin calls when the percentages vary on house requirements, but remember, a house does not want you to get below 25% so they will generally set a call for an earlier time, such as 30% or 35%, especially when there is a concentration in the account.

A customer can get a double pump from his money by going to a bank and borrowing some money as a non-purpose, general loan. He takes the borrowed money over to the brokerage house and uses that as the "equity" in his account to borrow another amount from the broker.

This is extremely dangerous, because any decline in the price of the shares will mean the customer may not be able to pay back the bank. He is losing the money they lent to him. If the broker knows the customer is doing this, the broker should stop it at once, or refuse to allow the account. It is too dangerous and violates the credit rules for the brokerage house and the Federal Reserve. A bad broker might tell you to go borrow the cash in the first place! Don't do it!

It is easy to see how this house of cards could crumble under pressure from market losses and bankers asking to be repaid. If the loan has been lost in the market, the bankers cannot be repaid.

A retail customer should never do this. It's dangerous and illegal.

Some brokerage houses do a variation of this monetary double pump.

That's right. They have their parent corporation go out and borrow money in its own corporate name. That cash, loaned from a bank, insurance company, or other institutional lender that theoretically knows what it is doing, is then placed in investments at the subsidiary broker. If the value of the investments goes sour, the parent may not be able to pay back the bank; in those cases the parent will try to make a deal for an extension of time to pay, letting the interest add on to the loan.

This is called capitalizing the interest on the loan. It was done with billions of dollars of interest on Latin American loans in the 1980's until banks finally had to start taking the losses on bad loans. Because of Latin America and the present Savings and Loan disaster, Federal Banking regulators, the FDIC and the Federal Reserve are closely scrutinizing the banks, so the banks have to be very careful about what they do.

They are slow to even CONSIDER capitalizing interest any more.

If the parent corporation can't pay on time, it better have hard, valuable assets to carry the loan for more time. Brokerage houses don't have hard, valuable assets. The parent can run into insolvency and the broker subsidiary could go as part of the corporate pyramid.

It can happen if Junk Bonds were used as the investment vehicle for the bank's loan money, or any other investment security that fluctuates widely in value.

Don't think that institutions are any wiser than you are now, this far into the book. They may have more facts at their command, which means they should be able to act sensibly, but they may not be able to make logical decisions. You know a lot of their tricks now. When you see an institutional loan debacle, where large amounts were loaned to a thinly capitalized business (or country) recall that paychecks and bonuses for the lending executives depended on the loan transaction. They are not debited for those salaries and bonus amounts if the deal fails later on. Lenders have to set up systems to make sure that loans are sound, that they make business sense now and in the long term. These committees are essential to normal banking operations. They may be called loan committees, commitment committees or other names in various institutions.

Nonetheless, the Savings and Loan Industry is reeling under bad real estate loans. The commercial banking industry is getting past its Latin debt bomb and dealing with its own real estate problems. The securities industry is beginning to deal with the debt situation.

Debt was popular in the 1980's. It was everywhere. It was used to buy all manner of things, including billion dollar companies. A lot of the debt is non or low rated - junk. What happens when investors stop buying this junk because they see a billion dollar company fail to pay on time? What happens when the bubble breaks?

What happens when the condo developers can't sell their condos?

Business failures.

Does your brokerage house exist as a subsidiary within a corporate holding chain? Does the parent borrow from institutions and then put the money into the brokerage house's investments? What are the quality of those investments?

If you ask your broker, he will know if his brokerage house is a subsidiary of a corporate parent, but he will not know if the parent is borrowing to put cash into the house's investments. He is "Chinese Walled" off from that as explained in the Chapter on that eastern mystery.

In my opinion, the double pump should be illegal. It would be foolhardy for a retail customer to do it. It should be illegal for a parent corporation to do it with its brokerage subsidiary. This is another reason why the firm's trading records should be fully disclosed to its customers every month, so that investors who have put their cash and securities in the house can see if the house is acting prudently with its own assets. A balance sheet will only tell you the amount of value in accounts, not what is actually there. If the accounts are filled with junk, the house is in for trouble if the value of the junk drops. Let people see what the assets are, not just the theoretical, aggregate market value, which can change on the moment.

This isn't radical. If the house doesn't want to disclose its investments, then it can drop its broker-dealer license and trade as a private institutional entity, without holding your assets in trust. If it holds your assets, why should it be allowed to trade and jeopardize itself?

Because over 20% of house income in 1987 came from trading house accounts, according to the SEC Annual Report for 1988? That's not enough justification. They should either be stopped from trading their own accounts, or made to disclose exactly what they have just done, which will allow you to think about what you should do.

Trading maniacs.

And you trust them with your money?

If you saw the securities in their firm accounts you might be pleased or terrified. If you buy a T.V. set, you pay and take the set with you. Do you care if the store files in bankruptcy the next day? No. You have the T.V. set.

If you wanted to buy a new car, you would go to a showroom and make a selection. The car dealer would want a deposit. New cars must be delivered. Even if the car is on the lot, preparation and registration will take several days. If you put a deposit down on Monday and the dealer files in bankruptcy on Tuesday, you do not get the car on Wednesday,and your deposit is part of the bankrupt's assets. You are stuck. Even if you don't worry about bankruptcy on short term purchases, you know that a deposit is a tricky item.

Your securities account is not at a bank. There is no "insurance" covering you. Be very careful about picking a firm. If you buy penny stock that has only a few small active market makers, you can lose your investment if the market maker disappears.

Bankruptcy happens fast. The firm runs out of money AND credit. Credit is the most important item, because it is the life-blood of business. Whether a brokerage files or not, if it is broke, it is effectively dead. Under SEC Rule 15b6-1, a brokerage is supposed to file a form BDW to withdraw from its license. The withdrawal takes 60 days. Business collapse does not give YOU 60 days. You can be hurt on day 1. Please, check out the house before you let them hold your account.

There can be an element of humor in most situations, however serious they might appear. Drexel is effectively gone (for now). By this point in the book, you understand the fleeting cash life cycle of a brokerage house. The New York Stock Exchange is rumored to be preparing a disciplinary case against Drexel, seeking 25 million dollars in fines. Oliver Cromwell, the Lord Protector of England, was a Puritan Powerhouse who toppled the English Monarchy in 1645, and took power. He died peacefully in 1658. After his death, the monarchy was restored. Cromwell was so hated, a mob dug up his body, cut it into pieces and displayed his head on a pike in London. By that time, Cromwell probably didn't care.

The NYSE should ask for 25 BILLION. They could then dig Drexel up, rip the remains apart like a dog shaking a dead rat, and proclaim moral victory. It's too late. Drexel fell peacefully. When the chips were down and times called for courageous action, the NYSE did what it has perfected over the last half century - nothing. Drexel, according to late reports, is going to try to make a small comeback in the investment business after a brief period of "reorganization."

CHAPTER SEVENTEEN

FRIENDS AND STRANGERS

The SEC
The SRO's

When you have a problem with a broker and you have tried to get it resolved in an orderly way inside the firm, where do you go? Who is your friend? Who is there to help you out before you have to go to the time and expense of getting a lawyer.

It's not the SEC. Within its bureaucratic structure, the SEC has a cadre of "consumer affairs specialists." When you complain to the SEC about your account, your letter is sent to this poor section.

Their job: they take your letter and send it to the brokerage house asking that the brokerage house respond to the complaint by writing to the complaining customer and sending a copy of the letter to the SEC.

The brokerage house sends you a letter that says they still think you're a crackpot, and they send a copy to the SEC.

That's it.

There must be a dimly lit, ivory white file room somewhere in subterranean Washington, DC, filled with stale air, with mildew growing on the sides of file cartons, stacked floor-to-ceiling, containing the pleading letters of abused brokerage customers, haunted by the anguish of past financial trauma. Every week more boxes go in, boxes of new letters, with the brokerage denials attached.

Go back in time. Chairman Douglas worked out the rule of primacy. In 1939 it was clear that the exchanges had the responsibility to deal with customer complaints, not the SEC. The SEC was going to watch the exchanges, but not deal with the public on individual matters. That has remained the policy, although the SEC now says it is going to change. It won't be able to change unless the SEC staff is greatly, greatly increased, which will not be the case.

According to its 1988 Annual report to the Congress, the SEC handled a total of 10 civil actions against brokerage houses involving fraud against a customer.

You may feel that is acceptable because of the hundreds of insider trading cases they brought. Wrong. In fiscal 1988, the SEC brought 21 civil actions involving insider trading. 21!

The SRO's brought 1,336 final disciplinary actions in fiscal 1988 covering many different kinds of infractions. Most were settlements.

So what does the SEC do with its staff? They review filings. Forget insider trading and all the headline grabbing. In fiscal 1988, the SEC reviewed 10,985 corporate filings including all kinds of reports from proxies to quarterly filings and 13-D control statements, covering 2,941 issuers. Don't they recognize the problem? Sure. This is a quote from their 1988 Annual Report to Congress:

> "Penny Stocks have become the subject of numerous manipulative schemes. Typically, these schemes involve "shell" companies, either newly formed "blank check" companies (companies which conduct registered offerings disclosing that the proposed use of proceeds is to seek business opportunities) or older companies with no assets or operations, but small trading markets. These companies are then merged with

private companies purported by the promoters to have great growth potential. Stocks in the merged companies are promoted through releases announcing the merger and marketed to the investing public through the use of extreme high pressure tactics. The securities may then be manipulated to reach inflated prices, at which point the promoters may dump shares they own, and move on.

Participants in these schemes may include promoters, broker-dealers, attorneys, accountants, and transfer agents. While the shares are low priced, often actually in pennies, profits of broker dealers involved in trading these stocks can be enormous, and investors can suffer major losses. These schemes have spread nationwide, and the Commission has commenced active programs to deal with them, including establishment of an in-house task force to propose regulatory solutions."

They know exactly what's going on, and they have commissioned a study to explain what is essentially ancient history, even as the problem rumbles along, nationwide. They don't have the people to do anything about it. The SEC got about 49,000 complaints or inquiries from investors in fiscal 1988. 49,000!

To deal with the penny stock problem, the SEC enacted a rule requiring brokers to send a risk disclosure to customers who purchase unlisted stocks costing less than $5 per share. Having passed a rule, the problem will politely go away. The bureaucrats think rules solve all problems. The problem will continue. Bad brokers will lie, steal and cheat. Rules have never bothered them. They forge margin and option papers - they'll forge these papers. People sign blank forms, "trusting" their broker. Clients will blindly sign such forms. What is the SEC doing?

They see the financials from the shells, but they do hardly any enforcement work. No staff, no money, no headlines.

If you read the reports from the SRO's about the kinds of cases that make up the 1,000+ actions mentioned above, it's usually something like churning or theft from an account by an individual broker, or bookkeeping problems with houses.

The SRO's are supposed to be policing the industry, but year in and year out, they keep turning up bad brokers who do illegal things to customers, such as churning, stealing, switching mutual funds and selling completely unsuitable securities to retail investors in order to take down high commissions. No one goes to jail for churning. The SRO's typically do not kick the wrongdoer out for life, and they do not touch the senior officers who are supposed to stop bad brokers from harming people in the first place. They let criminal firms stay in the business.

WHO IS REALLY OUT THERE TO PROTECT YOU?

The entity most on your side is the securities department of your state government. That department is a member of the North American Securities Administrators Association, Inc. The President of NASAA is Susan E. Bryant, a regulator from Oklahoma. Your state regulators are known as "Blue Sky" authorities from an old brokerage usage.

They may be part of the department of banking, or the insurance department, or in the state attorney general's office. My experience with state regulators was that they dealt with the grass roots level - you - as a constituency, not a statistic, because they are a working part of your LOCAL government. They have jurisdiction over anyone that does securities business in the state, and they'll use it to stop abuses and to try to help you as much as possible, remembering that fair play means they don't assume you are 100% right. They seem more patient, more willing to poke around to see if there is something to your complaint. They impressed me as fair.

Perhaps, because the state people do not have a Wall Street job agenda in progress, they are less afraid to ruffle the powers that be on the Street. The states are more prone to act to lock bad guys up when they find evil shell promoters hurting retail investors.

The state regulators get together in NASAA, which then deals for the group with the SEC and the SRO's on policy issues, although each state acts completely on its own in an individual case. The organization has a president, elected by the members, and an agenda of communication and education so that word can spread within NASAA that a problem exists, rather than waiting for victims in the respective states to show up. State regulators need your input. They want to hear from you when you have problems.

Most people who are harmed by bad brokers overlook this local, state office. Victims assume the SEC is there to help them, or that the NYSE will rush to their aid. Victims believe that in threatening to send letters to these famous regulators, the brokers will tremble and roll over. No way. The houses don't care if you publish a book, take out a full page ad, or rent a billboard to say what rats they have been. The usual response to a customer who threatens to write letters is, "go ahead!" It won't produce anything. It doesn't hurt, but don't hold your breath waiting for the cavalry, and don't waste time waiting for action.

Keep your securities business within your home state to the greatest extent possible so that if trouble occurs, you can contact your state regulators with your story. They will have the broker and branch manager under their microscope.

Please note that I have once again explained that penny stocks are dangerous. Don't buy stock under $5 per share unless you have considered the mathematics of roulette first and decided that a particular investment has better odds. Even then, consider betting on horses. Retail investors should not buy penny stocks, especially when they have a hot story behind them. They are dangerous, easily manipulated, and they appeal to one's sense of daring and GREED, not common sense! Sharp, modern marketeers may be at work. If you have been "tipped" on a hot, cheap stock, give a call to your state securities people to see if the stock can even be sold in your state. Securities are registered not only on the federal level, but on the state level, too. Most of the state registration requirements for securities that are listed on licensed exchanges are fairly automatic. That's also true if the company has regularly reported its financials to the public rating and reporting services such as Standard and Poors. Be suspicious of out-of-state cold calls from brokers who want to tip you to a hot stock.

New companies, partnerships, or companies that have come back from limbo have a more extensive registration process. The states do this to make sure that numbers are available to you locally, through a state office.

The state people can't tell you what to invest in - only you can decide that. But, they can tell you what is registered and available to you in that state, and they are always interested in hearing about what securities or deals are being offered to the public. If it hasn't been registered, they will jump into action to get the issuing company to comply with disclosure. Some companies comply, but it's a great way to discover and stop a scam from getting to you, because some will disappear once the state contacts them.

Absolutely phoney deals can be stopped at the state level. Completely fraudulent, non-existent matters can be caught early and stopped, if you call to check on the deal. The state regulators want to hear about all these deals so they can catch the bad ones.

Like a wave, criminals will start at one end of the country and make their way across, state by state, swindling people with completely phoney deals. I'm not talking about high-risk deals - I mean completely phoney ones. Your state securities people want to catch these criminals before they fade into the background. Call and check! It can't hurt. It takes a few minutes. The security and the salesman should be registered in the state or exempt because of specific legal reasons recognized by the state. If the deal can't wait a few minutes for your investigation, be on guard! Always think through your investments. If there isn't enough time, don't invest!

CHAPTER EIGHTEEN

JUSTICE AND REVENGE

Take Courage
Recognize Your Harm

By now, you see that there is no magic in the investment world, just a lot of specialty, which necessarily makes you feel like financial people must know what they are doing, that they are somehow more intelligent, more in control and more able to make decisions than you.

Rubbish! If you work at it, you can be as sharp as the Street. Probably the most difficult activity undertaken by civilized people is raising their children. The average two-year old is far more difficult to understand, faster on their two-year old feet, more fickle, and mysterious than the wildest days on the New York Stock Exchange. Any debate would be superfluous.

If you have not managed to go to the local library, you have let me down. You must go; you have to! Turn off the TV at night and go on down to one of America's great institutions, one of the beacons of a free society - the library. If you don't study, you are conceding an advantage to the Street: knowledge. The bad guys on Wall Street depend on <u>your</u> ignorance to abuse <u>your</u> money.

Recognizing you've been "had" is hard to do. It takes courage to deal with fraudulent reality because you can come to a hard question: how could I have let him (the broker) do that to me?

It bears the cloud of embarrassment, doesn't it? Consumers get beat all the time by bunko characters such as the con man that sells phoney silverware, super deluxe tires that wear out after a trip around the block, rodent repellents that fizzle in the face of repeat appearances of rats, paint that flakes, and one of the worst - screwdrivers with pot metal tips that shear when you are wedged under your car at night, surrounded by parts and wires, suffering cut fingers.

I once saw a Detroit auto jack buckle while holding a car up to change a tire. A factory issued jack. Smash! Fortunately, the tire was still on, although unbolted, and no one was underneath.

The trouble with brokerage accounts is that the damage happens right out in the open, over time. It's not a one-shot deal where you feel a desire for revenge against the con man, his ancestors, and all persons in his orbit.

Brokerage "fallout" is not apparent when you are dealing with the broker. It happens quietly, reflected by the mail, not by any specific noise or product failure. People that get worked over feel a sense of personal frustration in having let it happen.

They usually didn't know it was happening, but when they complain, the brokerage house will tell them that they got confirmations of each trade, statements of monthly activity, that they signed numerous documents which agreed to give the broker power to go on margin and that the customer bought the "oil well" or other deal after signing a form that said he knew what he was doing, could afford the risk, and wanted, on his own, to do it.

High pressure sales turns into higher pressure defense when you make an accusation. The broker reacts with umbrage, disdain, that you as a customer would dare to complain. Why, they contend, it was your own greed as a conniving customer that got you to this point, not the work of the poor broker!

After all, the broker didn't make the decisions - you did. He was only your agent; you were in charge. How dare you even question the integrity of this staid old brokerage house where everyone tries so hard on your behalf.

GO ahead, write to the SEC, the NYSE, the NASD! Write to your Congressional Representatives and Senators. The house lawyers will respond in the future.

How do you feel? It's like looking up the side of a skyscraper while you stand at the entrance door - you can't see the top. The structure seems to touch heaven.

Take heart.

Throw the embarrassment syndrome into the trash. Get it out of your mind! People, as consumers, get destroyed every day in the finance business. They usually find out when they have to round up a lot of cash for an emergency, retirement, to buy a house, pay for a wedding, etc. The cash isn't there! The other way is when they get a notice that the account is being sold out to pay off a margin debit.

The money, your money, is gone, in whole or in part, and it happened through the efforts of your "friend," the broker.

Customers get beat, and beat, and beat, and beat. They will continue to get beat because the industry has no reason to change, and no one is going to force them to change.

Let's do a little inspection of your brokerage materials and overall market portfolio, not for the sake of maximizing your profits, but to see if it's time to call for help. This is a private, easy, self-test. Make a note of your answers on a separate piece of paper.

Let's Do a Review

Get out your brokerage materials right now!

1. How much did you pay in commissions last year?

2. How much did you pay in bond mark-ups and on principal trades with the brokerage house?

3. Are you on margin? Does your statement show that you have paid any interest to the brokerage house, at all, last year or this year?

4. Do you own any stocks worth less than FIVE Dollars?

5. Do you own any stocks worth less than TEN Dollars?

6. Do you own any bonds from any issuer at all?

7. Do you know the S&P or Moody's ratings on your bonds?

8. Are any of your bonds rated BBB (triple "B")or less?

9. Do you own any mutual funds?

10. Are your funds loaded or no-loads?

11. Did you buy the funds understanding what a breakpoint, right of accumulation or letter of intent was?

12. What kind of funds have you bought in the past five years: are they Aggressive Stock Funds, High Yield Bond Funds, US Government Funds?

13. What did you pay to get into these funds?

14. Did you switch the same principal from a Loaded Stock Fund to a Loaded Bond Fund during the past two years?

15. Do you own any limited partnership interests?

16. What activity does the partnership work in - horses, gold, oil, etc.?

17. What did you pay to buy in?

18. How much of that payment went to work on the deal and how much was eaten up by promoters' fees in the first year?

19. Can you read an annual report for a corporation, or just a simple balance sheet?

20. Do you understand how the directors and officers are elected by any of the corporations whose stock you own?

21. Do your companies have staggered boards?

22. How much of the stock is owned by the officers and directors?

23. How much is owned by institutions?

24. Have you voted in any of the corporate elections by using a proxy or by attending the meeting?

25. Has your broker ever sent you material about the balance sheet of companies he recommends?

26. Has your broker ever sent you material about the makeup of company boards, or the breakdown of who owns large blocks of the stock?

27. Do you save all the materials that your brokerage house sends you?

28. Is your broker your "friend?"

29. If you noticed an unauthorized trade in your account, would you be prepared to fire your broker?

30. If you decided the recommendations from your broker were unsuitable for your economic needs, ability and experience, would you be willing to fire your broker?

31. What would it take for you to fire your broker?

32. Have you ever spoken to the branch manager of the office that handles your account?

33. Have you ever attended a seminar put on by a brokerage house, financial planner or money manager?

34. Have you ever made an investment recommended by a brokerage house seminar?

35. Was it your idea or their recommendation?

36. Have you given general discretion to your broker to make investments on your behalf?

37. Have you ever given written discretion to your broker?

38. Have you ever read a margin agreement?

39. Have you ever signed a margin agreement?

40. Are you on margin?

41. Can you read and understand your brokerage statement?

42. Can you tell from your statement if you are on margin?

43. Do you pay full commissions at your brokerage house?

44. Have you ever asked for a discount on commissions?

45. If your broker won't give you a discount, either because he simply won't or because he claims his branch manager won't allow it, would you fire the broker and move your account?

46. Do you believe your broker does his own research?

47. Do you do your own research?

48. Do you read the financial press?

49. Do you have a family accountant and lawyer?

50. If you were confused by your investments, where would you go for help to understand what happened?

Now What?
Grade the Exam!

How did you do? It's not a matter of having a right answer, but of having ANY answer. This is exactly the kind of information you need to be in control of your account. It's not hard to gather the facts.

This list of fifty questions goes to the heart of the matter, helping you figure out who is in charge your finances. If you don't have the answers to these questions, you should start working on solutions by re-reading this book and hustling down to the library.

No, you don't have to go back to school to learn how to read a financial statement, but you could pop into a bookstore to get a copy of a book that tells you how to do it. Get some annual reports. You don't have to own stock in the company to get their report. Determine the report you want. Would you like Ford's or G.M.'s, or how about IBM? Call their home office and tell the general switchboard that you want a copy of their annual report. They will put you in contact with either the corporate secretary's office or the shareholder relations people. Most public companies are happy to send reports to get the word out about how the company is doing. It might attract more investors, making the stock more liquid. It's good for business. If you go to the library and read financial magazines, you'll see ads asking if you would like a copy of a company's annual report.

You don't buy the report - it's free.

I keep coming back to discretion and margin, then I re-emphasize the idea of suitability. Most accounts that are abused suffer from these torments.

Does your broker use discretion? Do you want him to? Why does he have to use discretion? In reality, he doesn't need discretion unless you are heavily into options, which I hope you are not. Brokers that say they want or need discretion are giving you a warning signal, like a wolf showing it's teeth. A bad one might be getting ready to eat you up! A professional can control discretion, understanding the danger.

Are you ready to fire your broker if he gets out of line? You have to make that policy decision now, before you go any further. Brokers are not ordinary salesmen; they work in a special, licensed industry and they are required to know what they are doing before they get hold of your assets. They know the rules. When a bad one breaks the rules, he knows he is doing something wrong. A lot of morality is built into the rules to protect individuals from getting destroyed by a bad broker, but a good deal of common sense goes in to keep customers coming back to do more transactional business.

What I'm really getting at is this: if you and your broker discuss IBM common and decide to buy it after looking at the real numbers and prospects for the company, and if you really direct the trade, you have no complaint against the broker. If he recommended it and it goes down, that's tough. You might tell him, "Rasputin, I want all winners," but no broker can guarantee success. If you want to fire him or give him several chances to come up with a winner, it's up to you.

If a bad broker uses wrongful discretion in your account, he knows exactly what he is doing. It doesn't just happen. He has to fill in an order ticket, give it to his cage, enter the trade in his posting book, and wait to get paid. He gets the confirmation for the trade, just as you do. Fire him.

Don't wait. Repeat - fire him. Don't waste your time talking to him, offering him a chance to get out of the jam he put himself in, fire him! Call his branch manager, get that trade out of your account and get an explanation from the manager in writing. But, fire that broker! Get his greedy little hands off your assets.

If you let him get away once, he could destroy you the next time because he knows you have no guts. If he can talk his way out of a trade made on wrongful discretion, he'll laugh at you and think you are a dolt! He'll wait, and when the time is right, he'll walk over you again.

If the trade he did is profitable, but he did it using wrongful discretion, fire him!

Got it? Wrongful discretion is easy - fire the bum!

Revenge

Forget revenge. In business, revenge is a waste of time and usually makes people spend a lot of money for nothing remotely connected to a tangible result. Revenge sells novels and fills legends with a grand momentum of passion. It fulfills the requirement of plot in second rate plays, but it is hardly productive in real life.

It doesn't pay the rent, taste good, walk, talk or take out the trash. It doesn't undo what happened.

In the money business, if someone harms you, what good is revenge? Does it give you your money back? No. Does it make you feel better? My experience says "no;" people think it does, but it really doesn't. Revenge produces nothing that matters, adds nothing to honor, and glorifies small minds who can't tell the difference between right and wrong.

Justice

Justice accommodates the best in all of us. If someone runs over your foot, nothing on this earth can undo the fact that your foot was run over. It happened. It's history. It can't be rewritten.

Justice looks at the event and tries to figure out a solution to a problem, but cannot make the event disappear. In our culture, if someone runs over your foot without justification or legal excuse, they are liable to you for your damages, which might include having to pay for your medical bills.

Justice tries to right the wrong by using money as the equalizer.

If the fellow who runs over your foot has no money or insurance, you cannot recover. There is no debtor's prison, no slavery. People don't go to jail for accidents.

One of the worst things you can do is threaten to get someone locked up if they don't pay for your damages. In some places that kind of threat may be a crime in itself, and it's just plain dumb. What good would it do if you had to follow up and get someone thrown in jail in order to squeeze money out of them? Are they really going to pay any quicker? No. Violent felons and drug animals rarely go to jail as it is. Do you think a district attorney is going to waste his time acting as your collection agency when he's chasing dope gangs?

In order for Justice to work, you have to make some decisions. The first is to act.

You have to keep control of your accounts. It's your money. When you find something bad has happened, hopefully you will discover it early, before it has time to fester and wipe you out. When you find something bad, you have to be willing to fire your broker.

You have to be tough. Bad brokers will try to talk you out of doing something. They'll try to confuse you; if that doesn't work, they'll plead with you. Some will try to pay you off on the side and promise they'll never do it again.

When they plead, they tell you that, yes, what they did was wrong, but if you turn them in, they will get fired, their family will have no income, and they will be thrown out in the gutter. The kids, the dog: they will become street people! Are you willing to do that to them?

Do it!

Pleading is a line of hot air. Soft hearts fall for it, and the bad broker does it again, bigger. Don't wait.

If there is a key, it's "DON'T WAIT!" You have to watch over your assets and when you discover something bad, spring to action! Demand explanations IN WRITING. Now that you understand how they will use confirmations and monthly statements AGAINST you, you see that a timetable emerges built around the monthly statement.

30 days.

A branch manager and a broker can do remarkable things when it comes to their money. They can adjust commission accounts, split fees, and transfer enormous amounts of data in a day. They can take a telephone call, open an account, execute trades and send the confirmation - all in the same day. Brokers and the sales chain negotiate all the time about commissions and net payouts due. Adjustments are common, requiring computer assistance. Errors are frequent. They are regularly fixed. It isn't hard for the industry to act.

Remember our little discussion of firm capital? Every day, the firm computes its position. It can be trading away in its own account, sending stock out, and taking it in.

Therefore, if they say you have to wait for them, you're getting a line. If they tell you that adjustments are hard to make, you're getting a line. If you wait, you lose. They will then claim that the time you waited indicates that you ratified the activity - you accepted it.

You get a confirm in the mail. You didn't authorize the trade, so you call your broker. You have the confirm in your hands and he tells you on the phone that it must be a computer error, because he can't see it on his video tube right in front of him in the office. He says that the monthly statement will probably be correct.

You wait.

The monthly statement comes and shows the trade. You call the broker. He's a bad one. "What," he says! "Impossible!" He says the trade simply isn't on the video, and that he will fix it and call you back in five minutes. He calls back and lies. He says he has spoken to the Operations Department. It's all fixed. Computer error. It should be off the monthly statement next month, but it could take two months because it apparently happened when they installed a new software program and it takes 30 days to get that fine-tuned, but he, the broker will follow this and make sure that you don't get stuck with the trade.

From the time you got the confirm to the time you finally realize the broker lied to you, 90 days pass. The first 30 days went by waiting for the monthly statement. Then the broker said it might take two monthly statements to get passed the "computer" problem. After 90 days you call the branch manager. He says it looks like you ratified the trade and the reason there is a loss is that you sat on the trade and played the market and are now complaining because the trade is a loser. The broker will deny ever telling you to wait for a monthly statement. He'll say the whole trade was your idea, and there should be telephone records to show discussion of the trade not only on your telephone records, but on his records at the brokerage house. Remember, there ARE telephone records.

What should you have done?

When you saw the trade, forget talking to the broker. Call the manager, direct. Complain about the trade. Tell them to get the unauthorized trade out of your account right away. Demand a confirmation of the "fixing" trade, and a written explanation of what happened from the manager. Give them five days to get that letter to you. Federal Express, UPS and the US Postal Service deliver overnight. The brokerage house does all kinds of things overnight. They can get to you, in writing, in five days.

Send a letter to the branch manager that describes your conversation with him, making sure it goes out by US Postal Service, return receipt to you.

No response by your deadline - go see your lawyer. If you can't afford one, go to the state securities regulators and tell them the story.

Remember, firms don't have to have much capital to stay in business, especially small houses that clear through other houses. Fast action may be required before they close up shop and file for bankruptcy, leaving you with no place to go. The bad broker drifts to another house and cold calls for new accounts, making all the usual outlandish promises.

The longer you wait, the longer it looks like you agreed with the trade. Don't wait.

If you want justice, you have to act.

Don't waste a few weeks writing to the SEC or the NYSE. Go see your lawyer. Let him write to the regulators while he sets a few wheels in motion.

Don't get emotional - it's business. Treat it like business. The object is to get your harm fixed as fast and expeditiously as possible, with as little grief as possible. If your lawyer can't get the matter resolved in thirty days, you are going to have to consider suing the house.

30 days is a very long time in a brokerage house. In a sense, each month is like a little year to the house. They add up compensation, send out statements and pay their various rents. If you can't get any result in thirty days, you may have to force the issue by litigation. I urge you to reject the brokerage house's promise to discuss the matter running past thirty days. This is a typical tactic - keep them talking.

Don't. All you need do is raise the issue. Get it fixed fast or hand it over to your lawyer to get it fixed. Talk doesn't get it fixed past your complaint and further identification of the harm you may have suffered. Brokerage houses expect to have a lot of litigation, so they are not frightened by the threat of a lawsuit. The big ones have an in-house staff to handle the cases as they roll in. The sales chain of command, which runs the firm, doesn't care about lawsuits, except that suits cost money to cover lawyer's costs and paying judgments if the house loses.

There are times where integrity and good business sense will evaporate before your eyes. The brokerage house you thought was so wonderful turns into an animal. Its advertising is shown to be hollow garbage, with no relation to how they conduct their everyday business. You hold that confirmation in your hand, a little piece of reality, and the brokerage house acts like it doesn't exist. You expect a logical response - you get no response. I know, I know, everyone hates lawyers. But, where else do you go? Is there some champion on your side that can get you a result? Don't be lulled into wasting time or placing your hope in false heros.

Use Appendix F to send letters to the brokerage house to get information about your account NOW. Use the Question List in Appendix C to test yourself: do you know what's going on?

Become the MASTER!

APPENDIX A.

REGISTRATION INFORMATION

Public companies issue securities, stocks, bonds or other devices, to the public in order to get money as capital. The issuer uses the funds for a number of purposes. How can you find out what they are up to? Here is a list of some of the information documents that the US Government requires public issuers to file.

Form S-1 is the generic filing document required for an "issue" of new securities by an "issuer" that is going to the public for the first time. An initial public offering will be filed on an S-1 with the SEC. It is a public document, and it discloses the who, what, when and where of the company. Get it from your friendly, neighborhood SEC reading room, or call them and ask how you can get a copy. Don't confuse this with the prospectus. The S-1 is THE form. It's full blown and expensive to put together. THIS IS THE FORM THAT THE SHELL MANIPULATORS DON'T WANT TO FILL OUT SO THEY BUY AN OLD, BROKE, PUBLIC COMPANY.

Form S-2 is used by mature companies that want to go back to the public to sell securities. The issuer has to have been filing for at least 3 prior years under the 1934 act, so it has already filed an S-1 sometime in the past. The S-2 is a lot shorter than an S-1, far less expensive to put together, and can be filed in a flash. If IBM wanted to sell some new stock, they would use either an S-2 or an S-3. It's also a public document, open for your examination.

Form S-3 can be used by companies that have been filing for a while under the 1934 Act, have kept their records current, have no trouble with the SEC. They have alternative capital reserves and are looking for some, but not a whole lot of new capital. The S-3 is simple to shape up and file.

Form S-4 is used quite a bit these days because it discloses what happens in mergers. What is the acquiring firm paying in security value for the acquired company? This form tells you.

Form S-6 is for people that put together unit trusts. A unit trust is a closed pool of municipal bonds that allows you to buy a piece of the pool by buying a "Unit." You don't own an individual bond within the pool, but you have an interest in the whole. Pretty boring? Not so. Unit trusts can be excellent investments provided the bonds are of good quality, and the managers know what they are doing. Unit trusts have small management fees each year, unlike mutual funds which might charge up to 1% per year to manage their fund. Want to see the guts of the Unit Trust - read the S-6.

Form S-11 is the required filing for Real Estate Investment Trusts or REITS as they are called on the Street. This is like a unit trust that invests in real estate, not municipal bonds. Bonds can be pretty straight forward because they are rated and can be traded if they have quality and a good rating. Reits are not like that. Real estate is subject to great swings, as the nation well knows. If your broker wants to show you a REIT for an investment and you are not a professional investor, you should re-consider your relationship with this broker unless he is willing to help educate you at great length on the topic. REITS are very risky. Beware. Get the S-11 before you invest. Read it. If you can't understand it, don't buy the REIT.

Form N-1A is used to register open ended mutual funds, the ones you see advertising in the paper. As we discussed earlier, these companies are registered under the 1940 Investment Company Act. Further, the fund investment adviser is registered under the 1940 Investment Adviser Act. More information appears on that Investment Adviser Registration form, the ADV Form filed with the SEC. Mutual funds disclose their workings more than any other entity. It's all available to you. A lot of funds won't tell you who their adviser is. Why? They don't want to make the advisers rise like movie stars, then leave to form their own companies. Hollywood used to work the same way - no star billing! Some funds want you to be attracted by the Adviser, so they tell you who runs the fund in the literature. Try to find out who runs the fund. It may not ring any bells, but it helps to see who the pitcher is when the baseball game is "on." Always look at performance, then tie that into the present adviser: did the present adviser produce those results? Does the present adviser make any significant difference?

Find out!

There are more forms depending on the kinds of issuers.

APPENDIX B

ONGOING REPORTS

Public companies have a tough life because they have to keep on telling the public what they are up to. Filing an S-1 is not the end of filing. There are three principal items you can get about a company that are great compilations of numbers and commentary. To make any sense of them, you have to be able to understand how financial statements work. Don't be put off. Financial Statements are not that hard. If you have a check book and periodically balance your accounts, you can track a financial. Try it - give it a shot. FDIC banks file different reports because they don't report to the SEC. They still put out annual reports, but their reports go to a different library. Get a few 10-k's under your belt and you can read an FDIC F-2, their equivalent of a 10-K.

The Annual Report is put out by the company every year after the end of the firm's fiscal year. This is the booklet with all the photos of smiling management standing around like one happy family. The Annual Report is the firm's most important piece of public relations to the rest of the financial community. They are expensive to produce. Some win prizes for their advertising artistry - for good reason! Forget all the smiles and color photos. Look at the numbers, read the commentary and the chairman's message. Read between the lines. If the company had a bad year and lost money, watch how the chairman tries to talk his way out of trouble. If the company has a new product line, read about it. Some companies have great, combative annual meetings.

When the fiscal year ends, independent auditors review the numbers and sign off on the financials. The annual report gets published and goes to the shareholders and anyone who wants one. The annual meeting is held to elect officers and take care of business. If the firm ends its business on December 31, the annual report will be out in early February, and the shareholder meeting will be held sometime in March.

The SEC Form 10-K is a required filing that most public companies have to publish. The reason the auditors have to run over the books is the 10-K. The annual report is nice to see, but the 10-K is required. A lot of the information, the numbers and commentary, in the Annual Report comes right out of the 10-K.

The Annual Report can't be printed until the 10-K is completed. Companies and their auditors sometimes fight over the statements in the 10-K, because the company knows that stock analysts use the 10-K. Management wants friendly analysts. Auditors know that the 10-K is the real McCoy and will be relied on by investors. If the auditors sign off on too rosy a report, or if they agree to bury a bad item or write it down below where it should be, they can be sued by investors who rely on the auditors evaluation in this official filing.

If you are going to put major dollars into a stock, tell your broker you want a copy of the 10-K. If he says, "the what?" get a new broker. He can get it for you, or you can get it yourself through the SEC, or the issuing company itself.

The SEC Form 10-Q is required of most public companies; it reviews the financials and activity for the quarter just past. This form is not audited like the 10-K, but the company has to be careful about misleading investors or it can get into real trouble with the SEC or by investors bringing lawsuits.

If you hear people referring to the "K" or the "Q" it's just slang for the 10-K and the 10-Q. Don't be impressed.

APPENDIX C

THE QUESTION LIST.

This list is extracted from the previous material because it is so important. Mark it and use it for your defense against bad brokers. Consider it your annual self-help exam. Please, please, please: USE IT! Get out a sheet of paper and write down your answers. Staple your answers into this book so you don't lose them.

1. How much did you pay in commissions last year?

2. How much did you pay in bond mark-ups and on principal trades with the brokerage house?

3. Are you on margin? Does your statement show that you have paid any interest to the brokerage house, at all, last year or this year?

4. Do you own any stocks worth less than FIVE Dollars?

5. Do you own any stocks worth less than TEN Dollars?

6. Do you own any bonds from any issuer at all?

7. Do you know the S&P or Moody's ratings on your bonds?

8. Are any of your bonds rated BBB or less?

9. Do you own any mutual funds?

10. Are your mutual funds loaded or no-loads?

11. Did you buy the mutual funds understanding what a breakpoint, right of accumulation or letter of intent was?

12. What kind of mutual funds have you bought in the past five years: are they Aggressive Stock Funds, High Yield Bond Funds, US Government Funds?

13. What did you pay to get into these mutual funds?

14. Did you switch the same principal from a Loaded Stock Fund to a Loaded Bond Fund during the past two years? Why?

15. Do you own any limited partnership interests?

16. What activity does the partnership work in - horses, gold, oil, etc.?

17. What did you pay to buy into this partnership?

18. How much of that payment went to work on the deal and how much was eaten up by promoters' fees in the first year?

19. Can you read an annual report for a corporation, or just a simple balance sheet?

20. Do you understand how the directors and officers are elected by any of the corporations whose stock you own?

21. Do your companies have staggered boards?

22. How much of the stock is owned by the officers and directors?

23. How much is owned by institutions?

24. Have you voted in any of the corporate elections by using a proxy or by attending the meeting?

25. Has your broker ever sent you material about the balance sheet of companies he recommends?

26. Has your broker ever sent you material about the makeup of company boards, or the breakdown of who owns large blocks of the stock?

27. Do you save all the materials that your brokerage house sends you?

28. Is your broker your "friend?"

29. If you noticed an unauthorized trade in your account, would you be prepared to fire your broker?

30. If you decided the recommendations from your broker were unsuitable for your economic needs, ability and experience, would you be willing to fire your broker?

31. What would it take for you to fire your broker?

32. Have you ever spoken to the branch manager of the office that handles your account?

33. Have you ever attended a seminar put on by a brokerage house, financial planner or money manager?

34. Have you ever made an investment recommended by a brokerage house seminar?

35. Was it your idea or their recommendation?

36. Have you given general discretion to your broker to make investments on your behalf?

37. Have you ever given written discretion to your broker?

38. Have you ever read a margin agreement?

39. Have you ever signed a margin agreement?

40. Are you on margin?

41. Can you read and understand your brokerage statement?

42. Can you tell from your statement if you are on margin?

43. Do you pay full commissions at your brokerage house?

44. Have you ever asked for a discount on commissions?

45. If your broker won't give you a discount, either because he simply won't or because he claims his branch manager won't allow it, would you fire the broker and move your account?

46. Do you believe your broker does his own research?

47. Do you do your own research?

48. Do you read the financial press?

49. Do you have a family accountant and lawyer?

50. If you were confused by your investments, where would you go for help to understand what happened?

This list will help you get your feet on the ground, but you have to remain constantly vigilant for custom-devised tactics intended to get around your fortifications. A sharp operator can swindle an institution and all it's experts, yes, right out in the open, right on their field.

I am extolling, pleading, demanding, urging and otherwise daring to hope that you will not stop at this list.

Question 51 is: How am I going to be "had" on this latest deal being dangled in front of my nose?

Another way of looking at it: As the hardened movie detective might say, "Every investment opportunity is a suspect in your upcoming financial murder."

No one leaves the room, please!

APPENDIX D

THE FULL GLOSSARY: YOUR DEFENSIVE ARSENAL

This is extracted from the prior material where it appeared at the end of each of the first eight chapters, grouped by concept.

The terms and explanations are listed here in alphabetical order, following this list of terms. As you go down the list, make a note in the space at the side of the page indicating whether you understand the term or not. You should understand these terms before investing through a stockbroker. Notice: churning is here three times, and there is a separate appendix on margin. Very dangerous topics.

This is a list of ONLY FIFTY terms. There are plenty more which is why you have to start going to the library and hitting the books.

1. 1933 Securities Act
2. 1934 Exchange Act
3. Betting
4. Branch Manager
5. Broker-Dealer
6. Cage
7. Cash Account
8. Churning
9. Churning
10. Churning
11. Cold Calls
12. Commission Schedule
13. Compliance Department

14. Confirmation
15. Direct Investments
16. Discretion
17. Educational Seminars
18. Fear and Greed
19. Financial Operations Principal
20. Fraud
21 Full Disclosure
22. General Counsel
23. Grid
24. Gross Production
25. In-House Research
26. Individualized Research
27. Investing
28. Investment Company
29. Limit Order
30. Manias
31. Margin Account
32. Market Order
33. Monthly Statement
34. Net
35. NYSE Rule 472
36. Obsession
37. Odds
38. Options Account
39. Outside Research
40. Published Research Recommendation
41. Regional Manager
42. Registered Representative
43. Sales Assistants
44. Sales Script
45. SEC Annual Report
46. SEC Department of Enforcement
47. Self Regulatory Organization
48. Stockbroker
49. Supervisory Analyst
50. Wrongful Discretion

1. The 1933 Securities Act is a federal law that requires a series of public disclosures from issuers of securities. The whole idea is to have as much information as possible out in the public area before allowing companies to go to the public to get funds. Various registrations apply before securities can be distributed in an underwriting. This law mandates the "prospectus" when new stock comes out. Most investors and brokers have never read the law, which is, unfortunately, quite complex. More unfortunate, however, is that many investors don't understand that an incredible amount of information is made available to them under this marvelous statute. It's all there for the asking: registrations, applications, prospecti, amendments, etc. This law is referred to as the "Truth in Securities Act."

2. The 1934 Exchange Act is a companion to the 1933 Act. It provides for the licensing of the various Self Regulatory Organizations or "SRO's" such as the NYSE, and has all the licensing provisions for BD's and individual stockbrokers. It discusses margin, net capital, books and records and includes the various anti-fraud provisions that the SEC relies on for enforcement work. It's a highly technical piece of work that gets amended from time to time. Most recently, the Congress amended it to provide for tougher anti-fraud provisions including bounties or rewards for people who turn in bad guys. If you want more information on the bounty provision, contact the SEC for particulars on their program, which is still evolving. Extensive Regulations are in effect covering the industry, in addition to the statutes. Look for the law in title 17 of the US Code. The Regulations appear in Title 17 of the Code of Federal Regulations, which is available from the US Government Printing Office.

3. Betting is not what the markets are about. Firms go crazy when they see brokers using this word because it is demeaning to the industry. The NYSE gets very upset when the markets are referred to as a casino, or the word "bet" is used because it hurts their image. Betting means you put down money on some event you have no control over, choosing one possible outcome as your "bet." Someone else puts down money on another outcome for his "bet." The key is you have no control. The event will happen. You are not supposed to have control, only a guess. If you have control, it's not a bet. The NYSE feels that if

you believe the market is a bet, you will not invest. How much control do you have over the markets? Are all traders really bettors?

4. A Branch Manager is the local supervisor of a Stockbroker in a branch office of a brokerage house. The Branch Manager must have special licenses from the NASD and the NYSE if an NYSE member firm. He is responsible for watching what the stockbroker is doing, for approving new accounts of all kinds and for receiving customer complaints. He recruits from other firms. He trains new brokers in his office.

5. A Broker-Dealer is a licensed entity under the 1934 Exchange Act. Because it has a license, it can buy and sell securities in transactions with the public. It can lose its license if it violates the law or various regulations concerning how it does its business, how much capital it maintains or if it fails to keep the correct books and records. A "BD" is licensed by filing with the SEC. It must also be a member of the NASD if it does public business. It may be a member of the NYSE, but does not have to be an NYSE member. Most securities firms, or "BD's" are not members of the NYSE. The firm also has to be BD licensed in the state where it is doing business. Additional licenses are required by each broker at the BD. The broker files a form "BD" with the SEC and most states to get its license. The form is public information, so you can get it. Before a bank lends a lot of money to a BD, the bank gets a copy of the BD. So should you. Ask the house for it, or get it from your state securities examiners. The SEC has it, and it is available from them.

6. The Cage is located in each branch office. It contains an electronic wire system where an operator puts all data from the order tickets submitted by the brokers to get execution. It has restricted access because it may have cash, checks and securities on hand. Branches deposit cash daily to their bank, and they ship securities by secured courier to their home office each night. If you need to get a check from your account, the firm may mail it to you, or you can get it from the

office. Don't let the broker deliver it. Either get it mailed from the home office or get it at the cage in the branch. The branch manager has access to the cage - the brokers can't get in. The manager will go into the cage to review order tickets, review the wire traffic to and from the home office, and review the efficiency of the wire operators. Mistakes in the cage do happen, and they can be costly. The difference between 100 shares of IBM and 1000 shares of IBM is one keystroke. With option trades the danger goes up dramatically. Understanding this, you have to examine your confirmations very closely to see that you had correct execution.

7. A Cash Account is a securities account where no credit is used. If a security is bought, the money must be in the account or deposited within five days of the trade. The securities must be segregated by the brokerage house and may not be used by the house as security against bank loans to the house.

8. Churning occurs where a broker takes control of an account, acting on either written discretion or unwritten discretion, or by so dominating the customer relationship that trading occurs of such a frequency and for no apparent legitimate reason other than to generate commissions for the broker. The account does not have to have any losses. Churning is often marked by marginally profitable trades.

9. Churning is an abuse of your account, a fraudulent practice, wherein a broker causes trades to occur for the purpose of generating commissions. Profit or loss on the trades doesn't matter, just that the transactions generate commissions. You can end up with a profit and still be a victim of churning. It is one of the traditional forms of abuse in the securities industry.

10. Churning occurs when the transactions in your account are primarily intended to generate commissions to the broker. It's illegal, fraudulent conduct. If you find it, stop it!

11. Cold Calls are made by brokers or their assistants to random numbers or to numbers from lists that they or their brokerage house have bought from list brokers. Did you buy a car last year? If so, you're on lists. Are you a homeowner - you're on lists. There is nothing sinister about being on lists, just be aware that you are on lists somewhere. When you get cold calls from brokers you don't know, don't be polite: hang up! Learning to hang up is difficult. Here's a practice technique for people with brokerage accounts: call up your brokerage house, get your broker on the telephone, and hang up in the middle of a conversation about the weather. Need something easier: call a local, FREE info number about sports, weather - anything. Call them up and when the tape starts, wait ten seconds, then hang up. Telephone manners don't apply to cold callers - learn to hang up. Don't let them "into" your house on the telephone. Cold calls are supported by interesting statistics about the success percentage per so many calls, so when you hang up, the caller is already onto the next potential victim. Hang up. Hang up. Hang up. Hang up. Hang up. Hang up. Hang up. Hang up. Hang up. Hang up.

12. The Commission Schedule is the list of potential charges for your transactions. It will be based on the number of shares and the dollar volume of the trade. Any reduction from the official commission schedule is called a discount. Your broker may or may not have the power to discount. His manager can. Always ask for a discount when you do business with a full service firm. Big customers never pay full commissions. No discount? Use a discount firm!

13. The Compliance Department is the internal cop in the firm. In large NYSE firms, the department has many employees under the leadership of the Compliance Director, who has to be certified as competent by the Exchange. The department is supposed to look for trouble in all areas of the firm by use of computer surveillance, interpretation of data and personal interviews with brokers, managers and other personnel. If you have a problem with your account, don't hesitate to call this department. Ask for the director. Make a note of the person you talk to. Follow up with a letter. If you find wrongful discretion was used in your account to put on trades you didn't

authorize - call the Compliance Department. If you get a confirmation with white-out used to cover an entry - call the Compliance Department. Calling can't hurt. Bad brokers can't stand the Compliance Department. They'll do anything, say anything to get you not to call when there is a problem with the account. Call. Follow the call with a letter to the Director. Drag him into the problem. Brokerage houses are run for profit by the sales area, but you can get action from the Compliance Department, even if you have to drag them in, kicking and screaming. Unfortunately, a corrupt firm will have a Compliance Director who keeps his job at the pleasure of his masters, chained by his paycheck to his liability. In that case, you need a lawyer - FAST!

14. A Confirmation is printed and sent to the customer after every trade and after every order is put into execution. It is usually put together in the home office, but the branch may be able to print them on special occasions. Sometimes the home office will send the information electronically to the branch office where the confirmation is printed and mailed. You get the confirmation in the US Mail. It looks like a credit card receipt. Because they are printed by computer, be very careful if your confirmation has any overstrikes or erasures. It is supposed to be printed very carefully, not "fixed up." If it is fixed up, call the firm's compliance department at once. Bypass the branch manager - go right to the compliance department. If you deal with a small firm, go right to the president: tell him you have a suspicious confirmation. Demand an explanation. Don't just ask - demand. You have to read your confirmations carefully. If you don't, be prepared to be a victim. If you get confirmations for trades that you didn't authorize, go to the compliance department or president right away. If you directed a trade but you don't get a confirmation, get in contact with your broker's branch manager right away. If you don't get the confirmation in short order, then go to the compliance department or the firm president. Study the small codes on your confirmation, because it tells you if the firm acted as your agent, or as a principal, whether the trade was solicited by the broker or not and the price, commission, etc. Study the confirmation. It will be waved in your face by the firm if you later complain about unauthorized trades to indicate the firm told you about ALL the trades. The confirmation isn't there to help you so much as to

help the brokerage firm. Don't be a fool and a victim at the same time. Get the confirm; understand it. If it's wrong, suspect foul play!

15. Direct Investments are securities a broker can sell to you aside from stocks and bonds. These items usually have a higher payout to the broker, often approaching 50%. Take a $1,000 transaction. You buy a piece of an equipment leasing deal for $1,000. The brokerage firm takes 8% as the gross sales charge, or $80. The broker gets 50% of that, or $40. That payout is too small to make the sale worthwhile, so the product is sold in larger blocks of $5,000 or more to make it attractive to the broker. When the broker can't get you to buy stock and bonds, there are always the direct investments or mutual funds. Some also sell insurance. They don't sell cars - yet!

16. Discretion is given by a customer to the broker to allow the broker to make trades in the customer's account without calling the customer before the trades are entered. Discretion is usually required to be in writing, except where a customer gives discretion as to time and price of the execution. Don't give discretion to the broker because you don't understand how trades work. That's exactly the wrong reason to give discretion. The reason to give discretion is your necessity. That's right - your necessity. Don't trust your broker to do the right thing while you are ignorant of the style of trading, how the security works, or how the account is set up. You might get killed. At the least, you may be surprised! If you have positions in your account and you are going on vacation, only give discretion in writing. If you travel on business a lot and can't get to your broker, only give discretion in writing. If your broker asks for discretion but says he doesn't need it in writing, don't bother talking to the broker anymore about it - talk to the branch manager right away and report the conversation. "Time and price" unwritten discretion is only for professionals - people that know exactly what they are doing and are limiting the situation to one or two trades that are going to happen shortly in a volatile market. It's not for you, unless you are one of those sophisticated few.

17. Educational Seminars are put on by brokers to get you to use them as your investment broker. Sometimes the house will split the cost of these seminars with the brokers, but some very good brokers do this with their own money. Don't be afraid to go to one of these, but be prepared to say "No," to any solicitation of your account business based on one seminar. A lot of big firms have motivational speakers from the research department who are supposed to come in and impress you at these seminars so that you bring the account to that house. Ultimately, your commission dollars pay for the seminar even if there is no admission fee. You can learn something from these seminars, but don't be impressed with them. If you want to learn about finance, there is no substitute for the PUBLIC LIBRARY, where they aren't trying to sell you anything but unlimited ideas.

18. Fear and Greed are the rhetorical underpinnings of a lot of market theory. Somewhat demeaning in concept, it is a loose term used to indicate that retail investors, you, are motivated by fear and greed, that you don't think logically, and that retail investors are like sheep. Fear and greed do motivate a lot of things, not just in finance, but throughout life. Politics, philosophy, investments and more are influenced by these concepts, but there is, or should be, more. Fear and greed do motivate institutional investors, especially the ones who are "marked to the market" each month by calculation of their performance to the third decimal place. When the market drops a hundred points at a shot, you are seeing institutional fear and greed, not retail. Retail usually doesn't know what's happening until after it has occurred. Institutions and professional traders do panic. Some are the ones who try to convince you that they can calmly advise on your trades. Real fear is an "autonomic" reaction; it happens, and you can't control it because it is an instinctive reaction of the body to danger, such as jumping back when you are startled. Investment fear is an abandonment of thought. It is not autonomic, but for some brokers, it is automatic.

19. Financial and Operations Principals are specially tested and licensed by the NASD. The treasurer of a brokerage firm is a "finop," and is referred to as the chief financial officer. The head of the operations area is a finop, too. In smaller firms, the treasurer and the head of the operations area may be the same person. The first person to know what's really going on with the firm's revenues is the treasurer because he sees the income from each day and the value of the firm's accounts. He sees the expenditures, the taxes, the settlements - he knows exactly where things are going. He is usually a board member and composes the firm's financial reports and computes net capital. The head of operations has responsibility for safe keeping of all securities and for making sure that executions are reliably sent into the correct channels, that buys and sells are correctly entered in the correct accounts, and that floor personnel are working efficiently.

20. Fraud is the deceptive practice of intentional dishonesty where someone takes advantage of you to get your money or goods. The most sophisticated business people and firms are the VICTIMS of fraud at times as evidenced by the number of recent lawsuits by banks against their real estate developer customers who pledged property to the banks as security for loans, but gave false information about the property or their business assets in their applications. Fraud isn't an accident. It doesn't happen by the position of the stars or the moon. People do it. To you!

21. "Full Disclosure" is a term which generally describes the whole thrust of all the forms and licenses required for public filing by the 1933 and 1934 Acts. There are reams of paper available about brokerage houses and the brokers. It is available to you, but you have to make the effort to get it. Research people use this material all the time, and your broker can get it for you if he's serious about offering "full service." The SEC has regional reading rooms for your use. You can use the Freedom of Information act to get information. The Congress has put a great deal of thought into shaping Full Disclosure. Don't be bashful. It's yours. Use it!

22. The General Counsel is a lawyer who works for larger brokerage houses as an in-house employee. He usually has the compliance department reporting to him, and perhaps a few other departments in the firm. He may also have a staff of attorneys in a legal department handling a lot of the firm's lawsuits, advising the firm's management and figuring out what the compliance department is up to. The GC will be on the broker's board of directors, be involved in the most upper level discussions of firm policy, but will usually not have any significant gross production. No "book." When things really go bad at a firm, the GC goes. In a smaller firm, there will be no GC. They use an outside law firm. The brokerage house may not want a lawyer around inside because they can't control one as readily as they might like. A lawyer can quit and go into practice elsewhere, unlike a broker who has to work for an employing firm that is a member of the NASD, or else start a whole new firm requiring numerous licenses and at least a little capital.

23. The Grid is the way the firm figures what to pay the broker. It is made of a series of dollar amounts of gross production; for example, if a broker does $50,000 gross production for the year, he might get a payout of 25% as his W-2 income. If he does $250,000, he might get a payout of 38% as his W-2 income. The brokers watch their gross production to the penny because the impact on their pay is very direct and predictable.

24. Gross Production is the term applied to the total amount of revenue generated by a broker in all forms, from all products, whether it is from stock and bond transactions, sales of mutual funds or special, direct investments. In baseball, you would ask a player, "How many home runs did you hit last year?" In the brokerage business, you judge the success of a broker by, "What did you gross last year?"

25. In-house Research is the free material you get from your broker, published under the house masthead as a newsletter.

26. Individualized Research is something your broker might do just for you. It's legal and might be very good. It might be junk. Be very careful about this kind of literature. Professionals who manage big mutual funds or pension funds use this private material all the time. They understand its limitations. They know how to reject it or to use it in a context of other information. It will not appear as printed, newsletter-style material. Be very careful about using it unless you understand how to do your own research.

27. Investing means you think out your financial actions before you pay, looking at an opportunity as one where you might make some money because of a number of factors. In the markets, it means you will probably hold on for a while, that you are not a trader. Investors are long term. Traders are very short term.

28. An Investment Company has a separate license under the 1940 Investment Company Act. It is not a BD license. Sometimes the same company may have a series of licenses, such as a BD, Investment Adviser, etc. This should not impress you. You can become confused as to which hat the entity is wearing when you deal with it. You are most familiar with mutual funds as licensed Investment Companies. Some BD's have their own mutual funds, or captive Investment Companies. A lot of Investment Companies are set up as Massachusetts Trusts for administration purposes.

29. A Limit Order is issued to buy or sell a security at a specific price or better price. If an order to "buy 100 shares at 100, Limit" is given, the shares can be bought for 99, but not for 100 1/8. A sale order works in the reverse. "Sell at 100, Limit" means the sale could go off at 101, but not at 99 7/8. This is not a stop or stop-loss order which is used to try and limit losses. A stop loss is an order to close out a position if a price goes against you to a certain amount. If the threshold

adverse movement occurs, the stop-loss becomes a market order to get you out as fast as possible. A stop loss is not a guarantee that an execution will take place at any specific or better price.

30. Manias are very intense desires to get something or do something that goes beyond logical sense. People trying to quit smoking experience a mania for a cigarette. You have to stand back to understand a mania, looking to see if your thoughts are logical. Whole groups of people can get caught up in manias. It doesn't mean they are crazy. It means that something has become impulsively attractive beyond its logical level. Brokers can be involved in manias - sometimes they advise investing in electronics, or, alas, bank stocks to the exclusion of all else. Then the mania fades, the enthusiasm withers, and, in the cold light of logic, no one is excited about the industry. Prices drop. It happens time and time again. The Dutch tulip craze is the classic mania.

31. A Margin Account involves the use of credit. The amount of credit available is determined by rules promulgated by the Federal Reserve. It can vary. When an account is on margin, the customer uses leverage which involves a higher degree of risk and sophistication. If the account is on margin, it must pay interest each month.

32. A Market Order is an order to buy or sell a security at the prevailing price available in the market. There is no limit on the execution price, except that it must be the prevailing price in the respective market at that time.

33. The Monthly Statement is sent to you by your firm to show you what happened in your account. It will show the way the accounts looks at the end of the month, after the dust settles from any activity. The brokerage month is not exactly a calendar month because of the five-

day settlement rule, so the June statement from your firm may show all activity that occurred from May 26 through June 25. The exact dates depend on when holidays fall. When the monthly statement comes, look at it closely. If you can't read and COMPREHEND your statement STOP EVERYTHING. Learn to read it! You cannot be in a position where the monthly statement is unintelligible. Are you embarrassed if you can't read the monthly statement? Don't be. I have examined witness from the operations area, branch offices, regulators and lawyers who couldn't read certain entries on monthly statements. Statements are designed by your firm, not the SEC, the NYSE or NASD. Firms change the format for marketing purposes by adding color and flash - seldom clarity! They are printed by computer at the home office and you should get them in the US Mail. Examine the statement: there should be no erasures and strikeouts. You should recognize all the entries. Are you on margin? Can you tell from the statement? Learn how to read every entry. Keep all the statements.

34. The Net is what the broker gets paid from the grid. This is the amount that hits his paycheck. While you are figuring profit and loss from a transaction, the broker is thinking "Net."

35. NYSE Rule 472 covers "Communications With the Public." It is an excellent idea, intended to limit NOT the amount of information, but the manner of publication and therefore the quality of information that gets out to you for use in selecting investments. It does not apply to NASD firms. There are no guarantees in investing. Research can give a recommendation, but it can "guess" wrong. Rule 472 requires the house to have a good reason for the recommendation, that is, a file full of data and work notes. Read the hedge clause at the bottom of recommendations. Further information is usually available. Ask for it! See what you get as the additional material, if anything.

36. An Obsession is a constant, relentless preoccupation with an idea, thing, activity, person, etc. Even in the face of failure or rejection, the obsession continues. Some retail investors can't stop. They shouldn't be

in the market, they keep on losing but they can't say "no." The test: pull out for a few months. Don't do any trading. If you can't stop, you shouldn't be in the market. Some brokers get obsessed. When they lose, they can't accept they were beat. The tragedy is where they lose your money by their futile attempt to better the markets by their humble input. An obsessed broker doesn't care if he gets caught, or what the consequences are. He doesn't really care about his income. He wants to beat the system, to score and win. He can't stop. Manias fizzle and die. Obsessions keep going.

37. Odds are used to bet sports and other occurrences. Odds in football or basketball use "The Point Spread" method. If New York is favored in a game over Los Angeles by 5 points, you can lose the bet on New York to win if they DO win, but only by 3 points. You win but you lose. When you hear investments discussed with "the odds" as a factor, watch out! You can win, but lose. Be careful about brokers that tell you "the odds."

38. An Options Account is used where a sophisticated customer elects to use options as part of an investment strategy that is suitable for high risk. Options are not suitable for most investors. All option customers must read a brochure from the Options Clearing Corporation that discloses the risks involved in this trading. Options accounts must be approved by the branch manager and by the firm's Compliance Registered Options Principal or Senior Registered Options Principal.

39. Outside Research is done by firms that are independent and usually don't sell stock. Some is excellent; some is junk. Some of this so-called research is actually paid for by the company being "researched," which should cause you to question the independence of the report. A research firm does not have to be licensed as a broker or dealer, and does not have to be a member of the NASD or the NYSE. In-house research staff is expensive to maintain in slow markets, so Wall Street lays off analysts in droves when the market slows. Firms then use

materials prepared by some of the independent houses. Firms can also buy the research of another firm and distribute it to their clients. Watch out for that - while it is "independent" of the house handing it out, it is "in-house" for the firm that composed it.

40. Published Research Recommendations are usually done by retail firms as newsletters intended for your consideration to get your business. There is a "hedge clause" at the bottom that tells you there are no guarantees. This is intended for you, the customer. The research department may also be doing other research for sale to other firms, to Investment Advisers and to special customers. Research is also done for the firm's own trading account and the corporate finance department. Don't think that a research department publishes all its work.

41. A Regional Manager works in a larger brokerage house and has control over several branch offices. He watches to see what the branch managers are doing. He also recruits stockbrokers from other firms, and deals with the big producers in his region on special issues, following their production closely.

42. A Registered Representative is what we commonly call a stockbroker. They go by many different titles for marketing purposes. In the past, a stockbroker was known as a "customer's man," but today they are "account executives," "financial consultants," "investment executives," and other exotic, meaningless titles. The RR has to pass the Series 7 exam, a 6 hour test, given by the NASD, and he has to work for a firm that is responsible for what he does. In some firms that specialize in the business they do, the registered representative may not handle the full range of investment products, therefore he may have taken another, less extensive examination to cover only the product he is selling. Some brokers only sell variable annuities - they don't have to take the full Series 7. In the business, the registered representative is referred to as the "broker," or "rep," or "RR." Forget the titles and use the industry terms. He has to be licensed by the states he does business in.

43. Sales Assistants work for brokers. A big producer, that is, a broker that does a lot of gross production may have several sales assistants to help him post his book, keep track of order tickets and take calls from customers. Once the big broker has you as a client, you may end up dealing with the sales assistant more than the broker. That may be fine. Some sales assistants are great! The broker usually gives them a small split on his commissions - otherwise they are on salary as employees of the branch office. A good sales assistant working for a good broker will move with the broker when he changes firms. It's a kind of partnership. The sales assistant can get you research pieces from the firm, discuss activity in your account, get you copies of monthly statements, explain how to read your statements, and, if he is registered as a broker, take your orders. Get comfortable about dealing with a sales assistant. Because they work for salary from the firm and a derivative split on gross commissions, they are not as aggressive. They don't make a lot more if they take you to the cleaners, and they can always get work in the securities business, in banking, or with the government. Try dealing with a sales assistant for a while - they won't recommend hot items, because there is no pressure on them to use the hard sell. If you work with them, you're on the way to using a discounter! A discounter does the same thing, except they don't make any recommendations. They just give service. Some Sales Assistants go on to be brokers, while others are content to remain as sales assistants where they don't have the pressure to sell, where they can get jobs in many industries at their pleasure making about the same salary, and where they can go in and out of business to suit family needs. Low-grossing producers don't have sales assistants. Some brokers don't like to use them preferring to deal with all their clients direct, but big producers who handle a lot of small accounts for individual customers have to have them because they can't take all the calls or fill in all the forms. With computers, the need for sales assistants to do mailings and post accounts has decreased, but the increased reliance on cold calling telephone sales techniques has absorbed the brokers' time which has given more emphasis to the sales assistant.

44. A Sales Script is literally a script, in writing, down to the last word and blank space for the target's name. It is used by brokers to make fast sales calls. Professional motivators put these together to get the maximum marketing bang for the least time. A good script leaves you hanging, asking for more, and works in 30 telephone seconds. The brokerage houses put these together, the product wholesalers make them available, and the brokers invent them on their own. When your telephone rings and you get a sales pitch from a broker, he is probably reading it for the 100th time that day or week. He's fishing. HANG UP. Don't bother with a telephone dialer. I get calls at home and the office because I am on mailing and telephone lists (unfortunately) all over the country. The typical entry: "How would you like to have some great information about the exciting possibilities for terrific investment returns now available to investors who take fast action and take advantage of the 1992 European economic shakeup?" You can substitute anything in the press for the European economic part. The caller will make it seem that if you don't act NOW, the opportunity will pass. Don't fall for it. Let "it" pass. Telephone pressure sales are bad for your financial health.

45. The Securities and Exchange Commission Annual Report is composed each year and sent over to the President of the Senate and the Speaker of the House of Representatives to explain what the SEC has been up to for the preceding year. The report has general discussions about policy matters and how wonderfully the SEC has performed for the prior year, but it also has great statistics about what the SEC really does. What is their budget? How many employees do they have? How many exams do they conduct? Get it from the Superintendent of Documents, US Government Printing Office, Washington, DC 20402. The 1988 report cost $5.00. It's a great bargain.

46. The SEC Department of Enforcement gets all the news headlines, but is only a small part of the SEC. It is located in Washington, DC at

the main SEC Office. If you have a complaint, you can send them a letter, but their mission is not to handle consumer issues. They run the cases where the SEC has decided something very bad has happened and requires a halt and some penalties. They don't have the manpower to handle a lot of cases, therefore they handle the bigger ones. The new chief of enforcement is William McLucas. If you have a problem and want to bring it to the SEC's attention, contact the SEC Consumer Affairs and Information Services Office in Washington, DC. When they get complaints about brokers, they put it into a data base to observe trends. In fiscal 1988, they got 49,000 complaints!

47. A Self Regulatory Organization, SRO, is a body licensed under the 1934 Exchange Act through the Securities and Exchange Commission. It has powers to license, investigate and discipline its own member firms and employees of those firms. There are many SRO's. A brokerage house may be subject to the jurisdiction of several SRO's at one time because it does business there, such as the American Stock Exchange, The New York Stock Exchange (NYSE), the National Association of Securities Dealers (NASD), and others.

48. A Stockbroker is an individual who works for a licensed broker-dealer. The stockbroker, no matter what the firm calls him, is a Registered Representative. He must be licensed by each state he does business in, by the NASD and, if he works for an NYSE firm, he must be licensed by the NYSE.

49. A Supervisory Analyst is a person registered with the NYSE who has demonstrated knowledge of financial analysis and compliance matters who is able to act as the supervisor of a research department. He must sign off on all research matter that is intended for distribution

to the public under NYSE Rule 472. This means he has to approve research pieces done at the department level AND put out by the brokers. Some brokers like to do mass mailings to all their clients of their own "research;" the "SA" has to sign off on this in an NYSE firm.

50. Wrongful Discretion occurs where the broker does a trade in your account that you did not authorize in advance. The broker can cause the trade to go off because the brokerage business works on the telephone and will continue to do so. The broker fills in the ticket, gives it to his cage, and the trade goes off. The broker gets paid his commission. The house can't tell that the broker used wrongful discretion. The branch manager has no way of telling from the execution that the broker didn't talk to you about the trade. The assumption is that the broker did have permission to do the trade. You'll know about the trade when you get the confirmation. If you miss that mail, you'll see the trade on a monthly statement. If you see a trade in your account that you didn't authorize DO SOMETHING. Call the compliance department or the firm president right away. Send a note in writing to make a record of the complaint, but make sure you COMPLAIN. Forget all the usual excuses from the brokers - get that trade out of your account, fast! If a trade goes off in your account and you don't complain, it will look like you ratified the trade. Ratification means you may not have authorized the trade in advance, but once you saw it you said, "O.K.," and you are stuck with it. If you find wrongful discretion, fire your broker. REPEAT. If you find wrongful discretion, fire your broker. No excuses, forget the apologies, don't be a sucker - fire the broker.

SPECIAL NOTE: "Churning" appears three times in the list because it is of paramount importance. Recall that the securities business works on the telephone. Very few papers are ever signed. Customers don't sign their orders. The securities markets would come to a grinding halt if customers had to sign for each order. A car dealer can't churn you by buying and selling cars for you; the idea seems crazy! A bad stockbroker can buy and sell in your account without your knowing it. He can try to talk his way out of it after the fact. Once you have an account you are a sitting duck, or, more accurately, your account is ready for action with or without your consent. Watch out for churning! The brokers know it's wrong. If you find it, take action! If you don't read your brokerage statements, you are vulnerable for abuse. Some churning is dramatic. The numbers speak for themselves and the manager can find and stop the activity by data review. Churning can be subtle. It can occur with stock OR bond transactions. On a bond trade, the house may be selling the bond directly to you from its inventory. They don't have to go to any market to get it. This is called a principal trade. They are selling their bond to you. It's direct. There is no commission on this trade - instead, there is a markup. The bond might be worth 92, but you pay 96. It has been marked up 4 points. You can be churned by getting in and out of bonds, just as with stock. Markups are used when you buy Over the Counter stock from your broker as principal. Add up your commissions and markups. Compare the total to the equity value of your account. Are you paying 10% of your equity in commissions? Ask your broker to show you the numbers.

Use the letters in Appendix F. Get the branch manager involved in your accounts.

Fast!

APPENDIX E

MARGIN IN THE SPOTLIGHT

This is extracted from the chapter on Bankruptcy. Margin is mentioned throughout the book because it is one of the most dangerous things you can do with your account. I urge you not to go on margin. With program trading, you can get murdered in the course of one day, and margin calls can hit you when you can least pay.

Margin is a trading technique; it's not for investors. If you are on margin, get off. If you think you can handle it, look at the houses that have disappeared in the recent past, the S&L industry and the Latin Loan debacle for the commercial banks. The cream of the academic, financial crop manufactured those situations. The big leaguers did it.

Margin is a very dangerous form of investing. You borrow value from the brokerage house in order to buy more stock than your cash allows. If Finegan Motors is selling at 100 per share, you can buy only 100 shares with $10,000. If you go on margin, however, you can buy 200 shares. The account has a total value at the moment you buy the shares of $20,000, but you have only $10,000 of equity in the account. You have borrowed $10,000 from the brokerage house, and you will pay interest on that money you borrowed. If Finegan Motors goes down 10 points, you have lost $2,000 or $10 for each of the 200 shares. You still owe the brokerage house the same money - the $10,000 you borrowed to buy your shares.

With margin, when you win, because you have used leverage, you can increase your profits. When you lose, however, you lose a lot, because leverage works on the way down, too. Under NYSE Rules at this time, you cannot go below 25% equity on stocks.

Remember how the account was set up - you put down 50% of the purchase price, or $10,000 on the total price of $20,000 for the 200 shares of Finegan Motors at 100 per share. If the value of Finegan Motors drops, it is your equity that drops. If all your account has in it is Finegan Motors, it is concentrated. Concentrated accounts are not allowed to get down to the 25% floor because it might drop right through to 0% in a flash.

In our example, suppose the price of Finegan Motors dropped to 50 per share. The account would have a total market value of $10,000 and the margin debit would be $10,000 which means all your equity has been wiped out and you are now risking the firm's own capital. You will probably get a margin call from the firm when the price of Finegan Motors got to somewhere around 15 per share. This would mean that your equity in the account was down to $5,000, and the total value of the account was $15,000. The house is free to require MORE than the NYSE floor of 25%, and in my little example they required 35%. They will call you for the money. If you don't pay it, they will consider selling out part of your position to raise the amount of equity in the account to a level they are comfortable with.

If the account got down to 25% maintenance of equity, they would have to sell you out. That would happen when the market value got down to 13,333.33 in this example.

How do you calculate the 25% call level?

First, find the total debit balance in the account. Here it was $10,000. Divide that by 1 minus the percent maintenance requirement, which was 25% here. Thus, the divisor will be 1 minus .25 which equals .75. $10,000 divided by .75 equals $13,333.33.

You can use that formula to calculate margin calls when the percentages vary on house requirements, but remember, a house does not want you to get below 25% so they will generally set a call for an earlier time, such as 30% or 35%, especially when there is a concentration in the account.

A customer can get a double pump from his money by going to a bank and borrowing as a non-purpose, general loan. He takes the borrowed money over to the brokerage house and uses that as the "equity" in his account to borrow another amount from the broker.

This is extremely dangerous, because any decline in the price of the shares will mean the customer may not be able to pay back the bank. He is losing the money they lent to him. If the broker knows the customer is doing this, the broker should stop it at once, or refuse to allow the account. It is too dangerous and violates the credit rules for the brokerage house and the Federal Reserve Board.

A bad stockbroker who tells you to do this deserves to die by slow torture because he intends to get the leveraged money and whip it around through numerous trades to generate gross commissions. When you suffer losses, you experience LEVERAGED LOSSES, and you lose your house. Maybe your mind.

And now, after you have read the book and been exposed to the method of calculating margin, could you calculate it? Get out your accounts!

Are you on margin? What is your equity? When will the calls start coming for more cash? Do you have stop-loss orders in to stop margin from eating up the equity in your accounts?

Margin does not offer greater opportunity to make money for retail investors, only greater chance to get financially killed.

Don't use drugs. Don't use margin.

Special Note:

Margin accounts make money for the brokerage house in two ways. The first is easy: commissions. The more money in the account, the more there is to trade. The second is interest rate arbitrage. When you borrow from the brokerage, the house doesn't have the cash. The house goes to a bank and borrows the funds at the " broker's call rate," a special interest rate figure you will see in the financial press. This is the interest rate that major commercial banks charge major brokerage houses for margin funds. The loans are secured by YOUR STOCK. If you go on margin to buy stock, the stock is pledged to the bank that lends to the brokerage. The brokerage house might borrow from the bank at 10% and charge you 12% as the margin rate. They make 2%.

That 2% can add up to significant profits. The brokerage house can have a huge loan from the bank when you consider all the margin accounts on its books. If the price of all the margin stock drops drastically, how does the brokerage house get more money into the accounts to keep them up to the correct percentage of debt vs. equity: margin calls! The house is ultimately liable for the loan to the bank. If the security isn't enough, the brokerage house may have to put up securities or pay down the loan with cash IF the house has any cash!

The brokers don't usually get paid any net on the amount of margin interest their accounts pay to the house. After all, the broker has more funds to invest and more potential commissions to generate.

A good broker will be careful about which customers can handle margin. Mutual funds can't. Billion dollar, super-sophisticated mutual funds managed by the professionals can't go on margin. Why should you? A good broker will let you go on margin when it is to your advantage and you know what you are doing. A bad one wants you margined to the hilt to generate more commissions. When a margin call hits, the house sends a telegram or overnight letter saying that you have to deposit cash OR securities in the account will be sold to raise cash. The price of the securities has dropped. You will have a loss. Worst of all: when you are sold out, you will be charged commissions.

APPENDIX F

HELPFUL LETTERS

A few letters are set out to help you in dealing with your broker. If you use them, your broker will have to do homework, but you will end up with helpful facts. Don't take the answers you get at face value. Look at them. Think about them. Are they correct? Do you agree with them?

If you don't agree with the answers, take action now, before something goes wrong and your account suffers.

People are too used to the telephone these days, and we accept unrecorded talk about important topics. The IRS still requires you to sign your tax return and file it because they want you to be responsible for it.

Someone is supposed to sign a child's report card.

It's time for your brokerage firm to sign off on your account. They may refuse to do it. That will tell you something. Vote with your feet.

One more note: when you send a letter, demand a letter in response. Forget the telephone. Get a response in writing. Brokers are trained to sell on the telephone and will be very uneasy with this material. That's their problem. Get answers, in writing, and study them.

Every letter is saved. If you need facts, ask! If you want documents, ask! The worst they can do is say, "no," in which case you can consider whether to move your account.

When you have a good broker, let him know you appreciate his work. Remember, a good broker is like a precious jewel, an object of beauty, to be complimented and specially thought of. A bad one is a voracious rodent.

If you think something is wrong with your account, assemble your papers and get thee to a lawyer. Some letters can help you with infirmation-gathering, and they can help put your thoughts in logical order for analysis of your fears, but if you feel something bad is happening, GET GOING TO YOUR LAWYER. Get your papers and thoughts together and get legal advice on what course of action to take.

The fact that you are confused by something does not mean something is necessarily wrong, and obtaining facts may help DISPEL your fears, but you must understand that the complications of brokerage accounts require expert advice. When you think something is wrong, contact your lawyer. Talk it over. Get some counsel. Your lawyer might want to recommend other action than mere letter writing, or he may recommend that he write to get faster answers, or meet with the branch manager or other staff from the brokerage firm.

No matter what, when you think something is wrong, don't waste time! The passage of time makes it look like you agreed with the situation, or that you ratified it after you understood it. Stale complaints look suspicious! You also have a legal obligation to mitigate your damages, that is, take reasonable steps to stop the harm as fast as possible. You can't hold your breath and let matters get worse.

A bad stockbroker hates to have the daylight hit him, just like a vampire. A good one doesn't mind. Always look for answers - but don't expect to get any unless you

ASK QUESTIONS!

LETTER ONE.
Precise information letter.

YOU________________________________

____

____

____

BROKER________________________________

____

____

____

Re: Account No.________________________________

Dear ,

I have been reviewing my account and would like to get some precise information from you. Please use this letter. After the Questions, jot down the answer in the space provided and send it back to me within the next two weeks. I want to compare it to my own records. It will be most helpful. If you can't or won't do it, please send me a letter telling me that. Your cooperation is greatly appreciated, and really needed.

1. What is the total, PRESENT value of my account?

2. Am I on margin?

3. How long have I been on margin?

4. Please send me a copy of my new account form, margin agreement, option agreement, cash account agreement, joint account agreement, tax withholding information forms and any other forms I have signed for your firm. That might include letters of authorization or transfer information, and discretionary power papers. I really mean everything I have signed.

5. Do I have an options account?

6. How long have I had an options account?

7. How much margin interest have I paid in each of the past three years?

8. What was the rough average of the interest rate I paid each year?

9. Have I used margin to buy any bonds?

10. Which bonds?

11. Have I used margin to buy any mutual funds?

12. Which funds?

13. Do you call me before each trade to get my permission to do the trade?

14. Do you use ANY discretion in my account?

15. How often have you used it?

16. Do I own any below investment-grade bonds?

17. Is your branch manager aware of the use of any discretion in my account?

18. How many trades have taken place in my account in each of the past three years? Please give me the total number, and then separate the number of bond trades, stock trades, mutual funds buys and sells, agency and principal trades.

total number of trades:
stock trades:
bond trades:
mutual fund trades:
agency trades:
principal trades:

19. What were the total commissions, mark-ups, and other fees which this account has paid to your firm in each of the past three years for all products and investments which I purchased in the account or directly from issuers such as limited partnerships or mutual funds?

20. Do I get a discount on my commission business?

21. What is the amount of the discount?

22. Can you send me a copy of your commission schedule?

23. If you can't send it, can your manager?

24. Who is your branch manager?

25. Who is your regional manager, and what is his office address?

26. Who is the compliance director of your firm, and what is his office address?

27. Who is the president or managing partner of your firm, and what is his address?

28. Are there any customer complaints outstanding against you?

29. Are there any lawsuits pending against you?

30. Are there any SRO or SEC investigations pending against you?

31. Do you have a securities account?

32. Do you trade the same securities as me?

33. Would you show me your account statement?

34. Am I suitable to have an account?

35. What do your records show for my income,
my dependents,
my net worth,
experience.

36. Has your branch manager ever reviewed my account with you?

37. When did that review take place?

38. Please send me a copy of your posting pages for my account, which I understand are kept in your Account Book.

Thanks! This will help me with my financial record keeping and future investment decisions.

Sincerely,

LETTER TWO.
Unknown trade letter.

YOU______________________________

____

____

____

BROKER______________________________

____

____

____

Re: Account No.____________________________

Dear Branch Manager,

I just got a confirmation for a trade that I do not recall authorizing. Please find out if this is my trade and drop me a written note about your findings. I would like to get this cleared up as soon as possible.

A copy of the confirmation is enclosed. It concerns the following trade:

Thanks for your prompt attention.

Sincerely,

LETTER THREE.
Request for Branch Manager Review.

YOU____________________________

____

____

____

BROKER____________________________

____

____

____

Re: Account No.__________________________

Dear Branch Manager,

I would like to you to review my account with your registered representative and get in contact with me after you have familiarized yourself with the history of the account, suitability standards, frequency of trading, and commissions paid.

I understand you periodically review accounts.

I look forward to your experienced assistance.

Please send me a letter with your findings when you have reviewed the account, so that we can discuss it. I will read it. Then we can discuss it. Thank you for your prompt attention.

Sincerely,

LETTER FOUR.
Gratitude.

YOU________________________________

____

____

____

BROKER________________________________

____

____

____

Re: Account No.________________________________

Dear ,

I have read Patrick Finegan's book Master Your Stockbroker, and I wanted to thank you for giving excellent service and straight answers to help me get maximum financial performance from my account.

I wanted to express my appreciation for your past efforts.

I hope the relationship continues, and I will be happy to recommend your services as an honest and ethical stockbroker whenever I can.

Thank you.

Sincerely,

cc: Firm President (send copies to these managers)
Regional Manager
Branch Manager
Compliance Director.

EPILOGUE

When in disgrace with fortune and men's eyes,
I all alone beweep my outcast state,
And trouble deaf heaven with my bootless cries,
And look upon myself, and curse my fate,
Wishing me like to one more rich in hope,
Featured like him, like him with friends possessed,
Desiring this man's art, and that man's scope,
With what I most enjoy contented least;
Yet in these thoughts myself almost despising
Haply I think on thee, - and then my state
(Like to the lark at break of day arising
From sullen earth) sings hymns at heaven's gate;
For thy sweet love remembered such wealth brings,
That I scorn to change my state with kings.

- Shakespeare, from the Sonnets.

Fellow Marketeers, there are far more important things in life than the pursuit of profits.

Friend William, thank you!

A breath of fresh air after a session in the arena. Mark this page! As often as you return to this book, enjoy his poem. No matter where you are, your predicament or challenge, be touched by its gentle summary, be rewarded by its endowment of timeless wisdom!

Adios!

INDEX

A - Z